P9-AGA-151

Mark McVann, FSC

Neither Victim
nor Survivor

Neither Victim
nor Survivor

Thinking toward a New Humanity

Marilyn Nissim-Sabat

LEXINGTON BOOKS

A division of
ROWMAN & LITTLEFIELD PUBLISHERS, INC.
Lanham • Boulder • New York • Toronto • Plymouth, UK

LEXINGTON BOOKS

A division of Rowman & Littlefield Publishers, Inc.
A wholly owned subsidary of The Rowman & Littlefield Publishing Group, Inc.
4501 Forbes Boulevard, Suite 200
Lanham, MD 20706

Estover Road
Plymouth PL6 7PY
United Kingdom

Copyright © 2009 by Lexington Books

All rights reserved. No part of this publication may be reproduced,
stored in a retrieval system, or transmitted in any form or by any
means, electronic, mechanical, photocopying, recording, or otherwise,
without the prior permission of the publisher.

British Library Cataloguing in Publication Information Available

Library of Congress Cataloging-in-Publication Data

Nissim-Sabat, Marilyn, 1938–
  Neither victim nor survivor : thinking toward a new humanity / Marilyn Nissim-Sabat.
     p. cm.
  Includes bibliographical references and index.
  ISBN 978-0-7391-2822-0 (cloth : alk. paper)
  eISBN 978-0-7391-3928-8
  1. Victims. 2. Victims in literature. I. Title.
  HV6250.25.N57 2009
  305.9'06—dc22

                                                             2009013050

Printed in the United States of America

∞ ™ The paper used in this publication meets the minimum requirements of American
National Standard for Information Sciences—Permanence of Paper for Printed Library
Materials, ANSI/NISO Z39.48–1992.

Contents

Foreword

"Are you Lewis Gordon?" The querying voice, marked by a Brooklyn Yiddish accent, came seemingly from nowhere.

Of what am I accused? I wondered. Even worse, having recently written quite a bit on bad faith and on Jean-Paul Sartre, the straightforward question stimulated many possible responses. So much could flash through our minds in a single moment. I was on my way to a session at the Society for Phenomenology and Existential Philosophy meeting in Chicago in the fall of 1996. When I turned around, I at first saw no one, until the source continued:

"I see your name tag. Are you *the* Lewis Gordon who wrote *Fanon and the Crisis of European Man?*"

Looking downward, I saw a short lady whose dark eyebrows were curled, her eyes intense, as she leaned forward in a balancing-act of holding up her pocketbook and a large, plastic bag of books.

". . .Yes," I said. After all, I *was* guilty of what I was accused, and in the context of SPEP, which was by then nearly hopelessly trapped in the mire of Derridianism and Heideggerianism, to be guilty of authorship was no small offense.

She smiled. "That's a terrific book. It's quite original. It's really new philosophy. There should be a session on it."

I didn't know what to say since by then I had received a variety of comments on that book ranging from much praise to vitriol. In England, there was even a reviewer who asserted his vehement hatred of blacks and Arabs through making sure to voice opposition to nearly anything I wrote, and I mean *anything*. For instance, if I were to say that the sky was blue, he would object and assert a correction—no, it was *aqua!* (I later discovered that he was writing a very thick book on Frantz Fanon that was designed to discourage any engagement with Fanon's *ideas*.) So I said the obvious:

"Thank you."

"No, I mean it," she added. "It's excellent phenomenological work."

I was pleased to meet someone who understood that the book was not *on* Fanon but instead an engagement with some concepts he offered, which I used in the service of developing my own thought. I asked her name, and she responded: "Marilyn Nissim-Sabat." We shook hands, and there began one of the most important friendships of my life.

This book is aptly entitled *Neither Victim nor Survivor: Thinking toward a New Humanity*. Nissim-Sabat's commitments, as a philosopher, therapist, and activist, are against the stultifying social forces and interpretations of reality that, as Fanon once observed, make life "brittle" and block the path of action and imagination, which led to her struggle *for* thinking about the future, of future thinking, of responsibilities faced each generation for those who succeed them. In the course of such thought, the constitutional paradox comes to the fore, where we in effect make that which we are trying to find. This effort, in which our humanity haunts our failings, demands our not collapsing into a state of permanent ruin. There is a sense in which ruin is unavoidable, since, at least in psychoanalytical terms, the separation from the womb is a loss for which we seek external reconciliation in our cultivation of a home. History, however, reveals that although such a journey is shared by all, the obstacles placed on the majority of humankind renders its prize, not only coming home but also *having a home*, available to few. The human condition reveals a common goal that's an uncommon achievement.

This book could very well have also been entitled *For Love of Humanity* or *For Love of Ideas* since Professor Nissim-Sabat sees ideas occasioning their best through being in the service of humanity. She expects thought to be emancipating. With such high hopes, it is no wonder that she suffered a period of despair a few decades ago. The situation was so bad that she had left philosophy during those years, even though she was an academic. The worlds of theory and practice were for her hopelessly divided, and the behavior of many professional philosophers hardly offered much for such a meeting. Worse, the networks of phenomenological philosophers seemed to have taken a path of textual-philia, where "the things themselves" were of little concern over "the words themselves" and their meticulous translation. Whatever phenomenology intended to look at in efforts of conscious clarity, many practitioners by the 1980s seemed to have been approaching it as one would a government manual. That malediction unfortunately persists. Alienated by such circumstances, Marilyn Nissim-Sabat, Ph.D., became, as well, Marilyn Nissim-Sabat, M.S.W. There, in the practice of psychotherapy, she was able to engage a world that, in the best of times, grew progressively better and in the worst of times was always worth the effort.

Yet, Professor Nissim-Sabat, Ph.D., M.S.W., had a secret. In spite of her call for practical engagement with the world of suffering souls, her heart carried an ongoing, deeply devoted love of the thought of Edmund Husserl. She found herself living in two worlds that were seemingly incompatible. And what a time to be harboring such a secret love! The idiosyncrasies of politics and knowledge are such that odd contradictions reigned. The very people who were attacking Husserl and Jean-Paul Sartre were at the same time extolling Heidegger, sometimes in the name of feminism and the formation of a postmodern cultural conception of left-leaning politics. A weird environment of liking whomever Michel Foucault liked, admiring whomever Jacques Derrida admired—in other words, the worst forms of the fallacy of appealing to popular authority—dominated the times, and Husserl, with his fatherly appearance, penchant for foundational thinking, and heavily European commitments as a member of the assimilating German Jewish population of the late nineteenth and early twentieth centuries, many of whom converted to Lutheranism, was a ram ripe for the slaughter. And such sacrifice was attempted. I recall an eminent administrator, after listening to one of my talks, griping, "I really liked your talk, although I cannot forgive you for being a phenomenologist."

When I wrote *Fanon and the Crisis of European Man*, it did not occur to me *how* some readers would listen to my call for a genuine *post*colonial dimension to the decolonization of knowledge and a renewed effort to articulate processes of maturation in contemporary society, and especially so among those espousing revolutionary praxis. There were silly postmodern responses of valorizing childishness with a Peter-Panish declaration of never wanting to grow up. But, for therapists and philosophers such as Marilyn Nissim-Sabat and others who wanted a meeting of philosophy and psychotherapy, such a call was a godsend. Their two worlds suddenly met under the rubric of *postcolonial phenomenology*.

The meeting of her two worlds was enabling for Professor Nissim-Sabat. It brought her "out," so to speak. She began openly to speak and write about Husserlian phenomenology not as a relic of intellectual history but as a *living, breathing form of intellectual praxis*. The result is a series of essays that are breathtaking in some cases, poetic in others, and illuminating in all.

Thought and thinking, as any good phenomenologist knows, are sparks, wedded to the symbolic power of language, that inaugurate a world liberated from the shackles of grunts and the entrapment of the immediate. In thought, whose correlate is ideas, time itself is transformed into the temporal, wherein the object of thought is, in a sense, in constant vigil. I have characterized this phenomenon as the subjunctive dimension of theoretical work. It is what is set in motion by that extraordinary act of faith and commitment, which, paradoxically, is the decision to suspend the ontological backing of commitment itself. Its roots are familiar in the history of modern Western philosophy in the work of Immanuel Kant. It was he who demonstrated that existence lacked predication, that the being of a concept adds nothing to its coherence. Eliminating the question of the being of a concept does not affect the meaning of the concept, except, of course, where the investment in its being constitutes its value. How many of us, for instance, would desire a G-d without being? Yet, ironically, phenomenology offers just that, and in many ways, that places it in stream with some of the most complex theological demands of our age. I am thinking of Paul Tillich's call for a G-d above G-d, or perhaps Keiji Nishitani's Zen Buddhist demand for a G-d without being. All this is different from the challenges posed by Nissim-Sabat and my common ancestry, where, for Jews, there are prohibitions on naming G-d, which subverts these formulations. In that tradition, there is a being for whom naming is inappropriate, which challenges what we are speaking about as we take on responsibility for the words that unfold in Torah. For some contemporary Jewish philosophers, this has meant a path into negative theology. Ontological impositions demand so many attachments. Yet Nissim-Sabat is not seeking G-d, with or without being. Hers is a journey much like Kierkegaard's call for works of love. She is willing to give up much precisely because she wants to be able *to give*, which means she must also retain enough to present offerings to her clients, students, readers, family, the world. The immediate may be demanding, but it is tomorrow's connection to yesterday that enables the continuity of intersubjective relations, of, in other words, a social world standing on that fragile, always reaching and constituted reality simply called, in a word, love.

This is not to say that Nissim-Sabat is sentimental. Her love of knowledge and others demands both compassion and strength. She finds putting one on, conning others, contemptible. Woe the soul who stimulates her wrath in that regard. Stories abound of her furled eyebrows, interrogatives marked by a rich background in Socratic dialectics and the psychoanalytical interpretations of verbal slippage: Marilyn Nissim-Sabat has no tolerance for phonies.

Truth, which for phenomenologists requires a paradoxically magnificent yet mundane act of suspending prejudices by recognizing them as such, requires, as well, an act of trust, faith, and, given the challenges posed by such an offering of the self, the risk of love. As a therapist, Nissim-Sabat is aware of how damaged many people are in the modern world, and she is aware of the complex, sadistic web of complicity demanded by a world in which harm collapses into a spirit of victimization and responsibility becomes an increasingly anonymous phenomenon. In many ways, echoing Fanon, another philosopher guided by the insights of therapy as a professional, her work asks,

"How can dehumanized subjects become actional?" How, in other words, can people reclaim their agency in a world that prefers their souls to be, as Michel Foucault observed in *Discipline and Punish*, prisoners of their bodies?

Marilyn Nissim-Sabat is a phenomenologist. Her commitment is not, however, ideological, for her commitment to truth requires her to be concerned by her own practice, whether as a therapist or a philosopher. The continued credo of rejecting the unexamined life applies, as well, to any unexamined thought. Each phenomenological act turns upon itself, as did the proverbial Sankofa bird of the Akan community of Ghana, as it simultaneously moves forward. This process eventually reveals itself *as a radical project*. What this means is that it takes itself on to the point of going to its own roots, of recognizing its conditions of possibility beyond which there cannot be anything else but the absurd. Yet even absurdity is not without its own challenges. After all, the fear of jumping into such an abyss is that all may be lost; survival may not be possible. It is, after all, a realm of contradictions.

The meeting of psychotherapy and philosophical reflection offers for Nissim-Sabat an understanding of what it means to have a healthy relationship with life's contradictions. It is, in effect, what is involved in growing up. To do so requires much courage in our age. For the paradox of maturation is not only in the recognition that life is not fair, but also in the realization that it demands gains through processes of loss. To grow, something, as in our initial expulsion from the safety of the womb, must always be left behind.

The value of survival requires clinging tenaciously to a version of reality that leaves little room for change or growth. Placed on individuals, it means that one *must* exist, even at the expense of all others. And if drawn to its logical conclusion, it means that anything that places the surviving self at risk must fall to the wayside. The world that emerges is one so obsessed with its maintenance that it closes off all possibilities of change, and where change knocks on the door, it must be punished, cast out, or eradicated. Where is there recourse in such attachment but to the value of hate? Even where "*we* must survive at all cost" announces itself in the humiliation and destruction of others, that dimension of *them* that makes them *others* would emerge in *us* as that faces its logical disintegration into *me* and *you*, which is that "*I* must survive at all cost," and I need not spell out where that leads.

Building a world on love instead of hate requires, at some point, reaching out without expectation of receiving anything in return. Professor Nissim-Sabat has given much for which she has expected nothing. In a way, her life exemplifies the structure of phenomenological movement itself, for she has rejected the ontological payoff for the sake, simply, of understanding. Yet this act of love has not gone unseen and unheard, and its reverberations continue through the ideas she has stimulated in the work of others. It was she, for instance, who encouraged me to connect my thesis of narcissistic attachment to discussions of narcissistic rage. And it is she who continues to work across identity formations in the hope of them working together as much as possible—in her case, through the Husserl Circle, the Phenomenology Roundtable, the Caribbean Philosophical Association, the Association for the Advancement of Philosophy and Psychiatry, the Chicago Association for Psychoanalytic Psychology, the Society for Women in Philosophy, and many more. In each, she issues queries, constantly, for their *convergence* without a demand for any of them to lose any dimension of their distinction, for them, in other words, to be in genuine dialogue with each other.

Her former students, Carolyn Cusick and Michael R. Paradiso-Michau, who wrote the Introduction to this volume, are extremely grateful for the acts of love that she has shown them. Nissim-Sabat remembers that message from Plato's *Symposium*, that wisdom does not at first appear to be beautiful. Think of Socrates' face versus the ideas he emanates. Nissim-Sabat's students are grateful for how difficult Nissim-Sabat was, of how she introduced them to the world of fighting for what really matters. I, too, am grateful for that. I am grateful for the bevy of philosophical arguments since our meeting, of travels, both intellectual and geographic, marked by ideas spreading as proverbial fire, of symposia saturated with good rum and Nissim-Sabat's orated selections, by heart, from Herman Melville's opus. But mostly, I am simply thankful for Marilyn. The essays gathered here are, in many ways, intervening acts of love. Their aim, like those of their author, is simply to provide some light as we, too, continue that perilous journey through which we hope one day to find that opening through which we can really appreciate what it means to stand together, as Dante reflected so long ago, and behold the stars.

Lewis R. Gordon
Providence, Rhode Island

Acknowledgments

A few years ago, one of my former students, Michael R. Paradiso-Michau, put forth the idea of publishing a collection of my papers that were written over the course of about twenty years. Very soon after, another of my former students, Carolyn M. Cusick, joined with Michael in the project. And, soon thereafter, these two stalwart young people gained the support of our friend and colleague, Lewis R. Gordon. This book is the result of their dedication and abiding support and encouragement.

Carolyn, now a doctoral candidate in philosophy at Vanderbilt University, and Michael, now Dr. Michael R. Paradiso-Michau, a postdoctoral fellow in Jewish Studies and Philosophy at the Penn State University, wrote the Introduction to this volume. As a perusal of their essay shows, I have been most fortunate in having the sense and direction of my work expressed with such insight and empathy. Their devotion to philosophy, or as Lewis Gordon would say, to 'thinking,' is palpable, and their generosity, scholarship, and acute intelligence are everywhere in evidence. And, working with young people who share my values and goals was not only the icing on the cake; it was one of the factors that made it all worthwhile.

Working on the project of this book with Carolyn Cusick was an inspiring experience for me. Her unflagging enthusiasm, critical intelligence, and belief in the value of this work gave me the courage to pursue it. Carolyn also did a great deal of the early leg work—scanning, photocopying, and so on, wrote the proposal, and sent it to prospective publishers. Carolyn is a brilliant young scholar and thinker whose future work I await with great anticipation. Dr. Michael Paradiso-Michau is a young man with a gift for friendship who has already made his mark as a scholar, teacher, and writer.

Lewis R. Gordon's work, as readers of this book will discover, figures prominently in my own. He has been for the last twelve years both a

xiii

constant source of inspiration and a very dear friend. His work, unique in its synthesis of Husserlian phenomenology, critical race theory, Africana Studies, philosophy of the Human Sciences, Fanon studies, and existential sociology, stands apart from virtually all other contemporary work in these fields and in philosophy, and it does so because it is shot through with both deep and open commitment to human beings and, at the same time, without compromise or contradiction, to rigorous thinking. This stands as a model for us all.

My dear friend of many years, Mark McVann, F.S.C., Professor of Religion at St. Mary's College of California, read several of the chapters and nailed me with my omissions and confusions, as only he can. I am also grateful to Patricia J. Huntington and Martin Beck Matustik (both professors at Arizona State University) for their friendship, encouragement, and intellectual companionship.

My husband, Dr. Charles Nissim-Sabat, has been supportive of my work in every way.

Finally, I would like to express my appreciation to the editors at Lexington Books for graciously accepting this book for publication and for bearing with me as I wrestled with completion of the manuscript.

Chapter 1, "What Is a Victim?," was originally published with the title "Victims No More" in the *Radical Philosophy Review*, vol. 1, no. 1, 1998. Reprinted by permission of the *Radical Philosophy Review*.

Chapter 2, "Freud, Gender, and the Epigenesis of Morality: A Critique," is a substantially revised and expanded version of a paper, "Freud on Feminism and Faith," originally published in *Listening: Journal of Religion and Culture*, v. 20, no. 3, 1985. Author holds copyright.

Chapter 3, "The Crisis in Psychoanalysis: Resolution through Husserlian Phenomenology and Feminism," was originally published in *Human Studies*, v.14, no. 1, March, 1991, pp. 33–66. Reprinted by permission of Springer.

Chapter 4, "Addictions, *Akrasia*, and Self Psychology: A Socratic and Psychoanalytic View of *Akrasia* as Victim Blaming," is a previously unpublished paper.

Chapter 5, "Fanon, Phenomenology, and the Decentering of Philosophy: Lewis Gordon's *Her Majesty's Other Children: Sketches of Racism from a Neocolonial Age*," is a substantially revised and expanded version of a paper, "Lewis Gordon's *Her Majesty's Other Children: An Invitation to Existential Phenomenology*," originally published in *The C.L.R. James Journal*, vol. 6, no. 1, 1998. Author holds copyright.

Chapter 6, "Race and Culture: Victim Blaming in Psychology, Psychiatry, and Psychoanalysis," was originally published as Chapter 16 (pp. 244–57) in *The Philosophy of Psychiatry: A Companion*, edited by Jennifer Radden

(Oxford: Oxford University Press, 2004). Reprinted by permission of Oxford University Press.

Chapter 7, "Autonomy, Empathy, and Transcendence in Sophocles' *Antigone*, with an 'Epilogue: On Lacan's *Antigone*,'" is a substantially revised and expanded version of a paper, "Autonomy, Empathy, and Transcendence in Sophocles' *Antigone*," that was originally published in *Listening: Journal of Religion and Culture*, v. 25, no. 3, 1986. The "Epilogue: On Lacan's *Antigone*" was not previously published. Author holds copyright.

Chapter 8, "Neither Victim nor Survivor Be: Who Is Beloved's Baby?" was not previously published.

Introduction

As the title of this volume suggests, in this world we do not only survive or "make it through" certain life-activities and events; in addition, we aim to thrive, to flourish. Indeed, as Marilyn Nissim-Sabat shows, survival is a necessary (though not sufficient) precondition for freedom, so it cannot be its full aim or measure. As Edmund Husserl, Nissim-Sabat's primary philosophical resource, showed, our freedom as humans is to become creators and bestowers of meaning. This necessitates that we assume responsibility for our acts of meaning bestowal: we assume, that is, that they are rationally motivated, that is, conducive to human well-being.

Certain obstacles block the path to actualizing this future; most stem from the pervasiveness of positivism and its concomitant dualisms, still rampant in our culture, our thoughts, and our actions. Scientism and naturalism are two such obstacles. Most important for Nissim-Sabat, though, is victim blaming, one of the most pervasive and harmful of these obstacles to realizing human freedom. The victim blaming stance, whether held by the victimizer, the victim, or anyone else, "posits either a decontextualized, abstract, and thus dehumanized notion of human freedom—agency as atomized willing ("Just say no!"), or an insuperable determinism—denial of human freedom" (Chapter 6: Race and Culture). Discovering and realizing that victim blaming is at the heart of racism, sexism, and all forms of exploitation is the first step toward constitution of a global, radical, agentic community.

Nissim-Sabat's work is interdisciplinary: from philosophy to psychology, critical theory to psychoanalysis, with forays into literature and the transcendental dimension, and motivated by the struggle for racial and gender justice, and the end of class based oppression. Nissim-Sabat is at the same time an honored teacher, a well-known scholar and writer, and a respected psychotherapist, and each of these existential activities informs and is shaped by the other. Her philosophical point of departure is Husserlian phenomenology because Husserl grasped, as no one before him had, the method that is able to restore meaningful subjectivity to the human subject. For Husserl, transcendental phenomenology is transcendental psychology. So, for Nissim-Sabat, the project of freeing humanity must address itself to both philosophy and psychology as phenomenologically construed and with the goal of eliminating the theory-practice divide.

Nissim-Sabat's psychology is psychoanalysis, because, beyond its historical dogmatisms and failures, Nissim-Sabat recognizes its contemporary promise and its liberatory potential. So, it is as activists, as teachers and students, as philosophers and psychologists, as scholars, writers, and thinkers that we read this book. Herein one can glean the conceptual and psychosocial motives for responsibly creating and bestowing meaning and value on the world. In focusing and deepening our understanding, these essays clear the path of obstacles to moving beyond survival.

The chapters contained in this book are representative of Nissim-Sabat's work. She has been thinking, writing, teaching, protesting, and counseling for many years. These essays were not written originally for a book; rather, they were written on separate occasions for different publications and various scholarly meetings. Each highlights a different aspect of the larger project, but all are directed toward the same end. Reminiscent of some aspects of Kierkegaard's method as a writer, Nissim-Sabat wishes to meet her beloved readers on their own terms, and to seduce them into further deepening inwardness so as to more fully realize their human subjectivity in an age where the prospects for authentic freedom and possibility seem dismal, at best.

Finally, when one's goal is the liberation of all of humanity (and what else is philosophy?) one should, and Nissim-Sabat does, worry, not just about reading-in, that is, about projecting assumptions onto others and other texts; equally importantly, one should worry about reading-out—that is, failing to see what is there in the text. The thoroughness and rigor of Nissim-Sabat's thought and writings successfully avoid both horns of this dilemma. In the chapters that follow, one thus also gets a sense of the way that Nissim-Sabat relates to other people and other scholarly work. Several of the essays in this volume developed in part as critical reviews of new and prominent work in various fields. Her direct engagements with these discourses show her worrying about and defending against dangerous misreadings, both in and out. This is not only good scholarship but also recognizes how much is at stake in interpreting texts. Although it is necessary, it is not sufficient to be a generous reader of others. Writers must be both clear and thorough, and they can hope for a cadre of defenders. Nissim-Sabat is herself that thorough, as these essays will attest—and her critical engagements with others demand they be similarly judicious. We could all only wish to have Nissim-Sabat dialogue with us—clarify and teach our writings—as she does Husserl, Marx, Freud, Fanon, Gordon, and others.

Chapter One, "What Is a Victim?" begins with a clear and important statement of Nissim-Sabat's interdisciplinary and liberatory vision. Here one finds some key definitions and a trenchant, theoretical-practical analysis of victim blaming and its pervasiveness in our culture that is crucial for understanding subsequent chapters and this project as a whole. The essay begins with a unique taxonomy and analysis of types of victim blaming extant in the contemporary world, continues with a motivated proposal for a new view, and ends with appreciative summaries of the radical activist positions of two existential phenomenologists, Fanon and Lewis R. Gordon, and Marxist philosopher Raya Dunayevskaya, three key influences on Nissim-Sabat's conception of her project. With courage and compassion, Nissim-Sabat confronts existential problems including violence against women and oppression of those living in the Black ghettos of inner-city America. She critiques interpretations of those problems by various feminists and race theorists that do not adequately preclude victim blaming.

"Freud, Gender, and the Epigenesis of Morality," Chapter Two, and "The Crisis in Psychoanalysis," Chapter Three, delve directly into the problems of psychoanalysis, specifically its positivism and misogyny, bringing to bear on these a feminist phenomenological perspective. Chapter Two is a both an appreciative review and a radical expansion of the critique of Freud in Judith Van Herik's highly regarded book, *Freud on Femininity and Faith* (1982; reprinted 2004). In this essay, Nissim-Sabat, using Van Herik as source, examines the intricacies of Freud's views on religion and gender and makes some startling inferences that call into question the viability of Freud's notion of the origin of morality in superego development. This clears the way and points toward views of transcendence like the one Nissim-Sabat outlines in other essays, one that is not hostile to issues of human psychosocial development. Also, in Chapter Two she shows that and how patriarchy—certainly in its Freudian instantiation—is another version of the Sophists' claim that might makes right. But this is not to say that Freud and psychoanalysis must be rejected *tout court*. To the contrary, they must be rescued such that we can access the liberatory potential therein. One attempt to free ourselves from the image of Freud's use of psychoanalysis as a rationale for patriarchy comes in the next chapter.

Chapter Three is a phenomenological-feminist intervention in the ongoing, unresolved debate as to whether psychoanalysis is a hermeneutic or scientific discipline. Nissim-Sabat shows that the resources of Husserlian phenomenology integrated with feminist critique can resolve this problem which has severely compromised the development of a progressive, liberatory theory and practice of psychoanalysis. Husserl's great last work, *The Crisis of European Sciences and Transcendental Phenomenology*, is engaged as necessary for transcendence of the hermeneutic-science dichotomy, and the work of feminist philosopher of science Evelyn Fox Keller is engaged to show that and how phenomenology can be enhanced not so much through feminist correction of the philosophical perspective as such, but by showing and filling in the gaps and openings in that perspective. For example, Husserl raises the question but does not provide a full account of the motives that led Galileo to believe the mathematization of the sensory plenum reveals true being with no loss through abstraction from experience. Thus, this chapter shows the correctness of Keller's view that psychoanalysis suffers not only because of the problem of naturalism in science but also because of the masculine bias of naturalistic science.

Chapter Four, "Addiction, *Akrasia*, and Self Psychology: A Socratic and Psychoanalytic View of *Akrasia* as Victim Blaming," challenges mental health practitioners, philosophers, and the public in general on some basic and mistaken assumptions about rationality and health. The chapter is a powerful argument against the belief that persons with addictions act against their known own best interest, that is, they exhibit *akrasia* or weakness of will. Nissim-Sabat explains that *akrasia* is a paradoxical and counterintuitive idea in that it fails to acknowledge the rationality of seeking pleasure as the good. Here one can find a more complete rationale for the claim in Chapter One that an assumption of weakness of will inheres in all forms of victim blaming. Nissim-Sabat shows this through an analysis of Plato's *Protagoras* and a critique of the work of Alfred Mele, one of the leading philosophical authorities on and defenders of *akrasia*. This provocative chapter, through an original and important engagement with Mele, gives rise to a view of all persons, including those whose behavior seems to indicate otherwise, as inherently rational, i.e., acting always in accordance with their beliefs about what is in their own best interest. This chapter is also an unmistakable expression of Nissim-Sabat's compassion and vigilance as a psychotherapist and advocate for all those who are victims of victim blaming.

Issues of race and racism are the explicit foci of Chapters Five and Six, "Fanon, Phenomenology, and the Decentering of Philosophy: Lewis Gordon's *Her Majesty's Other Children: Sketches of Racism from a Neocolonial Age*" and "Race and Culture: Victim Blaming in Psychology, Psychiatry, and Psychoanalysis," respectively. The first is a fitting tribute to fellow freedom fighter Lewis R. Gordon, an existential phenomenologist whose work and charisma have deeply influenced many working in the fields of philosophy and the human sciences, Nissim-Sabat in particular. Nissim-Sabat presents and interprets Gordon's work to show the need for a radical existential phenomenology, along the lines he proposes, to enact a new humanism free of all oppressions. In particular, Nissim-Sabat highlights the unique manner in which Gordon shows that Fanon's own perspective is phenomenological and how Gordon sees the grounding of critical race theory in Husserlian phenomenology to be essential to working toward the creation of a "new humanity" as envisioned by Fanon. This essay also illustrates the extent of Nissim-Sabat's vision of collaborative thinking in philosophy.

Specifically, a unique and important feature of Nissim-Sabat's understanding of Gordon's work is the way in which she advances his critique of postmodern modes of thought through an extended discussion of the postmodern critique of the notions of center, centering, and centration. Nissim-Sabat shows that Gordon's critique of the postmodern claim that all of Euro-civilization is nothing but Eurocentrism indicts postmodernism as caught in its own trap. Postmodernism fails to transcend the temptation to essentialize and thereby essentializes anti-essentialism. Nissim-Sabat goes on to show that implicit in Gordon's work is a decentering that presupposes a center, one that is never closed but can and must be recentered to make possible liberatory thought and practice. As Nissim-Sabat writes, "We can now see that to abandon . . . phenomenology . . . is to posit a binary pair, an either/or: either essentialism or centerlessness, i.e., uncenteredness, fragmentation. Phenomenology and existential sociology reject this binary as we struggle to reconstitute radical theory and praxis for a human future." Chapter Six, "Race and Culture: Victim Blaming in Psychology, Psychiatry, and Psychoanalysis," continues the discussion of race, but here psychology is indicted for its racism as well as its failure to understand cultural forces (including but by no means limited to racism) as factors in the genesis of mental illness. Nissim-Sabat begins this essay with a preponderance of evidence drawn from past and contemporary studies detailing the scope and depth of racist practices in psychiatry. She follows this with a presentation of three efforts to move beyond the racist paradigm in psychiatry—those of Fanon, Michel Foucault, and E. V. Wolfenstein—and critiques of these efforts. Through her critique of Wolfenstein's *Psychoanalysis and Marxism*, in particular his interpretation of Ralph Ellison's *The Invisible Man*, Nissim-Sabat shows that psychiatry will not be able to rid itself of racist practices until it discovers that it must combat cultural, institutionalized racism in the consulting room itself and on the part of the psychiatric practitioners themselves. The end result is a detailed analysis of Husserlian transcendental phenomenology which shows that this perspective can bring about a synthesis of Marxism and psychiatry in a praxis that is as relevant in the consulting room as it is to society.

One of Nissim-Sabat's concerns inherent in but not yet made explicit in the preceding chapters is the unnecessarily rigid distinction between the inner and the outer, the individual and the social. Chapter Seven, "Autonomy, Empathy, and Transcendence in Sophocles' *Antigone*, with an Epilogue: On Lacan's *Antigone*," takes up that dichotomy directly as evidenced in the conflict between needs and rights of individuals (inner) and communities (outer). The chapter takes a reflective glance toward ancient Greece and at the same time propels us into the problematic present, where genuine inter-human empathy exposes the illegitimacy of such an uncrossable divide. This chapter proceeds by calling into question the interpretation of *Antigone* that is most pervasive in the historical and contemporary literature. The standard interpretation sees Antigone and Creon as equally justified though opposed moral agents. To see Creon in this way, Nissim-Sabat argues, is to exonerate the oppressor and blame the oppressed. This new interpretation is one where love is simultaneously and inseparably an autonomous and an empathetic act, where agency is an expression not only of a free will, but necessarily and inseparably of a socially embedded person. Nissim-Sabat's thesis is, as she writes, in Husserlian terms, that Antigone herself embodies the facticity that "Autonomy and empathy are the mundane correlates of transcendental intersubjectivity." This chapter also has an epilogue in which Nissim-Sabat critiques Lacan's claim that Antigone is "inhuman."

Although implicit or indirectly addressed in many of the above writings, Chapter Eight, "Neither Victim nor Survivor Be: Who Is Beloved's Baby?" turns us to a vivid and concrete discussion of Nissim-Sabat's anti-survivalist stance. This chapter exhibits Nissim-Sabat's exemplary interpretive capacity that often steals into her work in philosophy and psychoanalysis. Regrettably, more of her literary analyses did not make it into this volume, but this chapter is a beautiful engagement with Toni Morrison's *Beloved* which demonstrates the need to move beyond survival to a place of thriving. Or, to put the point another way, Nissim-Sabat shows that an aspect of Morrison's vision is that recuperation from trauma requires that we reconnect not only with our pre-traumatic selves, but with our free creativity, our inherent desire to create a more human future for ourselves and our progeny. Here again Nissim-Sabat offers us an original reading of a literary masterpiece in which she reveals the incisiveness of previous readings and at the same time shows that they do not go far enough to capture the fire of a telos toward a more human future.

What Nissim-Sabat shows in her own unique way is that the struggle for authentic freedom and for a non-racist, non-sexist, and non-classist society, is one such that, in Marx and Engels's famous formulation, "the free development of each is the condition for the free development of all"[1] —this struggle must be, simultaneously, a struggle against the defeatist ideology of survivalism that ever and always enacts its defeatism by blaming victims instead of exposing and opposing oppression.

Nissim-Sabat's life and spirit have been and continue to be examples of the compassion and empathy that, if expressed by each of us, would contribute to ending oppression everywhere. In Fanon's terms, ending dehumanization and constructing a "new humanity" are Nissim-Sabat's explicit goals and hopes for our future. But, it is not enough for her to express these goals: she must try to show the rest of us the way. For Nissim-Sabat, the possibility for a better, because more human, world is what philosophy and the humanistic disciplines, for example, psychology, critical theory, and critical race and gender theory, are about. Her vision for our human future is a world in which subject status is recognized by and for all.

Carolyn Cusick
Nashville, Tennessee

Michael R. Paradiso-Michau
State College, Pennsylvania

NOTE

1. Marx and Engels, *Manifesto of the Communist Party*, in Robert C. Tucker, ed. *The Marx-Engels Reader*. 2nd ed. New York: W.W. Norton, 1978: p. 491.

Chapter One

What Is a Victim?

INTRODUCTION

In the critique Marx made in *The Manifesto of the Communist Party* of his "critical-utopian" socialist predecessors (Saint-Simon, Fourier, Owen), he pointed out that the utopians were unable to bridge the gap between their ideals and the transformation of the world necessary for the realization of those ideals. Marx explained the inability to come to grips with this problem, that of the relation of theory to practice, as a function of the contemporary historical situation in which the proletariat, even after the rise of the bourgeoisie, was still a relatively undeveloped class. Unaware of the depth of the antagonisms nascent in the class structure of capitalist society, the utopians believed that all classes would immediately realize the rationality of their ideas regarding a better society. Consequently, they opposed revolutionary activity and turned their backs on the movement of revolutionary forces from below, for example, the Chartists. Marx sought to overcome the utopians' failure to come to grips with the all-important and most vexing problem of the relation between theory and practice; however, he saw that this could not be achieved merely by exposing the roots of human misery in the capitalist system, a task which the "critical utopians" had already taken up and for which Marx singled them out for recognition.[1] More important, inherent in Marx's, but not the utopians', analysis of capitalism, and explicit in Marx's writings, is an explanation of the means by which capitalism can be thrown off and a new society created. Thus, at the very heart of Marx's thought there is an explanation of the relation between theory and practice.

In moving beyond the limitations of utopian socialism, Marx, deeply immersed in the philosophy of Hegel, developed a critique of capitalism that is inseparable from a theory of the subject. Marx's analysis projected a

1

historical development such that the internal contradictions within capitalism would precipitate a series of more and more destabilizing crises. As a result, the most exploited and oppressed group in society will develop a consciousness of itself as a class, as the proletariat. At the same time, the proletariat will become aware of the unity of theory and practice. The new class consciousness will consist in the conviction that the proletariat can remake the world so as to eliminate its own dehumanization and thus eliminate the dehumanization of all humanity.

The outline of Marx's ideas just presented is not at all unique; however, it is often the basis for the conclusion that Marx was dead wrong. The proletariat, anti-Marxists contend, has not been constituted as a class conscious of itself as the agent of a total transformation of society; class warfare is an obsolete notion; capitalism has not died of its own internal contradictions and crises; and, especially now, in the post-Soviet world, those who seek progressive change should realize that it is better to bear with, and seek to ameliorate, those ills that we have than to fly to others we know not of. These ideas suggest that a socialist society can come about only through reform of the existing system rather than through total transformation of it into a new society; or, in other words, that revolution, or total transformation, is an outmoded idea.

The problem with this view and with the outline of Marx's ideas presented above is that both ignore an essential component of Marx's theory, one which strongly suggests that the current rejection of the idea of total transformation of society (and often the rejection of Marx's ideas *tout court,* for example, by some tendencies within postmodernism) is a self-defeating stance. First, in both his analyses of historical events and his response to contemporary events, Marx showed that the forces of revolution, movements of people organizing to throw off oppression, historically have always existed. Such forces exist today, for example, in France (the labor movement), in Mexico (Chiapas), and in the worldwide struggle of all women, and of black women and men, for liberation. Second, Marx was hardly ignorant of the fact that, even in his day, or especially in his day when exploitation was virtually homicidal, and despite the continual, restless activity of revolutionary forces from below, the mass of people appeared to tolerate their exploitation and oppression, in short their servitude, and some even denied its existence, as do many today. Third, and most important, whereas current ex-Marxist opponents of Marx take this apparent tolerance of servitude to indicate that Marx's Marxism (*not* the "Marxism" of the post-Marx Marxists,[2] e.g., Engels, Lenin[3]) is a defunct, obsolete philosophy which cannot explain either the success of capitalism or the means of bringing about its demise; in fact, Marx's analysis is inherently also an analysis of how capitalism has maintained itself despite its despotic, brutal character. The concepts of base-superstructure, false consciousness, and alienation, and the analysis of ideology as a purely pejorative concept, including sexism, racism, and classism, all of which designate the means by which capitalism creates a distorted consciousness, are inseparable from Marx's critique of capitalism and his theory of revolution. Thus, despite the fact that Marx's alleged predictions have not materialized, his work contains powerful tools for understanding the prolongation of capitalist despotism.

In addition, and most relevant to my purposes here, the contentious history of the understanding of the nature of ideology from Lenin through Althusser to the present shows that Marx's analysis has not yet been fully comprehended, and it further suggests that to do so would enable us either to build consistently on his foundation or to make a constructive, radical socialist-humanist, that is, *nonideological,* critique of that foundation.

All of this notwithstanding, the fact remains that most people in the world today are afflicted with a distorted consciousness that is the product of capitalist ideology, and they seem unable at this time to take up a position outside that ideology in order to move beyond it and concretely revolutionize existing societies. This inability or disability persists despite the current manifestations of capitalism's drive to destroy freedom movements everywhere; indeed, to destroy the very idea of freedom. Examples of this are (1) current efforts in the United States to roll back whatever gains were made as a result of the civil rights, women's, and gay liberation movements, as reflected, for example, in the continued disavowal of the racist implications of the Katrina disaster and its consequences, and (2) the complicity of the United States and the European nations in the destruction of the multiethnic society in Bosnia.[4] Thus, we may say that most people, including the members of the ruling class ┼ themselves, are victims of capitalist ideology, and that Marx created a theory of how that victimization occurs and what can be done to combat it. Marx's approach is twofold. On one hand, it is crucially important to listen to the voices of the masses in motion and to acknowledge and join with their drive for freedom without which the revolution cannot occur and which historically has inspired revolutions; on the other hand, it is vital at the same time to join with those in the minority who form organizations to expose the ideology which victimizes people and thwarts total revolution. To put the point succinctly, Marx wanted to exonerate the victims.

This question, how to exonerate the victims, provides a context for attempting to discern the contribution radical philosophy can make in the twenty-first century toward combating capitalist ideology and thus toward the development of revolutionary, socialist-humanist consciousness. The task of combating capitalist ideology requires a twofold approach: first, socialist-humanists, both those who are and those who are not in the academy, should align ourselves more actively with liberation struggles everywhere; second, radical philosophy needs to find a way to concretize further the analysis of capitalist ideology as a form of victimization that shackles those who are subjects for a liberatory praxis. The purpose of this essay is to suggest a means of taking up the latter task. In what follows, I will describe and interpret the taxonomy of ideologically constituted categories of victims extant in the United States, and very likely in the rest of the world, in order to suggest a way to show more concretely than has yet been shown how capitalist ideology acts upon human beings. To pursue this project I will explore the status of the 'victim' in contemporary society.

The following analysis is not intended to be exhaustive. Moreover, the analysis is intentionally limited by, at times rather obvious, exclusions in order to direct the reader's attention along a specific path. For this reason, even though I believe it will stand up to expansion and to an impartial critique, the argument is schematic and at times takes on a polemical tone. My intention is not to provide answers to the questions raised; in fact, the analysis presented here will probably provoke more questions than it directly answers. My intention is, rather, programmatic: merely to persuade readers that the line of investigation presented here is worth pursuing.

WHAT IS A VICTIM?

It seems plausible to assume that in order to understand and master the overwhelming feelings of fear and helplessness evoked by human suffering, people construct categories that function both to describe and explain that suffering. In American public life today, three ways of categorizing victims, which I shall designate as V-1, V-2, and V-3, are extant. As I will show, V-3 represents an effort to move beyond V-2, which deployers of V-3 view as victim-blaming. V-3 is, however, "metastable," to borrow a term from Sartre,[5] in that it is not secure against collapsing into V-1 or naive empiricism (in a sense to be explained below). I propose to show that progress in understanding how ideology acts to occlude awareness of human freedom requires that socialist humanism put forth and defend another conception of victimization, V-4. The point is, of course, that, inasmuch as it is a category cleansed, I believe, of ideological pollution, V-4 will embody a more accurate comprehension of the actual experience of victimization and, in so doing, enable a deeper comprehension of, and ability to speak to, the sources of human agency that will emerge in the struggle for a new society. I propose, that is, that radical philosophy develop a radicalized reconstruction of the concept of "victim," one that brackets and transcends the extant, dominant ways of categorizing victims and that critically builds upon Marx's ideas. I will begin with a description of the extant descriptive/explanatory categories and an explanation of the relationships that obtain among them.

V-1: Victims of "Natural" Disasters

The first category, V-1, has recently been deployed very frequently in the United States. Those characterized as V-1s are the victims of natural disasters, such as flood, tornado, or eruption of a volcano. To the extent that events resulting from human failure, for example, a plane crash, are viewed as inevitable because "we're only human," victims of such events are included in V-1. Those who suffer from such events receive national, even international, outpourings of concern, and they are viewed as deserving assistance. Victimized through no fault of their own, the victims of "natural" disasters need help. The general attitude is that, at the time of the disaster, no one reasonably could have been expected to have predicted, or to have acted to prevent, the disaster and consequent suffering. Victims of these sorts of events are rarely subjected to victim blaming; they are rarely held responsible in any way or to any degree for what occurred, for what they have suffered. Indeed, to attempt to do so would immediately bring charges of a hostile and unjust attempt to blame the victims for that for which they are patently not blameworthy. Moreover, judging by interviews with these victims as presented in the media, their remarks seem prima facie devoid of any tendency toward self-blame. These sorts of events and the response to them conform to the public attitude according to which (a) they are disasters that could happen to anyone and, furthermore and most important, (b) that anyone could fail to predict these events or fail to take preventive action to minimize suffering and loss of life.

V-2: The Victims Are to Blame

The second category, V-2, represents the notion of a victim who does indeed suffer, but, it is held, from self-imposed suffering: for example, people who live in depressed ghettos, people on welfare, or women who are abused by their husbands. Those cast into the V-2 category are alleged to have a "victim mentality." This notion of victim is inherent, for example, in remarks by conservative members of Congress to the effect that African Americans who seek positions through affirmative-action laws are people who have failed to internalize the value known as "individualism."

This suggests the dominant view that right-wing conservatives have an entirely different view of victimization than liberals have. For example, liberals maintain that people who live in depressed ghettos and are undereducated and unemployed need help. They need "compensatory education" and "job training." However, in his remarkable book *Blaming the Victim,*[6] William Ryan has shown that this sort of liberal ideology holds victims responsible for their own plight just as much as does the conservative, primitive, social-Darwinist view. Liberals, too, locate the cause of the victims' plight in the victims themselves, in their internalized "culture of poverty,"[7] for example, just as much as do conservatives who maintain that welfare recipients lack the desire to work. Indeed, for conservatives the very programs that "bleeding heart liberals" have designed to help the poor are simply in collusion with them, like enablers of addicts who do not create the addiction but are in collusion with it.

But, the point of the conservatives' remarks bashing welfare recipients and lauding "individualism" is that the perception by liberals that these victims were initially in need of help was totally misguided; rather, what they needed was precisely not to be helped, no matter what the circumstances that led to their exclusion from the mainstream of American society and compromised their chances for success. This reflects the standard social-Darwinist view that those who fail to succeed in a dog-eat-dog environment have inherent deficiencies, whether genetic (right-wing conservatives) or rooted in social conditions (liberals). As Ryan showed, in neither case is the cause related to the very foundation of society itself, its pervasive racism, classism, and sexism.[8] What Ryan maintained in 1968 is just as, if not more, valid today: V-2 is the dominant understanding of what it is to be a victim—that is, to be a victim of anything other than a natural catastrophe is to have a "victim mentality."

Deployers of V-2 hold that V-2s should never be confused with or taken to be V-1s, because, given that placement in V-2 is due to a deficiency in the person, not anyone can be a V-2, only those with the requisite deficiencies. Moreover, V-2s can overcome their genetic or socially induced deficiencies if they would only try, and it is reasonable to expect them to try, whether they do so totally on their own (conservatives) or with the assistance of various "programs" (liberals). Most importantly, deployers of V-2 deny that they are guilty of blaming victims by unjustly holding them responsible for their own suffering. For them, V-2 means quite the contrary: that the people so categorized are justly held responsible for their own suffering.

V-3: The Victims Are Not to Blame

The third victim concept, V-3, is frequently deployed by progressive theoreticians, feminists, civil rights activists, and others in reaction against V-2. For the deployers of V-3, the deployers of V-2 *are* blaming the victims; they *are* unjustly holding victims responsible for their own suffering, in particular certain types of victims. The V-3 notion of victim is inherent, for example, in the effort by some advocates in the women's liberation movement to destigmatize rape victims and victims of marital psychological, physical, and sexual abuse who have murdered their spouses or live-in lovers. These (for the most part) women are not self-victimizing; rather, it is claimed, they are victims of the actions of other persons, victimizers. The deployment of V-3 is an effort to counteract the strong tendency to blame the victim (as seen by the prevalent deployment of the V-2 category), and to do so by insisting that the victim is blameless and in no sense in complicity with the victimizer. From the point of view of the deployers of V-3, the V-2 category, contrary to the views of those who deploy it, is inherently victim blaming; in other words, deployers of V-2 unjustly hold those to whom it is applied responsible for their own suffering. Advocates of the V-3 view maintain, on the contrary, that anyone could be a victim of spousal abuse, and that these people are victims in that they could not reasonably have been expected to act in their own behalf. According to this view, the women who murdered were thoroughly brainwashed by their abusers and saw themselves as having no recourse but violence, and thus *de facto* had no recourse but violence against their abusers in their own defense.

Relation of V-3 to V-1 and V-2

That V-3, compared to V-2, is a more realistic and more humane descriptive/explanatory category is clear. Moreover, the critique of V-3 made here should not be taken as a justification for accepting any specific penalties as a consequence of actions taken by people against their victimizers. However, examination reveals a problem that must not be overlooked: V-3 is always in danger of collapsing into V-1 and, for this reason, is not adequate to the task of transcending V-2, the victim-blaming stance. That is, V-3 does not exonerate the victims.[9] The problem is that the move to V-3 does not recognize, and consequently cannot repudiate, the naive empiricism of V-1 that is also a dominant component of V-2.

Let us begin by reexamining V-1 to highlight its implicit naive empiricism. For purposes of illuminating the present context, naive empiricism designates an attitude that takes experienced events at face value, on the level of experiential immediacy. A person in this attitude does not ask questions regarding the experienced event, and believes her or himself to have a complete understanding of the event or, at least, an understanding adequate to the occasion of the event's causes, consequences, and meaning. In actuality, however, deployers of V-1 do not have any such understanding. For example, is it not evident to critical reflection that belief in the unavoidability of the human suffering wrought by V-1 type natural disasters is to a significant extent a function of the cost-benefit *modus operandi* of capitalism and consequent devaluation of human life? Is it not further evident to critical reflection that the public opinion subtext, according to which these traumas and consequent suffering are unavoidable and can happen to anyone, is a rationalization that stifles dissent and helps to sustain the priorities of the existing system? Is it surprising then that the system pours in massive amounts of aid to compensate the victims (often wealthy adventurers, as in, for example, boating or mountain-climbing accidents), whereas the system is constantly seeking to curtail programs for alleged V-2 type victims? A lengthy article in the *Chicago Tribune,* about the eruptive status of volcanoes, contained the following information:

> In the United States, the Cascades Range in Washington is under close monitoring because of the proximity of Seattle. Mt. Rainier is a particular concern because its top is covered with glaciers. An eruption would produce a *lahar,* an Indonesian word for a heavy mudslide caused by snow and ice that are melted in a volcanic eruption. . . . There are deposits of previous *lahars* around Mt. Rainier—deposits that can be found beneath the suburban developments that have sprung up in recent years. So far, according to Tilling, Rainier has stayed quiet.[10]

Real estate interests, like those building suburban developments over the Mt. Rainier *lahar* deposits, are not known for their concern for anything other than their bottom line. Moreover, the general attitude of those who buy such real estate seems to be, "If they're doing it, it must be OK." As we can see, both society's evaluation of the nature of the danger and society's response to V-1 disasters are significantly functions of the general interpretation of what the natural forces—and what people—are; and, as we know, in the present system, everything is evaluated in terms of exchange value, including, of course, the "value" of human life and misery.

The point is that naive empiricism, that is, the idea that nature is "out there," "objective," and perceived with a god's-eye purity just as it is, and that the massive suffering that results from earthquake, flood, tornado, and human failure is uncontrollable and non-preventable, occludes the fact that our range of options for dealing with these threats is, or can be, much broader than the cost-benefit analysis that capitalist economics allows for, and that much human suffering could be avoided if we lived in a society that put people before profits, that is, a humane society.

Another indication of the concealed, yet potent, ideological structure of V-1 is the way in which capitalism aims to cast many of its horrible creations into this category, for example, environmental pollution, as if they were "natural" disasters, which we cannot reasonably be expected to prevent or avoid. Another prevalent justification is that our "survival" requires that we allow industry to poison our air and water. Whatever is held to be "objective" within this attitude of naiveté is evaluated without any critique from the point of view of what ought to be and potentially could be. The deployers of V-1, in and through this attitude of consciousness, transmit capitalist ideology and create conditions that actually do threaten our survival.

The next point relevant to showing the metastable character of V-3, its perpetual danger of falling into V-1, is to show that V-2, which V-3 aims to transcend, does not depart from the naive empiricism of V-1.

What is the basis of the belief, in those who deploy V-2, that its members are to blame for their own suffering? First, those who deploy V-2 believe that people would not continue to live in those circumstances, for example, in a depressed black ghetto or with an abuser, unless they chose to do so, for whatever reason they so chose. According to those who deploy V-2, one is faced with a set of circumstances and one chooses either to accept or reject those circumstances. For example, residents of ghettos either choose to be gangbangers or they choose not to be gangbangers, and they then experience the consequences of their choices. Moreover, deployers of V-2 allege that the consequences of these choices are evident prior to the choosing. "Aren't the horrible consequences of becoming a gangbanger—prison, early death—obvious?" they ask.

Deployers of V-2 acknowledge that mental states are an intervening variable, or that the mental states of V-2s are a consequence, for example of having grown up in an environment of drugs and gangbanging. It is just these mental states that are among the factors leading to the alleged victim mentality. But V-2 deployers maintain that, despite mental states that are a consequence of the impact of the environment, people who have those mental states can, and some do, choose another way of life. This conception of the relation of subjects to their own mental states posits that, despite internalization of the trauma in the form of certain mental states, the victims' volition and judgment are unimpaired. This view is enabled by the notion that the events that led to those mental states, and the mental states themselves, afflict the individuals externally, or objectively, as if the subject, that is, the victim, and the object, that is, a trauma-like growing up in an impoverished gang and drug-infested neighborhood, and the consequent mental states, are radically split. Therefore, due to some isolated, unrelated intrinsic factor, V-2 victims are those ghetto residents who decide to fall in with environmental pressures rather than to resist them. The naiveté here, a consequence of viewing the traumatizing agent as radically external to the traumatized subject, lies in the consequent belief, a salient aspect of racism in the United States, that all residents of the ghetto have essentially the same experiences, and this includes experiences from earliest infancy and childhood: "Well, he grew up in the ghetto, but look at him, he's successful, etc. Why aren't you?" Thus, with or without the "help" offered by liberals, all those who lack whatever it is that leads them to succumb to defeat will rise out of poverty, and the others will remain in it, where they belong. Thus, the naive empiricism built into V-2 means that blame and self-blame are appropriate, because those individuals, for whatever reason, both internalized the traumatic events and allowed themselves to be dominated by them; i.e., they accepted a state of dependency. This view is naively empiricist too, in that it fails to move beyond what, to an ideologically constituted consciousness, appears to be the case to any consideration of what might actually be the case. In addition, the implied view of volition and judgment is equally abstract.

Now we can see that the naive empiricism of V-1 consists in the view that the object—a tornado or a volcanic eruption—is an event so radically external to its victims that blame (including victim self-blame) for loss of life and immense suffering is rendered unthinkable. Blame and self-blame are rendered unthinkable because of the understanding that the traumatic effect of tornadoes does not derive from a succumbing to internalized trauma inflicted by other persons, or trauma for which anyone is responsible. This mindset implies strongly that to experience or view oneself as a victim of an event that might be controllable by any individual person or the human race collectively is forbidden. It is forbidden because to be so victimized implies dependency, a degree of subjection to the control of other persons, and the internalized ideology of "individualism" and "self-sufficiency" will issue powerful sanctions, will produce intense feelings of shame and humiliation resulting in unbearably painful feelings of self-blame, if such dependency is believed to exist. One always has choices, after all, and one could have chosen to remain independent despite severe trauma inflicted by other persons; if one chooses to be dominated by internalized trauma, then one suffers from a primary deficiency that led to that choice.

However, since in actuality such dependency and interdependency do exist and are constitutive of our humanity, the most crippling effect of capitalist ideology is that it generates conscious and unconscious, chronic and crippling self-blame in those who are subjected to it. Thus, by imposing severe sanctions, including also ostracism, on the development of critical/speculative thought,[11] capitalist ideology forecloses the development of consciousness beyond the level of naive empiricism, of bland, unquestioning acceptance of what is. The result is a lifeworld dominated by a subject-object split or, more concretely, by a chronic depreciation of the value of the subject, the human being, in comparison with whatever is held to be objective. It is precisely from these consequences of ideology that Marx wished to free humanity.

We can now see that the V-3 concept is like the V-2 concept in that, just as deployers of V-2 acknowledge that trauma generates certain mental states in victims, deployers of V-3 acknowledge that the female victims of marital abuse have mental states that correspond to what their abusers want and what their abusers use against them. However, deployers of V-3 maintain that in effect, analogously with the V-1 concept, anyone would have reacted the way these victims did in that situation; anyone would have developed those mental states and cannot reasonably have been expected to react in any other way. Thus, V-3 differs from V-2 only in positing that victims had no choice. But, in neither case is any explanation proffered as to what led to the circumstance of either choice or no choice. No explanation is proffered, I submit, because deployers of both V-2 and V-3 accept events at face value, and simply incorporate their stance on choice in an *ad hoc* manner into their viewpoint on the events. That is, both V-3 and V-2 are locked in the naive empiricism of V-1.

Moreover, even if the deployers of V-3, of the notion that the victim is not to blame, acknowledge what is in fact the case, that a significant percentage of women sufferers of spousal abuse had been abused children, they do not thereby necessarily obviate the naive empiricism of V-1. This is because the link between abuse in childhood and abuse as an adult has not been fully clarified, and could be interpreted in an empiricist manner that feeds into conservative ideology suggesting deficiencies that are inherent and justify moral condemnation. How, one might ask, are we to explain the significant number of women who were abused as children and who do not experience abuse as adults, or who were not abused as children yet have experienced abuse as adults? As we have seen, the V-3 concept allows for the mental state of the victim—in other words, that these victims are victimized by the mental state that is their own mental state but which was nevertheless induced in them by the victimizer. Nevertheless, within the attitude of the deployers of V-3, the victimizers of V-3s are like natural disasters in that, it is believed, the victims cannot reasonably have been expected to have acted so as to avoid having become victims.

Thus, both V-3 and V-2 collapse back into V-1, the naive empiricist view with its essentially passive construction of the human subject. How can V-1, or the naive empiricism generated and sustained by capitalism and its ideology, be transcended? The V-3 concept cannot achieve this goal because it does not analyze why the same victims that are exonerated by V-3 are blamed by V-2; that is, it does not explain what enables deployers of V-2 to blame female victims of spousal abuse for their own predicament, nor does it have a coherent explanation of why such victims are to be exonerated. Indeed, those placed in V-2 by its deployers are notoriously subject to self-blame. But, most importantly, deployers of V-3 do not have a coherent account of why such victims ought not to be subject to self-blame. The only explanation proffered by deployers of V-3, as we have seen, is that these victims had no choice, and if they realize that they had no choice they would throw off self-blame. Yet, this claim that the victims had no choice not only can be called into question, but, as I will show, *must* be called into question if victims are ultimately to be exonerated. Moreover, V-3 does not provide any insight into the problem of reconstituting society so as to obviate victim-blaming.

V-4: Beyond Ideology

Let us begin by examining again the paradigmatic example of the female victim of spousal or "significant other" abuse in order to pose critically the key question. Usually, the abuser begins with a campaign to isolate the victim from acquaintances, friends, and family members. During the initial stages of this campaign, presumably, the victim is not yet thoroughly indoctrinated. How is it that she does not see and/or consciously experience (1) that the demands of the abuser are unreasonable and threatening to her, and (2) that she can opt out of the abusive relationship? Here, many psychosocial factors come into play: the socialization of females generates feelings of inferiority, low self-esteem, depression, and so forth. Now, in invoking these psycho-social factors, what in actuality are we saying? Are we not saying, to begin with, that in the context of, and under the duress produced by, these factors the victim herself gave her assent, i.e., that she *acted* in a manner that at the time appeared to her to be in her own best interest?[12] If this is denied, are we not dehumanizing the victim? One might argue that assent is given only by a person fully conscious of the potential consequences of, and alternatives to, their decision. But, why was she not so aware during the early stages of the relationship? To put the point another way, what is the impact of psychosocial factors in capitalist societies? Or, to raise the question more generally, what is the impact of capitalism on human psychosocial development?

   In response to these questions, and in view of the ground covered in this chapter, I submit the following: capitalism and its ideology occlude the understanding that human beings can experience or live their psychosocial development in a manner that *enhances,* rather than inhibits, their capacity to do what the abused women did not do—detect the potential for despotism and violence in the abuser at an early enough stage to prevent victimization. To say this is not to blame the victims, those who have not developed this ability, even though the victim-blaming standpoint of the deployers of V-2 also holds that the female victim of marital abuse should have been able to detect the potential for abuse, and the fact that she did not do so indicates that she is deficient and perhaps even desired the abuse. The approach I am suggesting to obviate victim blaming, contrary to the deployers of V-2 and V-3, is that indeed the abused woman potentially could have detected the abuse at an early stage; however, if she did not, this was due to failure to mature, that is, developmental arrest. How can this formulation avoid begging the question, and how can we understand the relevant factors so that we can grasp the sense in which victims are not blameworthy? To attain this, what is most important now is to attempt to conceptualize the relationship between capitalism and the developmental arrest that is the psychosocial state of the majority of people reared in capitalist societies.

The empiricism generated by capitalism and its ideology is naive and dangerous in occluding the understanding that, in the absence of viable norms of psychosocial health and maturity, human psychosocial development will fail to constitute health and maturity. The social norms promulgated in the United States today, norms of total self-sufficiency, for example, cannot be attacked or supported by claiming that they are simply relative to this culture, as, one might allege, are all norms relative to some culture. What is evident to critical reflection today is, rather, that the ideology of individualism and self-sufficiency (both of which normative standards are construed and deployed as abstract, atomistic notions) is profoundly and essentially victim blaming. This is so because these abstract normative standards are inherently anti-human, yet, since they are projected as norms, failure to attain them generates crippling self-blame in people who then view themselves as failures. Is it because we are self-sufficient individuals free of self-blame that the United States is now the Prozac (and Xanax) Nation? Is it because we are self-sufficient individuals that, in the wake of the campaign and election of Barack Obama as president of the United States, we are now experiencing the extraordinary and shocking depth and extent of the penetration of anti-black racism into our culture? Self-blame is a consequence of repressed or dissociated rage and it leads to victimization of others: they, not I, are to blame.

As mentioned above, the deployers of V-2 believe that all residents of deteriorated black ghettos, for example, have essentially the same experiences from birth to death. Moreover, since some in this group leave the ghetto and become highly successful, it is concluded that the traumas of life in such an environment do not impair will and judgment. As a matter of fact, it is entirely false that people in such environments have the same experiences. This is not evident, as it can and should be, to the deployers of V-2, because the very same factors that lead them to believe that people, including children, can experience severe trauma and yet be unimpaired in their volition or initiative and their judgment also render them profoundly resistant to experiencing empathy for human beings. The capacity to experience empathy requires a capacity to experience feelings of dependency and extreme vulnerability in oneself and others, and it is precisely this that capitalist ideology prohibits. Thus, capitalist ideology dehumanizes us by cutting us off from the springs of our humanity, our capacity to experience ourselves as beings-in-becoming, as beings who necessarily come to be in the context of an epigenetic process of psychophysical and psychosocial maturation that is either promoted or thwarted by internal and external factors.

The essential point here is to suggest that the goal of exonerating victims, a goal that motivates and underlies Marx's analysis of ideology, cannot be achieved in the absence of a framework acknowledging that there are norms of psychic health and maturity that transcend the patterns extant in societies like ours, societies that exist in the realm of necessity as contrasted with the realm of freedom; societies in which people work to live rather than live to work; societies in which hyper-pathological intolerance of dependency makes rewarding human relations impossible and generates anguish and raging conscious and unconscious resentment. Is it not clear that these factors have resulted in a pandemic of infanticide, homicide, suicide, psychotic depression, self-hatred, hatred of and violence toward blacks, toward workers, toward Asians, gays, women, and, indeed, have retroactively instantiated or revealed what was always already there: Hobbes' "war of every one against every one"?[13]

To return to the case of the abused woman, we need to understand, in the richest, most radical sense, the meaning of the statement that "she could have acted differently." I contend that it is true that she could have acted differently, and this truth flows from a telos or directedness toward certain norms of human psychosocial maturity. Moreover, unless this is the case, there is no possible way to transcend the victim-blaming attitude of V-2 and its inherent, naive, anti-human empiricism, and thus no way to move decisively and definitively beyond capitalist ideology. For this view, I claim transcultural validity, precisely on the ground that, as Sartre said, to be a human being is to be more than a rock or a stone. For the purpose of this chapter, I have simply dubbed this notion of victimization V-4: Beyond Ideology.

CONCLUSION

To present my point in reference to the question raised above, "What can radical philosophy do?" I posit the following: in order to move forward, radical philosophy needs to study the relationship between philosophy itself and developmental, psychodynamic psychology. This implies that thinkers on the left will have to put aside the hostility toward psychodynamic psychology that has imbued left theory and has prevented the development of a compelling synthesis between critical, left-social thought and practice and the understanding of human psychosocial development (though many have attempted to create such a synthesis).[14] A new attitude can be motivated by the insight which I have stated: psychosocial maturation of the person and the capacity of consciousness to progress dialectically beyond the level of sensuous immediacy (Hegel[15]), or "face value" experiencing, are inextricably linked. Moreover, it is just this decisive exoneration of victims, apprehended in and through the theory-practice unity, this freeing of victims from self-blame, that will release the energies and forces of revolution.

The following briefly discusses three recent and contemporary radical philosophers, and they are certainly not the only ones, *who* have said or implied much of what I have presented in this chapter.

1. Frantz Fanon

In Chapter Six of *Black Skin/White Masks,* Fanon raises this question: "Can the white man behave healthily toward the black man and can the black man behave healthily toward the white man?" Fanon then remarks: "A pseudo-problem, some will say." Fanon does not directly explain the motivation of those who will say that the question posed above is a pseudo-question. We can infer their motivation, however, in the light of Fanon's next statement: "But when we assert that European culture has an *imago* of the Negro which is responsible for all the conflicts that may arise, we do not go beyond reality."[16] Indeed, much of *Black Skin/White Masks* consists in Fanon's relentless expose of the existence and functioning of that imago. Thus, those who maintain that the problem of whether or not whites and blacks can behave healthily toward one another is a pseudo problem are just those who are unaware, due to repression, of the existence of this imago. They take imago for reality, and thus believe that it is unproblematic to assert without further ado that blacks and whites can behave healthily toward one another. This entire passage fits in with Fanon's avowed purpose: to disalienate the blacks by revealing to them the existence of this imago and their participation in sustaining it.

In this way, Fanon wanted to create the conditions for the emergence of a revolutionary consciousness in blacks. What is also evident is that Fanon understood revolutionary consciousness to be a commitment to a conception of what is psychic health and what is psychic illness. The validity of this perspective on Fanon is reinforced by his remarkable effort, in the concluding chapter, to encapsulate the meaning of all that he had already said. He does this by an exhortation to self-transformation through an accession of consciousness to psychic health. Echoing the quotation from Marx's *Eighteenth Brumaire* that he selected as a preface to the concluding chapter, Fanon construes psychic health as liberation from the dead weight of the degradations of the past:

I find myself suddenly in the world and I recognize that I have one right alone: That of demanding human behavior from the other. One duty alone: That of not renouncing my freedom through my choices. . . . I am not a prisoner of history. I should not seek there for the meaning of my destiny. . . . I am not the slave of the Slavery that dehumanized my ancestors. . . . I am my own foundation. . . .[17]

In this way, not only in *Black Skin/White Masks* but throughout his works, and through an existential psychoanalysis quite different from that discussed by Sartre, Fanon wanted to link a theory of the sociogenesis of black psychopathology with a psychoanalytic praxis that would engender disidentification with the aggressor, the victimizer, who, for Fanon, was himself a victim. An essential component of this process was a vision of how human beings would behave toward one another when human wholeness is achieved. Fanon implicitly addressed the question of what attitude is necessary in order to project the values of human inter-relatedness in the name of which the revolution will take place and which it will materially realize. Diana Fuss succinctly expresses Fanon's praxis of the inter-relationship of psychoanalysis and the political struggle for liberation in this way: "What Fanon gives us, in the end, is a politics that does not oppose the psychical but fundamentally presupposes it."[18]

2. Raya Dunayevskaya

When Raya Dunayevskaya, the founder of Marxist-Humanism, died in 1987, she left behind a large and rich legacy of published and unpublished writings that is still revealing her immense and unique contribution to radical thought.[19] Fortunately, her associates are continuing the essential task of making her writings available and developing her ideas in their own writings.[20]

In the discussion in the first part of this chapter, about the failure of theoreticians within the socialist movement to comprehend fully how ideology affects human subjects, I did not emphasize that theoreticians have also failed to emphasize another, related factor inherent in Marx's philosophy: the necessity to project a vision of what happens after the revolutionary transformation of society. The necessity for such a vision is at the core of Dunayevskaya's Marxist-Humanism.

The writings in which Dunayevskaya first conceptualized Marxist-Humanism were published as *The Philosophic Moment of Marxist-Humanism*. Included in this book are Dunayevskaya's 1987 revisiting, shortly before her death, of two early documents, dating from 1953, in which she expresses her initial insight into the real meaning of Marx's "new continent of thought." These documents are a profound and original reflection on the Hegelian roots of Marx's Marxism, in particular the meaning of the negation of the negation. In developing this meaning, Dunayevskaya quotes from Hegel's *Science of Logic* (my abridgement): "The second negative, the negative of the negative. . . . is no more the activity of an external reflection . . . it is the innermost and most objective moment of Life and Spirit, by virtue of which a subject is personal and free."

Dunayevskaya follows this with her own words: "Now stand up and shout personal and free, personal and free. . . ." The significance of this passage lies in this: that the reason for revolution is to bring to birth new human relations, and that to have a vision of a new society is precisely to have a vision of new human relations, that they shall be "personal and free."[21] Moreover, in her last works Dunayevskaya showed that unless this vision of new human relations is reflected through and through in those organizations that seek to bring about a new society, there will be, not progression, but inevitable retrogression, as the past history of such efforts shows.[22] My essential point here is that implicitly Dunayevskaya recognized that the norms of human psychosocial maturation, of what it is to be a person, are at the very least a significant aspect of the struggle for liberation.

3. Lewis R. Gordon

In his seminal book *Bad Faith and Antiblack Racism,* Lewis R. Gordon writes that "both Kant and Sartre are urging humanity to grow up. It is this aspect of Sartre's thought that locates him outside of what has come to be known as the 'postmodern' camp, although there are aspects of modernity that he rejects."[23] By suggesting that a vision of human maturity, and *ipso facto,* a vision of mature human relations, is just that which locates a philosopher outside of the postmodern camp, Gordon both indicts postmodernism as a retreat from the project of human emancipation and locates Sartre and himself within that project's tradition. In his next book, *Fanon and the Crisis of European Man,*[24] Gordon not only locates Fanon within the same perspective; in addition, as the title, reminiscent of Husserl's *The Crisis of European Science and Transcendental Phenomenology,*[25] indicates, he places Fanon and himself in the anti-relativist, global philosophical "camp." Indeed, in his Fanon book, Gordon establishes Husserlian phenomenology (which he insists is a necessary component for understanding Fanon's thought) as the philosophical framework for achieving insight into the nature of human, and human philosophical, maturity. This framework consists in grasping the existence of essences that are at once both open and not subject to a relativizing, naturalistic reduction. Gordon sees, correctly I believe, that Husserlian phenomenology is a philosophical framework which both encompasses the existential moment of human reality and allows for those creative ambiguities that are the constitutive ground for the maturation of humanity and of human societies.

NOTES

1. Karl Marx and Frederick Engels, "The Communist Manifesto," in: *Marx and Engels: Basic Writings on Politics and Philosophy,* ed. Lewis S. Feuer (New York: Doubleday, 1959), 37–41.

2. The category of post-Marx Marxism *as a pejorative* is one of the most original and important of the theoretical innovations of Raya Dunayevskaya. See her *Rosa Luxemburg, Women's Liberation and Marx's Philosophy of Revolution*, 2nd edition, with a Foreword by Adrienne Rich (Urbana: University of Illinois Press, 1991), 175–97.

3. For a recent interpretation of Lenin as a post-Marx Marxist, see Kevin Anderson, *Lenin, Hegel, and Western Marxism: A Critical Study* (Urbana: University of Illinois Press, 1995).

4. For a thorough analysis of the war in Bosnia from this point of view see *Bosnia-Herzegovina: Achilles Heel of Western "Civilization"* (Chicago: News and Letters, 1996).

5. Jean-Paul Sartre, *Being and Nothingness*, trans. by Hazel E. Barnes (London: Routledge, 1969), 50.

6. William Ryan, *Blaming the Victim*, rev. edition (New York: Random House, 1976).

7. Ryan, *Blaming*, 29–30; 119–20.

8. Ryan, *Blaming*, 1–30.

9. An interesting recent work which at least suggests that efforts to counteract victim blaming are inadequate is Sharon Lamb, *The Trouble with Blame: Victims, Perpetrators, and Responsibility* (Cambridge, MA: Harvard University Press, 1996).

10. *Chicago Tribune* (July 17, 1977), 2.

11. "Speculative propositions . . . are Hegel's attempt to unify theory and practice, and not the clumsy attempt to justify the political status quo that . . . critics have been pleased to see in it. All too often the speculative proposition that the rational is the real has been read as if it equated the natural law of reason with the existing positive law of the state. In fact the proposition summarizes Hegel's critique of Kant's abstract natural law . . . rational means *both* 'intelligible' and 'as it ought to be' for Hegel." Jon Stewart, *The Hegel Myths and Legends* (Evanston, IL: Northwestern University Press, 1996), 23.

12. Here the issue of what is a victim joins the issue of whether or not *akrasia*, or weakness of will, is possible. Space limitation prohibits discussion of the issue in this paper. However, for a defense of the impossibility of weakness of will, a stance implicit in the argument of this paper, see Chapter 4, this volume.

13. Thomas Hobbes, *Leviathan* (New York: Collier Books, 1962), 100.

14. For a history of such efforts, as well as a recent, highly interesting attempt to synthesize Marxism and psychoanalysis, see V. E. Wolfenstein, *The Victims of Democracy: Malcolm X and the Black Revolution* (London: Free Associations, 1990), and *Psychoanalytic Marxism: Groundwork* (New York: Guilford, 1993). See also chapter 6, this volume.

15. Recent interpretations of Fanon have shown that rather than locating white-black relations at the level of Hegel's master-slave dialectic, the colonial order constituted the black at the prior level of sensuous immediacy. See Lou Turner, "On the Difference between the Hegelian and Fanonian Dialectic of Lordship and Bondage," in *Fanon: A Critical Reader*, ed. Lewis R. Gordon et al. (Oxford: Blackwell, 1996), 134–51.

16. Frantz Fanon, *Black Skin, White Masks,* trans. Charles Lam Markmann (New York: Grove, 1967), 169.

17. Fanon, *Black Skin ,*229–231.

18. Diana Fuss, *Identification Papers* (New York: Routledge, 1995), 165.

19. For a concise summary of her intellectual history and body of ideas (along with a collection of some of her most important writings), see Peter Hudis' introduction to Raya Dunayevskaya, *The Marxist-Humanist Theory of State Capitalism: Selected Writings* (Chicago: News and Letters, 1992), vii–xxvi.

20. Dunayevskaya wrote four books, all of which have recently been reissued by Columbia University Press *(Marxism and Freedom,* 1988; *Philosophy and Revolution,* 1989); the University of Illinois Press *(Rosa Luxemburg, Women's Liberation, and Marx's Philosophy of Revolution,* 1991), and Wayne State University Press *(Women's Liberation and the Dialectics of Revolution,* 1996). For recent works by her associates, Kevin Anderson and Peter Hudis, see notes 3 and 17 above.

21. Raya Dunayevskaya, *The Philosophical Moment of Marxist-Humanism* (Chicago: News and Letters, 1989), 33.

22. For a discussion of the relation between radical philosophy and organization in the thought of Dunayevskaya, and its relevance to women's liberation, see, e.g., Olga Domanski, "Two Contributions by Olga Domanski," in *Woman's Liberation and the Dialectics of Revolution,* ed. Raya Dunayevskaya (Detroit, MI: Wayne State University Press), 91–109.

23. Lewis R. Gordon, *Bad Faith and Antiblack Racism* (Atlantic Highlands, NJ: Humanities Press, 1995), 86.

24. Lewis R. Gordon, *Fanon and the Crisis of European Man: An Essay on Philosophy and the Human Sciences* (New York and London: Routledge, 1995).

25. Edmund Husserl, *The Crisis of European Sciences and Transcendental Phenomenology,* trans. with an introduction by David Carr (Evanston, IL: Northwestern University Press, 1970).

Chapter Two

Freud, Gender, and the Epigenesis of Morality: A Critique

INTRODUCTION

The dilemma presented by Freud. . . might be a useful basis for asking further questions, within the context of feminist social theory, about how gender works in our moral economy and about how gender and uses of God are thereby intertwined.

In this chapter, I will take up one of the suggestions in the epigraph above and discuss "how gender works in our moral economy." The epigraph is taken from the last paragraph of Judith Van Herik's fine book, *Freud on Femininity and Faith.*[1] In her book, Van Herik showed that liberation of psychoanalysis from the prejudices against women and religion built into it by Freud requires exploration of the ways in which these prejudices are interrelated, imbricated one with the other, in psychoanalytic theory.[2] Van Herik's disciplinary sources—religious studies, psychology of religion, and women's studies, are evident in her book: she is interested in the development of a feminist psychology of religion, and of Christianity in particular. The focus here is different: it is, rather, on certain conceptual problems in Freud's schema of moral development, and how these problems are related to Freud's denial of the transcendental dimension of human existence. The disciplinary source for these concerns is philosophy, especially transcendental phenomenology as developed by Edmund Husserl.[3] The purpose of this essay is to provide another way of thinking about the genesis of moral development, one that is not compromised by the contradictory claims which inhere, as will be shown, in Freud's schema.

There is, of course, overlap between concern with the transcendental dimension—the dimension of the *a priori* conditions for the possibility of any knowledge,[4] and religious concern with the notion of God as creator of all things. One way to characterize the overlap is to point out that both God and the *a priori* are posited as atemporal, necessary origins of all things. Historically, however, there has been tension between these concerns, particularly regarding faith, and, this tension has characterized the histories of philosophy and religious thought. Both disciplines, like science itself, are invested in justifying their own claims to be sources of knowledge in one form or another: as the evidence of faith or revelation, of *a priori* truth, or of fact and law. These types of knowledge claims are not prima facie compatible or incompatible with one another. However, as a minimal characterization of the tension between religion and philosophy, one can say that while the philosophical notion of the transcendental is not antithetical to faith, it is not grounded, as is religious thought, in the presupposition of the existence of the divine. This presupposition is a given in Van Herik's critique of Freud's schema of the epigenesis of morality and its relation to religion, but not in the philosophical approach elaborated here.

Van Herik points out that Freud believed that morality must be undergirded by what he took to be the scientific worldview, which itself was undergirded by his asymmetric theory of gender.[5] For Van Herik, it is the asymmetric character of Freud's notion of gender, his privileging of the male, which determines his negative view of religion, and her masterful exposition shows this to be the case.[6] Consistent with her aims, Van Herik does not discuss the epigenesis of morality—which for Freud also depended on his asymmetric notion of gender—independent of religion, of relation to the divine. This is shown in the quotation above in which she says that asking about the working of gender in our moral economy "*thereby*" will show the intertwinement of gender and the "uses of God." In this chapter, I will show that when the epigenesis of morality is considered independent of religion, its dependence on the transcendental dimension of human existence is given evidentially.

In order to bring out the relevance of the transcendental dimension, I will show that Freud's rendition of the epigenesis of morality in the psyche is flawed by contradictory claims, and that the conceptual slippage that generated the contradictions necessitates an understanding radically different than Freud's of the epigenesis of the human capacity to make ethical and moral judgments. I will argue that the contradictory claims that obtain in Freud's schema of moral development serve to justify his misogyny. Put another way, the problem is not only that Freud's asymmetric view of gender led to his theory of the origin of morality; most important, the latter is for Freud a rationale for the former: his views on morality provide a rationale for his asymmetric theory of gender. I will further show that the internal contradictions in Freud's theory of morality reveal that his and psychoanalysis's divisive prejudices are not only confined to religion, as shown by Van Herik; additionally, Freud had an irrational, unfounded aversion to *any* non-materialist, non-reductionist philosophical perspective. Hence, it was not only religion that Freud railed against; in addition, he reacted negatively to any hint of the transcendental character of human being-in-becoming. In the conclusion, I will also discuss the implications of Freud's aversion to the transcendental for his concept of the unconscious.

As just noted, there is considerable overlap of Van Herik's concerns and those of this chapter, not only in regard to the overlap between philosophy and certain religious ideas, but also in regard to our feminist concerns. In what follows, first I will present a summary exegesis of Van Herik's analysis of the way in which Freud's notion of gender is deeply intertwined with his notion of religion. Second, I will develop a critique of Freud's notion of the epigenesis of morality, extending the scope of Van Herik's critical principle—Freud's belief in gender asymmetry, to his view of moral development independent of his views on religion. However, before beginning it is necessary to explicate a specific presupposition which Van Herik makes in reliance upon Juliet Mitchell's classic book, *Psychoanalysis and Feminism: Freud, Reich, Laing and Women.*[7]

Mitchell's justly famous book is a critique of those who, in their effort to repudiate Freud's misogyny, did so at the cost of transmogrifying or rejecting his notion of the unconscious. In this group Mitchell includes not only Wilhelm Reich and R. D. Laing, but also feminist theorists de Beauvoir, Greer, Millet, and others. Mitchell is a feminist and social theorist whose concern is social change, and who maintains that Freud's conception of the unconscious must be a component of any theory of social change because it provides what no other concept has provided or can provide—an explanation of the powerful resistance to change of ideological structures like misogyny. She shows that ideological structures resist change and extinction precisely because they are dynamically inscribed in the unconscious. Mitchell responds to those who dismiss Freud's prejudices as merely reflective of his culture by pointing out that Freud not only reflected and described accurately the prejudices of his day; in addition, he explained scientifically through exactly what psychodynamic structures and processes the personality types he described ("feminine" females and males, and "masculine" males) come into existence in the course of psychosexual development, that is, their epigenesis. For Mitchell, those personality types actually exist exactly as described by Freud. She concludes that social change vis-à-vis women can come about only through change in the content of the unconscious, of what culture demands that we repress, and this would involve a revolutionary transformation of those socialization practices which now, all too successfully, inscribe patriarchy in the unconscious of both men and women. However, neither Mitchell nor Van Herik do what I aim to do in this chapter: problematize Freud's conception of the relation between the unconscious and consciousness (as he himself did—see 41n33). Van Herik agrees with Mitchell's evaluation of the descriptive and explanatory validity of Freud's theory of gender. Moreover, as noted above, Van Herik implicitly shares with Mitchell's emphasis on retaining from Freud the postulate of the dynamic unconscious. At least, nowhere in her book does she raise any question regarding the strictly Freudian notion of the unconscious. Mitchell, however, did not focus on Freud's theory of religion, whereas, Van Herik's aim is to show that it is deeply undergirded by his asymmetric theory of gender. Through a meticulous analysis of his most relevant texts, Van Herik shows that Freud's theory of religion is a special case of his asymmetric theory of gender. However, she did not follow Mitchell's method entirely; if she had, this would have led her to discuss whether or not Freud's conception of religion accurately describes certain types of religious beliefs which may be associated with certain actually existing personality types. Certainly, Van Herik does not mean to suggest, turning the tables on Freud, either that all misogynists are, like Freud, atheists or irreligious, or that all religious are feminists. What she does show is that Freud's inability to conceive religion as other than a symptom of neurosis, that is, of a "father complex," was a function of his asymmetric theory of gender. Thus, Van Herik's book, like Mitchell's, is a critique of patriarchy, whether it is a function of individual psychic development, or is inscribed in society, or both, though Van Herik places much less emphasis than Mitchell on social ideology. Using Freud as her case study, Van Herik also implies a point of far reaching significance: that a consideration of the role of concepts of gender is essential to the psychology of religion and to religious studies in general.

Though Van Herik's book was originally published in 1982, she did not discuss any of the numerous critiques of Freud which were made by feminist scholars since the publication of Mitchell's book in 1974. Such discussions were not directly relevant because Van Herik's central theme was to show, through an exegesis of Freud's texts, the dependence of his theory of religion on his asymmetric theory of gender. Though Van Herik accepts Mitchell's critique of those feminist critics of Freud who either diluted or rejected his concept of the unconscious, it does not follow that either she or Mitchell would reject subsequent feminist critiques of Freud. However, in this chapter I will follow Van Herik in not alluding to extensive recent reevaluations of Freud from a feminist perspective, and I do so because, like her, in this chapter I am interested in the internal structure of Freud's theories.

However, one aspect of the contemporary feminist critique of Freud is directly relevant to the second part in which I challenge Freud's theory of the epigenesis of morality and the extraordinary degree to which he under-emphasized the role of the mother in the development of children. As one group of researchers wrote, referring to Freud: "But is it not more useful to see this blindness in so astute an analyst as the manifestation in him of a perversion—the repression of the mother—which lies at the root of Western civilization itself?"[8]

VAN HERIK'S ANALYSIS OF
FREUD ON FEMININITY AND FAITH

Van Herik's analysis of the interrelatedness of gender and religion in Freud's thought turns upon his asymmetric valorizations of two homologous dyads, with the more highly valued term placed first: masculinity/femininity and renunciation/fulfillment. The essential finding of her book is that Freud's theory of psychosexual development and his theory of religion are based upon, and inseparable from, his strong association of masculinity with renunciation and the scientific world view on one hand, and his association of femininity with fulfillment and religion on the other hand.[9]

Masculinity and the Superego

(This section is a summary and synthesis especially, but not exclusively, of relevant material from chapters 4–6, pages 55–104, of Van Herik, *Freud.)*

The superego, often referred to as the 'conscience,' develops, according to Freud, with respect to the relationship of individuals to their fathers. While all people love and identify with their mothers initially, their deepest wish, Freud thought, is for their father's love. The reason for this given by Freud is that the father, as the stronger, is the protector, and thus the authority figure, that is, the patriarch. In the oedipal situation, however, males develop ambivalence toward their fathers: they love them as protectors and hate them as rivals for their mother's love. According to Freud, in their struggle to undo this ambivalence and resolve the oedipal conflict, males go through a stage in which they develop a passive attitude toward their fathers: they attempt to win their father's love by being pleasing and non-competitive. Because Freud, who claimed that all people are originally bisexual, equated passivity with femininity (because of what he took to be women's passive role in intercourse), he referred to this stage in male psychosexual development as the feminine stage. (The term 'feminine' in this context does not suggest homosexuality because this stage occurs in all males and does not necessarily lead to development of a male erotic object choice.) However, the feminine stage provides only a temporary solution to the oedipal conflict because the father does not respond to the boy's solicitations and the boy still wishes for instinctual gratification of his love for his mother; the boy still experiences his father as a threatening rival and still wishes to eliminate him in order to have the mother to himself. At this point, the boy is threatened with both the father's retaliation in the form of castration and the dreaded loss of his father's love. In the course of further development, 'normal' males resolve their oedipal conflicts and ambivalences towards their fathers by thinking, in effect, "If I can't beat him, I'll join him." That is, they give up their desire to replace their fathers in their mothers' affection, and decide to grow up and be men, husbands, and fathers themselves.

What is of great moment in this developmental path is that resolution of the Oedipus complex involves a tremendous struggle: to achieve it, the male must effect a great renunciation—he must repress his desire, his libidinous wish, to love and be loved by his mother, a relationship that goes back to earliest infancy and which represents direct, immediate fulfillment of wishes, that is, instinctual gratification. Repression of this wish and the associated wish to eliminate the father diminishes the threat of castration. What enables the male to effect this renunciation is his maleness, that is, his ability, as a male, to iden-tify with his father and, through this identification, internalize the norms of so-ciety, especially the incest taboo. This internalization is the institution within the psyche of the superego. Thus, in Freud's conceptual vocabulary, a strong superego means maturity in the sense of the capacity to delay, and ultimately even to renounce, gratification of powerful erotic and aggressive drives.

However, as Van Herik shows, for Freud even the development of a strong superego does not enable males to attain the highest level of maturity. This is so because the institution of the superego takes place on the basis of a struggle that is fraught with great dangers, and which is ultimately repressed, that is, it becomes entirely unconscious (for Freud, portions of all three psy-chic agencies in his final, structural model of the psyche, the ego, id [drives], and superego, are unconscious). Due to repression of the oedipal struggle, ambivalence toward the father is never eliminated; rather, it lives on in the unconscious. As long as it does so, it continues to press toward reemergence into consciousness. Preventing reemergence of the oedipal conflict, which is associated with intense anxiety (fear of retaliation and loss of the father's love to compensate for unconscious rivalry), requires constant vigilance on the part of the ego and therefore drains off valuable ego energies. Moreover, because the conflict is repressed but not resolved, the need to seek the father's love long after the boy has become a man and a father himself continues.

The highest stage of maturity is reached when the individual is able to be-come consciously aware of his own past conflicts, his attempted resolutions, and his deep desire for his father's love associated with these. As a result of this lifting of repression, he realizes that maintaining this desire keeps him in a position of psychic dependency, and thus, instead of re-repressing it, he *consciously suppresses it.* For Freud, males who achieve this level of maturity and psychic independence no longer project their unconscious wishes onto the external world; that is, they are no longer afflicted with illusions based on the hope that their archaic desires, especially desire for their fathers' love, will be gratified. Having achieved the capacity for conscious renunciation, having tempered the pleasure principle with the reality principle, they are relatively free from the need to distort reality, and are thus preeminently suited to be scientists. For Freud, then, masculinity was powerfully associated with renunciation. With what did Freud associate femininity?

Femininity

(This section is a summary and synthesis, especially, but not exclusively, of relevant material from chapters 7–8 in Van Herik, *Freud,* pp. 107–139. Freud synthesized and summarized his views on female development in his essay, "Femininity."[10])

Freud associated femininity with fulfillment, with the wish for instinctual gratification that is the opposite of renunciation. The reason for this, according to Freud, is that women are incapable of renunciation because they do not develop strong superegos. Thus, they can achieve neither the unconscious renunciation involved in the acquisition of the superego, nor the conscious renunciation of the need for the father's love which was, for Freud, the highest stage of maturity. This inability on the part of females is explained by Van Herik as follows:

> The boy realizes that only the father can possess the mother, but the girl realizes that she, being like the mother, cannot possess her but rather must be possessed, in the passive mode, as she perceives her mother is. At this stage, the mother represents the girl's own limitation rather than her rival. The masculine attitude toward the mother, which prior to paternal intervention was held by both boy and girl, is submitted to the incest taboo in the case of a boy. In the case of a girl, it becomes psychologically impossible.[11]

Girls, then, do not develop strong superegos because they are never subjected to the pressure of the incest taboo, which is socially and psychically reproduced through the implicit threat of castration made by the strong father, the patriarch, to his son. This threat the father cannot make to the daughter because she perceives herself as like her mother, that is, already castrated.

Girls perceive themselves as already castrated when they learn the anatomical difference between the sexes because, according to Freud (and this is a point hotly disputed by feminists), all children believe that everyone originally has a penis. When, then, the daughter identifies with her mother as another castrated being, and consequently turns her libidinous drives toward her father, she establishes the psychic position in which she will remain for the remainder of her life: *she will seek to defer to him and to please him in order not to be abandoned by him.*[12] When she realizes that she cannot successfully compete with her mother for his love, she will seek another man to replace him. Since such "feminine" women do not need to identify with the father and internalize his authority in order to cope with ambivalent feelings toward him, they do not develop strong superegos and are not capable of instinctual renunciation.

The crux of the matter here is that Freud sees superego formation as entirely contingent upon the strong father as representative of society's norms, in particular the incest taboo, which originally ensured survival of the human species. Since, in the course of normal development, girls do not identify with the father,[13] they cannot develop strong superegos and cannot abandon their need for his love. In Freud's mind this meant that they seek immediate gratification, that is, fulfillment of wishes and, relative to "masculine" males, are not autonomous beings because they cannot temper the pleasure principle with the reality principle. The fact that women cannot renounce their wish for their fathers' love means that they will be unable to view reality objectively, that is, independent of their need for fulfillment of this wish; thus, it is impossible for them to adopt the scientific attitude toward the world. Since then the contribution of males to the survival of the species is far greater than that of females, who merely mother their sons in early infancy, males were more highly valued by Freud.

In the remaining chapters of *Freud on Femininity and Faith,* through an analysis of Freud's major texts devoted to religion, *The Future of an Illusion* and *Moses and Monotheism,* Van Herik shows unequivocally that Freud's conviction that religious belief is an illusion entailed that believing males are fixated at the "feminine" stage of psychosexual development:

> Just as his theory of gender carries on an implicit critique of the feminine attitude (at the same time as femininity is considered normal for women in a patriarchal context), his indictment of standard Viennese Christian belief is based on the critical principle that renunciation of illusion means developing beyond attachment to the caring father. The psychical qualities of the Christian believer and the feminine man or woman are the same: a weak superego, a poorly developed sense of morality, a restricted intellect, opposition to cultural advance, insufficient respect for reality, *Ananke* [Necessity], *Logos* [Reason].[14]

For Freud, then, the idea of God was unequivocally the idea of the patriarchal father. (Obviously, there is some rhetorical support for this view in religious literature.) Thus, as a projection of a father complex, religious belief, that is, belief in God, is critically evaluated by Freud on the basis of what Van Herik refers to as Freud's fundamental "critical principle": his asymmetrical theory of gender; that is, "masculine" males would not believe in God. It is interesting to note in this regard that, as Freud recounts in the opening paragraphs of *Civilization and Its Discontents,* when Romain Rolland suggested to Freud that perhaps religious feeling was more akin to the "oceanic feeling," that is, to the desire to merge with the universe, Freud dismissed this suggestion out of hand, insisting that only a father complex can explain theism.[15]

Freud's claim that the religious suffer from weak superegos is particularly odd in the light of the fact that, certainly in the Judeo-Christian tradition, religion is inconceivable without the moral and ethical concerns and principles which it encompasses. Rather than the strong negative association between them laid out by Freud, in this tradition there is a strong positive association between morality and religion. The claim of a weak superego in religious men reflects Freud's view of their immaturity, that is, their continued dependence on the father, rather than authentic concern for right action and avoidance of evil. For Freud, such concern is not possible in insufficiently developed men (who are in this respect like women), men with unresolved oedipal complexes. Religious morality, then, is an inauthentic substitute for Freudian "morality."

CRITIQUE OF FREUD ON THE EPIGENESIS OF MORALITY

Following Mitchell, Van Herik rejects the idea that Freud's version of psychoanalysis is a form of biologism.[16] I find her discussion of this point to be unconvincing. A reading of Freud's texts in the light of the pervasive influence of social Darwinism on his thinking, including survival of the fittest through natural selection, makes it clear that Freud viewed the instinct for survival of the human species as the origin of all values, including moral values.[17] Given this, what, we may ask, has ensured the survival of the human species thus far, and what will secure its survival in the future?[18] Freud's response to these questions was that the development in human beings of an intrapsychic agency which he called the "superego" ensured the survival of the species in the past, and, related to this, the continued emergence of scientists and development of science will secure it in the future. The main point regarding the issues at stake here is that in Freud's view two types of persons, along with concomitant social formulations, tend to thwart the development of science and are actually antithetical to the further development of civilization, and thus to the survival of the species: these types are women and the religious, with their respective social institutions.

It is important, then, to ask what are those social practices that ensure the survival of patriarchy. As we have seen, according to Freud, patriarchy reflects the fact that a child's greatest need is for the love of the father and this because the father, being stronger, is the protector of the family. Patriarchy, then, is a matter of maintaining the image of the father as strong. Strength is physical in nature and, theoretically, the male can physically overcome the females and children. In fact, Freud believed that only civilization, that is, the incest taboo, prevented all males from fulfilling their wish to violently seize females.[19] The institution of the incest taboo had the result that fathers no longer need to back up their authority with physical force, for the sons have internalized the fathers' authority, and have begun the process that led to the development of the superego. The authority of the father no longer rests directly or entirely upon his greater physical strength. With respect to child development, the authority of the father in a "civilized" society depends to a significant degree *on the willingness of the mother, the mother of his children, to defer to the father as the authority.*

Here, an insistent question emerges: precisely why, we may ask, does Freud think that women should accept their "femininity" and defer to their husbands, that is, their father substitutes, as to authorities? In Freud's attempts to answer this question, an unresolved ambiguity in his thought comes to the fore. When Freud claimed that men have stronger superegos than women, he also claimed that, in consequence of this, men have a stronger *sense of justice* than women, indeed that, "women have little sense of justice."[20] However, consistent with Freud's theory of psychosexual development and of the origin of morality, children, prior to the development of their own superegos and the final consolidation of them subsequent to puberty, know nothing of justice. What then is the meaning of patriarchy? *Is the father the authority because he is right, that is, just, or is he to be viewed by women and children as right, that is, just, because he is the authority?*

Certainly, for Freud, the father is the authority because he, having the stronger superego, and thus the stronger sense of justice, is right. What then did moral rectitude mean to Freud? There is no doubt that Freud subscribed to the great liberal, bourgeois values of freedom, justice, and "brotherhood"; on the other hand, his encompassing stance is that human unhappiness cannot be eliminated and that the survival of the human species is the highest value. If, then, patriarchy in the form of the authoritative father is, as Freud clearly thought, necessary for the survival of the human race, then it would seem that ultimately the father is right because he is the authority, that is, *because it is paternal authority itself which is what is right.* Thus, the child and the mother, having weaker superegos, or none, and a lesser sense of justice, or none, must accept the father/husband as right because he is the authority, and it is *precisely the mother's deference*[21] *toward him in and through which his position as authority is established.* The mother's deference to the father has a powerful impact on the child because the intense bond between mother and child has as one of its components great awe and high esteem for the mother on the part of the child. It is this deeply loved and highly esteemed being whom the child experiences as deferring to his father, rather than as behaving toward him as to an equal.

Since according to Freud morality does not pre-exist, but is rather *a consequence* of superego development, children cannot become moral beings until they develop the superego. Therefore, in performing any actions or making any statements which undermine the authority of the father, Freud's views entail that the mother is acting against the ability of the children to become moral beings. The next question, and the crux of my concerns here is this: *what should the mother do if she disagrees with the father regarding his behavior toward their children?* It is clear that the implication of Freud's views is that, since the children are not yet moral beings, the *nature and content of their father's actions is of less significance than the unimpeded manifestation of his authority.*

Here it is necessary to ask what the mother should do if her disagreement with her husband turns upon a moral issue. For example, suppose that the mother believes that the father's behavior towards his son is characterized by prejudgment, that this is painful and harmful to her son, and that her husband persistently disagrees with her and continues his prejudgmental behavior. Should the mother not only defend her son, but, as an equal, do so in her son's presence at the very moment the father's action occurs, by indicating her disagreement with his father to him? Can we take seriously the conclusion which Freud's views force upon us: that in the absence of a superego the boy will not suffer from the father's prejudgment and experience it as unfair, that is, unjust? Can we take seriously the claim implicit in Freud's views: that a "feminine" woman, lacking a strong superego, is thereby incapable of recognizing the injustice of such actions? Since physical survival was Freud's highest value, to which all other values must be subordinated, can we suggest that his views entail that women and children must be *indoctrinated* into patriarchy "for their own good," that is, for the good of the species?

Moreover, do not Freud's views suggest that it is precisely with respect to situations which evoke moral disagreement that the mother ought to defer to the father because it is precisely in overriding other ethical stances that the patriarch (like Creon in Sophocles' *Antigone)* can consolidate his authority? Furthermore, if this is the case, does not the consolidation of paternal authority require that the child already have a sense of justice? Is it not only then that the child can grasp that authority is strongest: precisely, as advocated by the sophist Thrasymachus in Book I of Plato's *Republic*, when it overwhelms justice?

To make my point most explicit, it seems that Freud's theories entail that in order for human beings to develop a moral sense they must experience both their mothers' insignificance and acts of injustice committed by their fathers. To the extent that children are defended by their mothers, to that extent it would seem, their morality is subverted. Is this not the "repression of the mother . . . at the root of Western civilization itself"? Thus, morality for Freud is derived primarily from the repression (oppression) of the mother, and the children, not from internalization of the strong superego of the father; that is, it is *intersubjective*, i.e., relational, not exclusively intrapsychic in origin. And, most importantly, does not the foregoing seem to suggest that Freud's patriarchal standpoint and its contradictions presuppose, in sharp contrast to his explicit theory of the origin of conscience, that *morality has another ground, a constitutive source other than patriarchy?* That is, Freud's schema of the epigenesis of morality presupposes what it claims to explain, and this suggests that the sense of justice cannot be explained by a reductive account of human development grounded in survivalism. Rather, it seems that the conscience and its origin must have a transcendental source as an aspect of the conditions for the possibility of being human. That is, conscience can be neither biologically generated nor materially determined.

As we have seen, both Juliet Mitchell and Judith Van Herik believe that Freud's theory of the epigenesis of gender identity explains the etiology of "feminine" males and females. Van Herik shows that Freud's theory of religion was a product of his theory of gender identity: belief in God is an illusion generated in "feminine" men and women by a father complex; that is, a distortion of the external world in an effort to gratify need for the father's love.

In posing an alternative to Freud's view of the epigenesis of morality, it is necessary to evaluate Freud's notion of repression, which is shared by both Mitchell and Van Herik. They accept Freud's conception of the dynamic, repressed unconscious as the other scene wherein the drama of patriarchy is inscribed and reinscribed.[22]

AN ALTERNATE VIEW: PHENOMENOLOGY

In this essay, taking as my point of departure a suggestion made by Judith Van Herik in the concluding paragraph of her book, I have attempted to begin the task of moving beyond both Van Herik and Mitchell by relating Freud's misogynist and reductionist dogmas to his schema of moral development and the survivalist stance upon which he based it. On this account, Freud's prejudices originate in his moral economy: his remarkable attempt to prove conclusively that morality is a consequence of superego development in order to preclude absolutely any other conception of the origin of morality, including all philosophical and/or religious conceptions. In this context, we see that Freud's scientistic, anti-philosophical, anti-religious stance, his Hobbesian conception of 'uncivilized' humanity (males) engaged in a war of all against all (in Freud, the primal horde—borrowed from Darwin—prior to the incest taboo) motivated him to invest his theory of moral development through psychosexual development with misogyny. However, Freud did not devalue only women; rather, he devalued all of humanity, males and females alike.

Thus, for Freud, morality was neither an *a priori* principle, as philosophers and theologians might hold, nor a concomitant of psychosexual development, as some contemporary psychoanalytically oriented researchers maintain,[23] nor a concomitant of cognitive development as the Platonist Piagetian Lawrence Kohlberg maintains; rather, for Freud morality is a *consequence,* a product, a result, of optimum psychosexual development. That is, morality is a product of the genesis of masculinity. Needless to say, for Freud, few people achieve this optimum psychosexual development.

As we have seen, Freud's theory of the genesis of morality in human beings is illogical and self-contradictory in that it presupposes that which it claims to explain—morality, the sense of justice. Moreover, Freud's view presupposes that survival is the highest value, but neither Freud nor Darwin provide a philosophical rationale for this presupposition, but rather justify it on the basis of an empiricist epistemology.[24] And, as will be discussed below, one of the claims of this chapter is that an empiricist epistemology, in order to be evidential in the fullest sense, in order to fulfill its potential, must be encompassed by the more radical empiricism of transcendental phenomenology. Finally, Freud's theory of the epigenesis of morality reflects, and, by situating it within a system, intensifies, the repression of the mother. This repression of the mother deforms the epigenesis of the human psyche because it does violence to the attachment from which flows the psychological birth of the child.

Finally, we can ask the following question: if, through an analysis carried out on the constitutive field, the very birth scene of psychoanalysis, that is, the scene of the Oedipus complex and castration anxiety, a question is raised as to the capacity of the psychoanalytic theory of psychosexual development to account adequately for the epigenesis of morality in human life, is the psychoanalytic concept of the repressed unconscious, in its relation to consciousness, called into question? After all, if morality is not a consequence of superego development, that is, of the resolution of the oedipal struggle, then repression (of that struggle) cannot play the ultimately determining role in human life attributed to it by Freud, for whom the unconscious was the true, and only, psychic reality. However, in Freud's schema, it was the original struggle of the primal brothers with their father for possession of women that began the process of formation of the unconscious as the repository of repressed ideas. Freud's notion was that that scene, the scene which led to the incest taboo, repeated over and over again through the millennia generated the culture that demands repression of the oedipal struggle, demands that the unconscious contain not only the instinctual representations of the drives, libido and aggression, but the specific content of culturally induced repression.

As noted above, Juliet Mitchell held that a revolution in the socialization practices that inscribe patriarchy in the unconscious of both men and women is necessary if patriarchy is to be overcome. For Mitchell, change in socialization practices will follow from a revolution that would bring capitalism to an end: "It is not a question of changing (or ending) who has or how one has babies. It is a question of overthrowing patriarchy. As the end of 'eternal' class conflict is visible within the contradictions of capitalism, so too, it would seem, is the swan-song of the 'immortal' nature of patriarchal culture to be heard."

Mitchell's point is well taken, and it underscores how radical a change in the conditions of human existence is necessary in order to end patriarchy, just as it underscores how damaging patriarchy is to human life. Nevertheless, Mitchell's stance here does not suggest that an end to patriarchy would mean a change in the unconscious/conscious structure, or, a change in our way and the psychoanalytic way of construing this structural relation. On the contrary, Mitchell unequivocally supports what she takes to be the Freudian notion of the relation between consciousness and the unconscious and the barrier of repression, and she does so in large part because she believes that it is the linchpin of Freudian psychoanalysis's explanatory power and, in this, she follows Freud's own view. [25]

Ricoeur, Freud, Phenomenology

In order to put forth an alternate view, the relevance of Husserlian phenomenology to the problematic of the relation between consciousness and the unconscious will be explored here. The primary reference point for this discussion is Paul Ricoeur's remarkable book, *Freud and Philosophy*. Though a full-scale critique of Ricoeur's interpretation of the harmony and disharmony in the views of Freud and Husserl on the unconscious cannot be undertaken here, the sense of such a critique can be suggested.

After an intense elaboration of three points of radical agreement between the two views of the relation between consciousness and the unconscious, in which Ricoeur, importantly, undermines the widespread, erroneous critique of phenomenology according to which it is a philosophy based on belief in the complete transparency of consciousness to itself,[26] Ricoeur concludes that "psychoanalysis is not phenomenology"[27] and that: "The unconscious of phenomenology is the preconscious of psychoanalysis, that is to say, an unconscious that is descriptive and not topographic [i.e., dynamic]. The meaning of the barrier is that the unconscious is inaccessible unless the appropriate technique is used . . . ." This is so, Ricoeur points out, because, while both phenomenology and psychoanalysis are concerned with relations of meaning to meaning, "the important thing, for analysis, is that this [unconscious] meaning is *separated* from becoming conscious by a barrier. This is the essential factor in the idea of repression"[28] (Ricoeur's emphasis). This is why, Ricoeur emphasizes, a special technique must be used, and, for Ricoeur, phenomenology does not provide such a technique. For this reason, and other important reasons that he adduces, Ricoeur, who was a philosopher of religion, and who in *Freud and Philosophy* advocates for a hermeneutic philosophical approach to psychoanalysis, claims that phenomenology cannot be the *philosophical* perspective appropriate for psychoanalysis.

The questions that can, and should, be raised in response are these: How, given Ricoeur's account of the barrier of repression, is it possible for the ideas in the repressed unconscious *ever* to become conscious, technique notwithstanding? How is it possible for the repression barrier to be breached or lifted at all? The barrier of repression was construed by Freud as the means by which the human species survived, biologically: it was instituted at the very same moment that the incest taboo was instituted—this was the moment of the coming into existence of civilization, morality, etc. as the means by which the human species would survive, would become "fit" (Darwin) to survive. In Freud's words, "Every *internal* barrier of repression is the historical result of an *external* obstruction. Thus the opposition is incorporated within; the history of mankind is deposited in the present day inborn tendencies to repression" (Jones 1955:455, letter of 1 August 1912; trans. Jones, and his italics).[29] The operative term here is "inborn." That is to say, the tendencies to psychic repression are inherited, and thus in some sense material rather than purely psychic, and therefore not as such meaning.

To clarify the point here, Ricoeur does *not* acknowledge that for Freud the split between consciousness and the unconscious in the form of the repression barrier was not at all a matter of meaning; rather, it was an entity conceived by Freud through his social Darwinist and Lamarckian perspective. Therefore, the justification for its existence as represented by Freud stands or falls on his Darwinian perspective on psychology and his biologism. Ricoeur cannot, therefore, consistently incorporate the repression barrier into a perspective that considers psychoanalysis to be a field of investigation restricted to the relation of meaning to meaning. For Freud, the repression barrier does regulate the relation of meaning to meaning, or, of conscious and unconscious meaning. Therefore, the repression barrier cannot itself be a phenomenon of meaning; it is, rather, as we have seen, a phenomenon explained by Freud's historically and culturally situated view of the evolutionary-biological roots of human psychic life. Thus, Ricoeur cannot both have and not have the repression barrier, that is, the Freudian conception of the unconscious in its inaccessibility to consciousness. Either psychoanalysis is encompassed entirely in a field of meaning and the relation of meaning to meaning, or psychoanalysis is based on Freud's 'discovery' of the barrier of repression which is not at all a matter of meaning. The biologism of Freud's manner of construing the repression barrier is a manifestation of the naturalistic attitude that he never abandoned. Finally, here I aver that Husserlian phenomenology, *pace* Ricoeur, does provide a philosophical foundation for psychoanalysis in that it accounts for the conditions for the possibility of moving beyond naturalism (positivism) in any form, including versions of evolution that, like Freud's, are reductionist.

In a telling comment near the end of his magisterial book, Ricoeur indicates his awareness of the problem of the epistemology and ontology of the barrier of repression:

> That Freud's topography requires a realism of the unconscious is beyond question. . . . But this disjunction with regard to my consciousness is not a disjunction with respect to all consciousness. The relationship of the metapsychological concepts to the actual work of interpretation implies a new kind of relativity, no longer to the consciousness which 'has' so to speak, the unconscious, but to the overall field of consciousness constituted by the work of interpretation. . . .[F]or this work and this field pertain to a scientific consciousness which it is important to distinguish, at least in principle, from any private subjectivity, including that of the analyst; this scientific consciousness must first of all be regarded as a transcendental subjectivity, that is to say, as the locus or home of the rule governing interpretation.[30]

Ricoeur, unlike other post-Husserlian philosophers (Heidegger) never concealed or even underemphasized the profound influence of Husserlian phenomenology on his thinking, or the degree to which he retained fundamental Husserlian notions in his own thinking and writing. Just so, in the quotation just cited, Ricoeur invokes the uniquely Husserlian notion of consciousness—the notion of transcendental subjectivity as the ground for the possibility of any science, including the science of psychoanalysis. The notion of scientific consciousness spoken of above by Ricoeur is the attitude of the phenomenologist who has suspended ontological commitments and thus left the natural (-istic) attitude and entered the phenomenological attitude, which enables consideration of evidence with the radical empiricism afforded by the suspension of ontological commitments, including both reductive materialism and immaterialism. What Ricoeur elides here, however, is the relation between the transcendental subjectivity or ego and the mundane consciousness or mundane ego, the latter referred to by Ricoeur as "private subjectivity." For, even the private "consciousness which 'has' so to speak the unconscious" mentioned by Ricoeur is, for Husserl, inseparable, and not just "in principle," but existentially as well, from transcendental subjectivity and intersubjectivity, including for the scientist. Grasping this requires transcending naturalistic reduction of the world to facts. Thus, in this context, it is markedly unclear what Ricoeur means by his phrase "a realism of the unconscious." Realism in what sense?[31] In other words, against Ricoeur, we can say that phenomenology in principle can provide an account of the unconscious because it and psychoanalytic psychology, *pace* Freud, are encompassed within the field of transcendental subjectivity, the field of meaning.

Ricoeur goes on in *Freud and Philosophy* to discuss Freud in relation to Spinoza and Hegel, and to return to his concern with the relation of psychoanalysis and faith. However, he does not in his Freud book thematize the encounter of the transcendental with faith in divinity—a perplexing omission, which, in the philosophical literature, is not merely omitted—it is repressed.

CONCLUDING REMARK

Perhaps that strange and tormented man—Freud—will be our Hermes yet, our herald of the end of the repression of the mother; then we might discover whether the end of the repression of the mother will be the end of repression, at least as it has heretofore functioned in human development, and the dawn of a new humanity: "Where id was, there ego shall be."[32]

NOTES

1. Judith Van Herik, *Freud on Femininity and Faith* (Berkeley: University of California Press, 1982), 200.

2. In her book, Van Herik does not refer to Freud's views on gender and religion as prejudices. Her primary reference point for her critique of Freud is what she refers to throughout as his "asymmetric theory of gender," which is the source of his devaluation of women and the allegedly 'feminine' men who turn to religion. My use of the term prejudice follows the usual definition: an adverse opinion formed without

just grounds. Van Herik eschews the terms 'prejudice' and 'misogyny' because she wishes to avoid any imputation of hostility on the part of Freud. She focuses on an internal analysis and critique of his writings. Other critics of Freud do use such terms, for example Philip Rieff who, in his renowned book, *Freud: The Mind of the Moralist* (Chicago: University of Chicago Press, 1959), writes about Freud's "animus" (257) toward religion and of his "misogyny" (185).

3. An explication of transcendental phenomenology can be found in Edmund Husserl's late work, *The Crisis of European Sciences and Transcendental Phenomenology*, trans. by David Carr (Evanston, IL: Northwestern University Press, 1970).

4. A thorough discussion of the meaning of the transcendental in philosophy can be found in Husserl, *Crisis*, 97–100. He writes: "It is the motif [the motif of the transcendental] of inquiring back into the ultimate source of all the formations of knowledge, the motif of the knower's reflecting upon himself and his knowing life in which all the scientific structures that are valid for him occur purposefully, are stored up as acquisitions, and have become and continue to freely become available. Working itself out radically, it is the motif of a universal philosophy which is grounded purely in this source and thus ultimately grounded" (Husserl, *Crisis*, 97–98).

5. Van Herik, *Freud*, 80–84.

6. Van Herik, *Freud*, 80–84.

7. Juliet Mitchell, *Psychoanalysis and Feminism* (New York: Random House, 1974).

8. Jerre Collins, et. al., "Questioning the Unconscious: The Dora Archive," in Charles Bernheimer and Claire Kahane, eds., *In Dora's Case: Freud-Hysteria-Feminism* (New York: Columbia University Press, 1985), 251.

9. In my exegesis, I will not repeat here the numerous references to Freud which can be found readily by consulting Van Herik's scholarly and unusually well-documented book. Also, I have interpolated into my exegesis of her text material relevant to my theme: the relationship between gender and the epigenesis of morality.

10. S. Freud, "Femininity" in *The Complete Introductory Lectures on Psychoanalysis*, trans. by J. Strachey (New York: Norton, 1966), 576–99.

11. Van Herik, *Freud*, 130.

12. See Freud, "Femininity," passim.

13. According to Freud, as Van Herik points out, girls normally go through a masculine phase in which they compete with their fathers for their mothers' love; however, this phase subsides as soon as they discover their "castrated" state.

14. Van Herik, *Freud*, 192. As Van Herik shows, because he viewed Judaism as a religion which imposed renunciation, Freud preferred Judaism to Christianity. He viewed Christianity as a regression back to matriarchal psychic structures which had been historically superseded, he believed, by patriarchal structures. Nevertheless, he repudiated all religion as based on illusion and as antithetical to the scientific weltanschauung.

15. S. Freud, *Civilization and Its Dis*contents (New York: Norton, 1961), 11–12.

16. Van Herik, *Freud*, 40–47. Van Herik marshals the work of several authorities on Freud, e.g., Juliet Mitchell, Jacques Lacan, and Paul Ricoeur, who claim that Freud separated psychology from biology and relegated psychoanalysis to the relatively independent domain of psychology. There is no doubt that this is correct. But, for

Freud, this was a methodological imperative: he could not show, as he wished to show, a one to one correlation between mind and brain, though he believed that eventually science would succeed in this task. Though Van Herik points this out, she, like Mitchell, denies that Freud's version of psychoanalysis is biologistic.

17. Freud's Darwinism is the subject of Frank Sullaway's magisterial 612 page treatise, *Freud, Biologist of the Mind* (New York: Basic Books, 1979). That Freud's Darwinism remains an integral aspect of the contemporary psychoanalytic worldview is evident in the following quotation from the eminent theorist of psychoanalysis, Arnold Cooper: "Any working psychoanalyst or any thoughtful psychoanalyst of course assumes that evolution has made our minds ultimately, if not made our minds up and that we are a product of it" (P. Brooks and Alex Woloch, eds., *Whose Freud; The Place of Psychoanalysis in Contemporary Culture* [New Haven, CT: Yale University Press, 2000], 289). Moreover, Van Herik herself cites an important statement by Freud regarding the father complex and evolution:

> The origin of religion in the father complex as a male achievement was emphasized in 1923 in *The Ego and the Id*, wherein the ego ideal, which "answers to everything that is expected of the higher nature of man" is shown to be a "substitute for the longing for the father." Because of this substitutive function, the ego ideal "contains the germ from which all religions have evolved." Freud continues:
>
> > Religion, morality, and a social sense—the chief elements in the higher side of man—were originally one and the same thing . . . [T]hey were acquired phylogenetically out of the father-complex: religion and moral restraint through the process of mastering the Oedipus complex itself, and social feeling through the necessity for overcoming the rivalry that then remained between the members of the younger generation. The male sex seems to have taken the lead in all these moral acquisitions and they seem to have been transmitted to women by cross-inheritance. (Freud, SE 19: 37.) (Quoted in Van Herik, *Freud*, 159n19).

Sullaway also deals extensively with, and thoroughly documents, Freud's later insistence that psychoanalysis be regarded as a purely psychological and non-biological field. Sullaway shows that this stance by Freud was a consequence of many motives, in particular Freud's great fear that psychoanalysis would be subsumed into a biology that was not sufficiently developed to do justice to psychoanalysis. As a result, Sullaway shows, Freud became a "crypto-biologist." See Sullaway, *Freud*, 419–44.

18. As is well known, Freud also postulated that human life is governed by an instinct that has the opposite aim, not survival but extinction: the death instinct, explained by Freud as the tendency for life to return to its earlier non-organic state. For Freud, moreover, the two instincts were in constant combat. Nevertheless, Eros, the sexual or self-preservative instinct, was for Freud the source of all values, and values were merely efforts by Eros to combat the death instinct. That is to say, the postulate of the death instinct, which Freud introduced in order to explain phenomena like the compulsion to repeat that he could not otherwise explain, is an equally biologically reductive notion. Frank Sullaway has a through discussion of Freud's views on life and death drives in Sullaway, *Freud*, 393–415.

19. What follows is Paul Ricoeur's rendition, in *Freud and Philosophy* (New Haven: Yale University Press, 1970), of Freud's conception of the origin of the incest taboo: "From Darwin and Atkinson he takes over a theory of the primal horde,

according to which the jealousy of the male is alleged to play the role of excluding the young males from sharing the females whom the leader wishes to monopolize . . . " (Ricoeur, *Freud*, 206).

Ricoeur goes on to quote from Freud (I have shortened the quotation):

> One day the brothers who had been driven out came together, killed and devoured their father and so made an end of the patriarchal horde . . . .Cannibal savages as they were, it goes without saying that they devoured their victim as well as killing him. The violent primal father had doubtless been the feared and envied model of each one of the company of brothers; and in the act of devouring him they accomplished their identification with him, and each one of them acquired a portion of his strength. The totem meal, which is perhaps mankind's earliest festival, would thus be a repetition and a commemoration of this memorable and criminal deed, which was the beginning of so many things—of social organization, of moral restrictions and of religion. (Freud, SE 13, 141–42.) (Quoted in Ricoeur, *Freud*, 207)

For Freud, the unconscious has two components: the drives and the content that is repressed, including, and primarily, the memories associated with the Oedipus complex. The drives are not repressed, they are not accessible to consciousness; only ideas, their instinctive representatives, are accessible to consciousness. Consciousness for Freud is just a thin layer, so to speak, of the psyche, and it arose as the register of perceptual experience in the service of the reality principle.

20. "The fact that women must be regarded as having little sense of justice is no doubt related to the predominance of envy in their mental life; for the demand for justice is a modification of envy and lays down the condition subject to which one can put envy aside. We also regard women as weaker in their social instincts and as having less capacity for sublimating their instincts than men" (Freud, "Femininity," 598). Here we see that Freud's fundamental philosophical stance regarding morality is Hobbesian in that he viewed virtue, i.e., justice, as a product of the necessity, to ensure survival of the species, to prevent us from killing each other. Justice, for Freud, was a product of superego development and thus male.

21. Freud argued that because women, unlike men, cannot overcome their need to be loved by their fathers, "normal" women have a lifelong fear of abandonment by him or by his substitutes in her life. Thus, she will always seek to please him by deferring to him. This is a consequence for Freud of women's sense of inferiority due to her perception of her biological, genital inferiority. See Freud, "Femininity," passim.

22. ". . . the theatre where our dreams are enacted is a different one from the scene of action where our ideas are generated in waking life." Sigmund Freud, *The Interpretation of Dreams*, trans. by Joyce Crick (Oxford: Oxford University Press, 1999), 349.

23. See, for example, Jane Loevinger, "Origins of Conscience" in Merton M. Gill and Philip S. Holzman, eds., *Psychology versus Metapsychology: Psychoanalytic Essays in Memory of George S. Klein* (New York: International Universities Press, 1976), 265–97.

24. Readers should not infer that I reject Darwin's theory of evolution. On the contrary, as a scientific theory of biology supported by a consensus of biologists,

I fully accept it. It is, rather, Freud's psychobiology and his sociobiology that I reject—his reductive application of Darwin to human psychological and psychosocial development.

25. S. Freud, *The History of the Psychoanalytic Movement* (New York: Collier Books, 1963), 50.

26. Ricoeur, *Freud*, 375–90.

27. Ricoeur, *Freud*, 390.

28. Ricoeur, *Freud*, 392.

29. Quoted in Sullaway, *Freud*, 370.

30. Ricoeur, *Freud*, 431.

31. Ricoeur goes on to explicate the sense of 'realism' that informs his thinking by recourse to Kant: "In the area of physics, Kant taught us to combine an empirical realism with a transcendental idealism. . . . Kant achieved this combination for the sciences of nature; our task is to accomplish it for psychoanalysis, where theory constitutively enters into the facts it elaborates" (Ricoeur, *Freud*, 432–433). This is surprising for surely Ricoeur was familiar with Husserl's compelling critique of Kant, i.e., that Kant failed to transcend empiricist naturalism and that his views flowed from unquestioned assumptions that disallowed him from discovering 'evidence' in the phenomenological sense. See Husserl, *Crisis*, 114–16.

32. "It is easy to imagine, too, that certain mystical practices may succeed in upsetting the normal relations between the different regions of the mind, so that, for instance, perception may be able to grasp happenings in the depths of the ego and in the id which were otherwise inaccessible to it . . . it may be admitted that the therapeutic efforts of psycho-analysis have chosen a similar line of approach. Its intention is, indeed, to strengthen the ego, to make it more independent of the super-ego, to widen its field of perceptions and enlarge its organization, so that it can appropriate fresh portions of the id. Where id was, there ego shall be" (Sigmund Freud, *The Complete Introductory Lectures on Psychoanalysis*, trans. and ed. by James Strachey [New York: Norton, 1966], 544).

Chapter Three

The Crisis in Psychoanalysis: Resolution through Husserlian Phenomenology and Feminism

1. THE PROBLEM AND ITS SOLUTION: PRELIMINARY DISCUSSION

The contemporary crisis in psychoanalysis reflects the following state of affairs: while on one hand, though it has not yet succeeded in getting its theoretical house in order, psychoanalysis has managed, thus far, to maintain its viability; on the other hand, it is now faced with more powerful challenges than ever before—challenges from neuropsychiatry and psychopharmacology, and from rival schools of psychotherapy, for example, cognitive-behavioral therapy, brief therapy, interpersonal therapy, and so on, whose practitioners maintain that psychoanalysis is not scientific, takes longer, is more expensive, and is not more successful than they are in achieving beneficial results. In addition, the emergence of feminist critical theory and feminist philosophy of science has forcefully augmented the traditional charge that psychoanalysis was from the beginning, and continues to be, a misogynistic theoretical structure.[1] These factors combined have generated a crisis in psychoanalysis that threatens its existence. To survive, psychoanalysis must get its theoretical house in order.

From its inception, psychoanalysis has embodied two opposed foundational models for theoretical work: (1) Freud's mechanistic and reductionist, that is, positivist, natural science framework which he dubbed his 'metapsychology,' and (2) his interpretive or hermeneutic framework. There is general agreement in the field that Freud's theories were inconsistent, at times supporting each of these conceptions of psychoanalysis's foundations. Because it resulted in a discourse which describes the mind as both mechanistic and purposive, this conflictual aspect of Freud's thinking is often alluded to under the rubric of his "mixed discourse." Though proponents of a positivist view of psychoanalysis are still active, many theorists have rejected it. Nevertheless, psychoanalysis is still bifurcated by rival constructions—a natural science model versus a hermeneutic discipline—of its theoretical foundations.[2] Another significant dimension of this problematic is the possibility of constituting a non-positivist natural science perspective, which some adherents of the natural science model affirm and others deny.

The positivist element in Freud's conception of psychoanalysis is comprised of the following components: (1) scientism, that is, Freud's belief that natural science is the only source of knowledge;[3] (2) his mechanistic conception of nature, that is, his belief in the so-called "billiard ball" model of causation; (3) his materialism, his belief that only matter as conceived by natural science exists;[4] (4) his reductionism, that is, his belief that the mental is reducible to the physical;[5] and (5) his belief in the subject-object split (and its corollary—the correspondence theory of truth), that is, his belief that a particular attitude of consciousness—the scientific attitude—enables one to acquire "objective" knowledge of the external world, the world construed as existing independent of subjectivity.[6] The opposed perspective, the hermeneutic view of psychoanalysis, will be laid out below in a discussion of the work of Roy Schafer.

This theoretical bifurcation has far-reaching implications, not only for psychoanalytic practice, but also for the future of psychoanalysis. If psychoanalysis is a natural science, its uniqueness is potentially undermined in that it might collapse into neuropsychiatry and psychopharmacology. If it is a hermeneutic discipline, its uniqueness is potentially undermined by the specter of relativism and by an inability to differentiate its method from fictionalizing.[7] Consequently, neither model, neither natural science nor hermeneutics, has succeeded in supporting the indefinite continuance of psychoanalysis as a unique field of research and practice, a matter of great concern to all in the field.[8] In this chapter, I will explore this controversy and I will propose an alternative, and, I believe, more fruitful, means of construing the philosophical foundations of psychoanalysis.

I intend to show that the bifurcation in contemporary psychoanalytic theory (1) is generated, in large part, by failure to understand the interrelation between positivism and misogyny (the unwarranted devaluation of the female); and (2) can be resolved through the development of a Husserlian phenomenological psychoanalysis[9] informed by feminism.

As I will show, Freud's misogynistic theory of psychosexual development and his positivist conception of science are inseparably intertwined, and for this reason psychoanalysis cannot be restructured as a nonpositivist domain of investigation, not unless, that is, the link between positivism and misogyny built into it is exposed and the misogynistic elements are eliminated. The link between positivism and misogyny, which sustains both ideological distortions, can be broken, I argue, through a phenomenological reconceptualization of the psychoanalytic field. This entails reconceptualization of psychoanalysis as a humanistic, rather than natural, science. In the perspective to be developed here, such a transformation does not entail loss of scientificity. Moreover, phenomenological reconceptualization of psychoanalysis's theoretical foundation must be augmented, I will show, by feminist philosophy of science.

Put another way, the crucial point here, which will be fully developed below, is not that the proponents of a non-positivist natural science are to be supported as over and against a hermeneutic model. I argue, rather, similarly to the proponents of hermeneutics, that it is at best highly questionable whether or not a non-positivist *natural* science is possible. The point here is that rather than a natural science foundation for psychoanalysis, what is needed is a foundation that eschews the specific theoretical limitations of both natural science and hermeneutics: a science that ensures the scientificity of psychoanalysis and is immune to positivist reductionism. This is the vision of the humanistic disciplines that is found in the work of Edmund Husserl, founder of post-Hegelian phenomenology. Most importantly, I will maintain further that it is precisely the misogyny that still inheres in psychoanalytic theory that prevents the move into phenomenology.

2. THE LINK BETWEEN POSITIVISM AND MISOGYNY IN PSYCHOANALYSIS

Freud's misogyny is expressed, feminist critics maintain, in three important claims. First, he claims to have demonstrated that "normal," that is, psychologically healthy women, owing to the vicissitudes of their psychosexual development, do not have the capacity to be scientists.[10] Freud's views involve a second, and, as we shall see, interrelated claim that has been contested by feminist critics: that the strongest wish of all people is for love of and protection by the father: "I cannot think of any need in childhood as strong as the need for the father's protection."[11] Third, Freud virtually eliminated the dynamic interrelation between infants, children and their mothers as a significant factor in psychosexual development. The same criticism is expressed by the now fully accepted charge that to the great detriment of psychoanalysis, Freud ignored the preoedipal stage of human development.[12]

In relation to his views regarding scientists, a great deal turns upon the emphasis Freud placed on the wish to be loved by the father. The crucial difference between male and female paths of psychosexual development, on this account, is that "normal" females, in contrast to males, neither renounce nor overcome in any way the wish fulfillment fantasy of winning their fathers' love.[13] For Freud, the only "normal" people who could become scientists were also, for him, the most highly developed and most mature persons: non-neurotic, "normal" males. It is by virtue of successful resolution of the oedipal conflict and the resultant ability consciously to abandon the quest for love from the father that, according to Freud, men win both secure masculine identity and the capacity for scientific objectivity. Mature males are capable of objectivity because, having consciously suppressed their wish for their fathers' love, they no longer distort reality by experiencing it in the light of that wish. In this framework, then, masculinity, secure male identity, and science mutually imply one another. Mature males can split subjectivity and objectivity; their capacity to experience the world as it is in "reality" is uncontaminated by unconscious wish fulfillment fantasies.[14] Only an "abnormal" female, one fixated at the stage of "masculine protest" or the "masculinity complex," the transient stage at which a girl afflicted with penis envy rejects her femininity and seeks her mother's love by imitating her father, would be motivated to be a scientist, and such a person is neurotic, that is, sick.[15] Only a woman who could not accept her femininity and the role prescribed by it would wish to become a scientist. Moreover, and most important, in Freud's formulations the science from which "normal" women, women capable of contentment, are excluded is science as Freud conceived it: positivism.

Significantly, as we have just seen, *in characterizing science as a male domain, Freud himself posited a link between gender and science.* This link suggests that the two historically pervasive critiques of Freud—critiques of his positivist framework and of his views regarding gender—can and ought to be interrelated. However, few of those who have mounted attacks on Freud's positivism have either seen or attempted to critique it in its intricate relation to a critique of his analysis of gender. Even though Freud's positivism has been rejected by many contemporary psychoanalytic theorists, they have not succeeded in eliminating its presence in their theories because they have failed to grasp the full theoretical and philosophical significance of the link between positivism and misogyny. In this chapter I will fill in, and thus eliminate, this lacuna.

In this chapter, the relation between gender and natural science will be discussed by focusing on the work of Evelyn Fox Keller, a philosopher of science as well as a theoretical physicist and molecular biologist. In her 1985 book, *Reflections on Gender and Science,*[16] Keller attempts to account for the fact that the vast majority of scientists throughout the history of Western culture have been male. She concludes that the operative forces generating this state of affairs were, and are, an interrelated nexus of psychological, historical, social, political, and economic factors.

Keller shows that the devaluation and delegitimation of the female was an integral aspect of the birth of modern science in the seventeenth century. She points out that social and economic conditions in seventeenth century England generated an ideology which would justify the privatization of family life and the dissociation of public life from family values. This justification involved the judgment that females were unfit for, and indeed a danger to, public life: "With the domestication of female power, sentimental regard and protective solicitude could safely displace the overt misogyny of earlier times."[17] Thus, the male genderization of science reflected and arose out the same conditions that generated misogyny. Women were devalued and relegated to the home, and this prevented them from playing a role in public life, including, of course, science. The masculine nature of science has had, Keller maintains, both historically and contemporaneously, misogynistic results: it generates both an institutional hostility to females and an intellectual climate inhospitable to certain modes of thought.

What is most significant in Keller's work and most germane to our concerns here is her view that, owing in part to these factors, natural science itself, qua science, in its epistemology and its method, was and is gendered male. This explains in part the continued predominance of males in natural science. Keller shows that natural science as presently constituted rests on epistemological and metaphysical presuppositions that are irrational in that they reflect an attitude of unwarranted exclusion. What is excluded is a point of view that would allow for mediation of the radical subject-object split, a split built into modern science when it came into existence in the seventeenth century. Keller shows that an attitude that permits only a radical subject-object (subjective-objective) split was and is culturally identified as male, and an attitude that allows for mediation is culturally identified as female.[18] The term she uses to denote the exclusion from science of attitudes identified as female is "masculinist." An excellent example of Keller's analysis of the negative effects on science of the radical subject-object split is her treatment of the theoretical impasse in quantum physics. Keller's discussion of this impasse will be explicated at length later in this chapter.

As noted above, Keller's aim was to demonstrate that science has acquired characteristics associated with maleness, with a consequent negative effect on both female scientists and on science itself. She used the insights of psychoanalytic, post-Freudian object relations theory to analyze the psychosexual, developmental aspects of the origin and continuance of masculinist science. However, while Keller does not at all deal with the relation of masculinist science to Freud's positivist model of psychoanalysis, and while she relies on post-Freudian object relations theory (Winnicott) to explain her notion of masculinist science, one of the principal claims of this chapter is that in Freud's model of psychoanalysis the link between misogyny and positivism became explicit. Let us examine more closely the link within psychoanalytic theory between the male genderization of science and misogyny. (In this paper, the relation between masculinist science and misogyny will be addressed only in relation to Freud's version of psychoanalysis; however, though undemonstrated here, I make the claim that these findings are generalizable to all of the sciences, *Geisteswissenschaften* as well as *Naturwissenschaften*, as presently constituted.)

Freud, child of the Enlightenment, viewed natural science as the highest expression of human reason. However, as we have seen, in Freud's model of psychosexual development women cannot be both happy, that is, relatively free from the unnecessary suffering brought about by neurosis, and scientists. That is, women cannot live the life of reason, the most highly valorized life, and be happy. For Freud, an ardent Darwinian, "normalcy" was the most desirable state because it ensured the survival of the species. Normal men can, and will, both produce children, and, if so inclined, become scientists. Science serves survival of the species by enabling human beings to bend nature to human needs. Science is thus the preeminent realization of the reality principle, and the reality principle serves survival because it enhances adaptation to the external world.[19] For Freud, since normal women cannot both produce children and be scientists their prime role is to ensure the survival of the species by bearing and rearing children, especially male children who could, and some of whom would, become scientists. As a result, since a normal life for women excluded a life of reason, Freud viewed females as inferior to mature males who can both engender children and be scientists, with the help of their child-bearing and rearing wives, naturally.

Most important, however, is that Freud's conviction that normal women cannot be scientists was a function of his masculinist conception of science. This can be shown in the following manner: positivism presupposes the radical subject-object split, and this is precisely that which, for Freud, normal women are incapable of achieving. Unlike normal males, who, as we have seen, consciously abandon the need for paternal love when they successfully resolve their oedipal conflicts, normal females are destined, like their mothers, to live for the love of their fathers/husbands.[20] For Freud, in order to guarantee the survival of the species, which requires that women desire to bear and rear many children, women must identify with their mothers' identification with that role. Such an identification meant, for Freud, renunciation of any other ambition, especially any ambition outside the home. Identification of women with women rather than with men is biologically guaranteed because the anatomical difference between the sexes makes it impossible for women to develop "normally" and simultaneously identify with the male.[21] Consequently, "normal" women cannot fully internalize the norms of society, including moral norms, and cannot abandon the wish for the love of the father. Therefore, normal females can never cease projecting their wish-fulfillment fantasies, especially of attaining their fathers' love, onto the world. In projecting this wish, they are rendered incapable of grasping "objectivity" as that which exists independent of human wishes; that is, women cannot achieve the radical subject-object split. In this way, the Freudian version of psychoanalysis reveals that for him positivism, masculinist science, was inseparably linked to the devaluation of women, the claim that women cannot live the life of reason and cannot achieve the fullest actualization of human potential. Thus, the Freudian version of psychoanalysis put the capstone on the legitimation of misogyny by showing that the (positivist) science of psychoanalysis can prove that women are inferior. (With regard to the central theme of this book, we might say that Freud sacrificed women on the altar of the survival of the species, a form of survivalism that victimizes women as persons.)

It is obvious today that Freud's theories are replete with unexamined philosophical presuppositions, most notably belief in the existence of the radical subject-object split. It seems likely that at least some of these presuppositions were defensively held by Freud and were unexamined because of a conflict that generated resistance. However, this claim will not be substantiated in this chapter with respect to Freud. It will be substantiated, as we shall see, with respect to the theories of a contemporary psychoanalyst-theoretician, Edwin Wallace.

This chapter is an effort to provide more persuasive grounds than have yet been put forth for the claims (a) that psychoanalysis, despite significant theoretical advances, still has a positivist-misogynist core, and (b) that the goal of contemporary psychoanalysts to eliminate positivism from psychoanalytic theory will not be achieved until and unless this core is eliminated. Positivism is an ideological distortion of the nature of science and, for Husserl, founder of post-Hegelian phenomenology, of philosophy as well: "Positivism . . . decapitates philosophy."[22] This is the central insight of Husserlian phenomenology. Misogyny, similarly, is an ideological distortion of the meaning of gender and its role in human existence. This is the central insight of feminism. Keller's work, unique in the extent to which it focuses on and reveals the masculinist nature of the positivist version of science, is nevertheless inadequate to overcome the natural science versus hermeneutics bifurcation in psychoanalytic theory because it is inadequate as a means of grounding a reconceptualization of psychoanalysis as a nonpositivist science.

The reason for this, as will be shown later in this chapter, is that outside the framework of Husserlian phenomenology, the psychic field cannot be conceived nonreductively, that is, nonpositivistically, as a domain of scientific investigation. Finally, though the focus here is on the relation of positivism and misogyny in psychoanalysis, this focus is intended as a case study that can generate interest in this issue in relation to the problem of the foundations of the humanistic disciplines in general. Before proceeding, however, it will be helpful to have a fuller understanding of the hermeneutic and natural science models of psychoanalysis.

3. FOUNDATIONAL MODELS OF PSYCHOANALYSIS

The powerful reaction against Freud's mechanistic reductionism that set in after his death took the form of a rejection of what Freud had called his "metapsychology." This term refers to the extra-clinical, theoretical framework of psychoanalysis as presented, for example, in his *Project for a Scientific Psychology*[23] in which he attempted to reduce the psyche as dynamically described by psychoanalysis to physical substances and quantities, and in the famous seventh chapter of *The Interpretation of Dreams*.[24]

One of the results of the rejection of Freud's scientistic metapsychology has been an emphasis on what is called "clinical theory."[25] Clinical theory attempts to do what Freud advocated but did not do: base all generalizations directly on clinical experience and nothing but clinical experience and refrain entirely from reliance on extra-clinical, experience-distant concepts. Some proponents of the natural science model, like Edwin Wallace, work we will shortly examine in detail, also accept the criticism that was made of Freud's natural science model insofar as the latter was alleged to be mechanistic and reductive. Many of the contemporary proponents of the natural science model also affirm the necessity, in order to secure the viability and survival of psychoanalysis, to continue to develop a rich clinical theory, and that any extra-clinical, theoretical constructs must be based in clinical theory and clinical experience. Thus, there has emerged within psychoanalysis a consensus regarding the clinical setting, a consensus that has both theoretical and clinical implications and which rejects not only Freud's mechanistic reductionism, but aspects of his clinical practice as well.[26] However, even though Freud's positivist metapsychology has been rejected, no consensus has been reached regarding the necessity for a metapsychology as such.[27] Even though contemporary proponents of the natural science model reject Freud's mechanistic reductionism, they think that psychoanalysis requires grounding in a metapsychology. Those who reject metapsychology in toto believe that a conceptualization of psychoanalysis as a hermeneutic discipline obviates both the possibility of any metapsychology at all and the need for any generalizations that could be universal in the natural science sense. Significantly, both viewpoints share the notion that natural science is the only type of science and thus hold that any metapsychology must be of the natural science type, whether mechanistic and reductionist, that is, positivist, or not. The hermeneutic standpoint is that any conception of psychoanalysis as a natural science is ipso facto reductionist.[28] The contemporary proponents of the natural science model, including Edwin Wallace,[29] argue that a metapsychology could, but need not, as was the case for Freud, be mechanistic and reductionist, or positivist. As I will show, however, Wallace does not succeed in eliminating positivism from his conception of psychoanalytic theory.

The most influential and systematically developed version of the hermeneutic model of psychoanalysis is found in the work of Roy Schafer,[30] who, in his more recent book, writes that, "What has been presented here amounts to a hermeneutic version of psychoanalysis. In this version, psychoanalysis is an interpretive discipline rather than a natural science."[31] In general, the hermeneutic perspective denies the radical subject-object, subjectivity-objectivity split and affirms that the relation between human beings and the world in which we find ourselves is interpretive. On this account, nothing can be known independent of some interpretation. Interpretation, moreover, is always relative to factors that are intrinsically historical and changing. Most important, the hermeneutic perspective implies that no universal, nonrelative constituents of human "being in the world" can be discovered, and thus that there can be no science of interpretation or meaning.[32] Some of the proponents of hermeneutics deny that it entails the radical relativism that is indistinguishable from reduction of human experience to meaninglessness. However, I maintain that the theoreticians of hermeneutics have not succeeded in refuting this charge, and that hermeneutics is in fact a form of relativism.[33]

Explicit details of the hermeneutic viewpoint are provided by Schafer. In his view, psychoanalysis is and can only be a narrative or interpretive practice and is thus describable in the same terms as all other forms of narrative. For Freud, belief in rigorous psychic determinism was the defining standpoint of psychoanalysis. In line with his hermeneutic standpoint, Schafer rejects psychic determinism and substitutes for it, as the defining characteristic of psychoanalysis, emphasis on human persons as free and active agents:

> . . . interpretations will redescribe . . . conflicts that the analysand has unconsciously defined. . . ; to say this is to say that, through interpretation, the great extent to which the analysand is unconsciously the agent or author of his or her life gets to be established beyond doubt.[34]

What has been presented here amounts to a hermeneutic version of psychoanalysis. In this version, psychoanalysis is an interpretive discipline rather than
a natural science. . . . Interpretations are redescriptions . . . of actions along the
lines peculiar to psychoanalytic interest. Action can only be . . . described from
one or another point of view. . . . A simple positivistic conception of analytic
work is inadequate. The facts are what the analyst makes them out to be. . . . In
many ways, the second reality of psychoanalysis is more akin to the reality constructed in poetry, story. . . . It both supplements and competes with pragmatic
conventionalized reality. Both kinds of reality are constructions.[35]

Note that Schafer implies that a natural science model of psychoanalysis is
ipso facto a positivist model.

The discussion of the natural science model of psychoanalysis herein
focuses on an analysis of Edwin Wallace's book, *Historiography and Causation in Psychoanalysis* (see 77n29). There are several reasons for working
with this text. First, unlike many psychoanalytic theoreticians, Wallace engages the issues philosophically and attempts to back up his positions with
philosophical argumentation. Because he rejects mechanistic and positivist
versions of natural science, Wallace, again unlike other proponents of a
natural science model, makes a serious effort to defend his position without
lapsing into positivism. Furthermore, Wallace has framed his arguments as a
response to Schafer's hermeneutic model of psychoanalysis. Thus, in engaging the work of a highly philosophically knowledgeable and sophisticated
psychiatrist and psychoanalyst who believes that psychoanalysis can be a
non-positivist natural science, we can begin to see the contradictions that
emerge from such a project, on one hand, and, on the other hand, the reasons
why the move into phenomenology is necessary.

According to Wallace, the fundamental distinction between his and Schafer's views centers on the issue of determinism or causality. For Wallace,
psychoanalysis is a natural science, yet is not mechanistic or positivistic because, while it insists on psychic determinism—strict causality in the psychic
domain—it nevertheless accepts as well a significant role for chance. Human
life is interpersonal; encounters with other persons, as well as other life experiences, can be quite fortuitous. Moreover, since Wallace views psychoanalysis also as an historical science, he maintains what Schafer rejects: that it is
possible for analysts to reconstruct the patient's past: ". . . denials of historical
objectivity result from the conflation of a procedural proposition—that one
cannot resurrect historical occurrences themselves or reconstruct them with
total accuracy—with an ontological one—that the events had no structure
other than that the practitioner imaginatively provides them."[36]

Wallace claims, furthermore, that natural science is nomothetic, that it
aims at the discovery of regularities, and that regularities can be discovered

to be operative in the psychic field: "If psychoanalysis abandons the concept of determinism, must it not also relinquish its claims to be a nomothetic science demonstrating certain universalities in human development and certain regularities between antecedent conditions and subsequent behaviors?[37] In fact, for Wallace, if it abandons determinism, psychoanalysis will cease to exist. In his view, because human life is historical and interpersonal, and because interpersonal life inevitably involves chance occurrences, maintaining psychic determinism as its defining concept does not render psychoanalysis a form of positivism.

From the point of view Husserlian phenomenology, the proponents of the hermeneutic approach are correct to claim that any natural science version of psychoanalysis is necessarily mechanistic and reductionist. On the other hand, phenomenologically viewed, the proponents of the hermeneutic interpretation of psychoanalysis are incorrect in their belief that science is inherently equivalent to natural science. That is, they are in error in concluding that investigation of the psychic field can never yield knowledge of universals and regularities. Before continuing the discussion of Wallace's views, an excursus into phenomenology is necessary.

4. PSYCHOANALYSIS AND PHENOMENOLOGY

As we have seen, there is today a consensus among psychoanalytic theoreticians that both the natural science and hermeneutic models were present in Freud's theories and that the two models imply incompatible claims. Parties to this consensus hold that the future of psychoanalysis depends on determining which model is most appropriate and adopting it as the foundation for theoretical work in psychoanalysis.[38] Since the purpose of this study is to show how a Husserlian phenomenological standpoint informed by feminism can contribute to the resolution of this conflict, it is appropriate to indicate which of the two incompatible models is most homologous with phenomenology. In fact, however, neither model can be reconciled with phenomenology. Most important, partisans of both models agree that science is coextensive with natural science. Since the hermeneutic standpoint rejects in toto the idea that psychoanalysis is or can be a science, the two models are irreconcilable with each other and with phenomenology.[39]

Thus, since both models delimit science to be coextensive with natural science, both are incompatible with phenomenology, for, phenomenology grounds the possibility of a science of the lifeworld, the prescientific world in which we are always already embedded. Given the shared natural science-hermeneutic delimitation of science, if psychoanalysis is a science, it must be a natural science; and, if psychoanalysis is not a natural science, it cannot be a science at all. Husserlian phenomenology is a far reaching, systematic critique of this delimited concept of science. Within the framework of phenomenology, psychology, and thus psychoanalysis—is construed as a science, but not as a natural science—a science of the natural world, the world of space, objective time, and matter, where matter is construed, as in physics, as that which is known to exist independent of consciousness. Rather, for phenomenology, psychology is a science of meaning, and it is the central one of the humanistic disciplines. Thus, because it recognizes a concept of science broader than natural science, phenomenology is incompatible with both the hermeneutic and natural science models currently espoused by psychoanalytic theoreticians. Moreover, given that the object of investigation of the natural sciences, the natural world, is the product of a specific attitude—one that abstracts from experience as a whole, phenomenology aims to examine the world as immediately given in experience prior to any abstractive acts— the *Lebenswelt* or "lifeworld"—as a self-sufficient domain that is the proper object of investigation of the humanistic disciplines.[40] The lifeworld comes into view when the phenomenological reduction—the voluntary suspension of all ontological commitments, is performed.

As noted above, the natural science and hermeneutic models developed within psychoanalysis share the notion that science is coextensive with natural science. According to Husserl, this stance is the same as natural science's own self-understanding, a self-understanding that developed simultaneously with the development of modern natural science in the seventeenth century. Husserl termed this self-understanding of science "naturalism,"[41] and showed that the nature of natural science as such did not necessitate this self-understanding, that is, that it was a self-*mis*understanding. For natural science to understand itself as coextensive with science, as the only possible type of science, was and is an ideological distortion. From the phenomenological standpoint, psychoanalysis today, including both types of foundational models, is afflicted with the same ideologically motivated distortion that was constituted simultaneously with the constitution of modern natural science. A resolution of the theoretical impasse of psychoanalysis cannot be found, therefore, because the two parties share the same distorted conception of the nature of science. It is precisely this problem which generated and continues to generate opposed models which are unable to render psychoanalysis immune to the charges of reductionism and relativism and which impede the progress of psychoanalytic theory. Thus, even if I succeed in disclosing incipient motives toward phenomenology in contemporary psychoanalysis, these motives will not reach fulfillment unless the underlying conceptual problem is revealed and corrected.

From a Husserlian perspective, psychoanalysis (along with all of the humanistic disciplines) could obviate this Scylla and Charybdis dilemma by construing itself as legitimately and properly scientific, yet not scientific in the same sense as natural science. To construe psychoanalysis in this way would not eliminate either natural science or hermeneutics; rather, it would disclose the proper relation between natural science, phenomenological science, and hermeneutics. If the practitioners of the humanistic disciplines understood the nature of the ideological distortion involved in the origin of natural science, they would gain self-understanding as specializations within another, equally legitimate type of science—phenomenological science. Moreover, since within the phenomenological attitude experience is relative to universal structures of subjectivity, they would then see that phenomenological science encompasses hermeneutics, the theory of interpretation, yet is neither reductionist nor relativist. In order, then, to show how the phenomenological standpoint can assist psychoanalysis in resolving its theoretical impasse, I will both disclose motives toward phenomenology within psychoanalysis and attempt to dislodge the ideological distortion which prevents those motives from moving psychoanalysis toward phenomenology.

In his last work, *The Crisis of Human Sciences and Transcendental Phenomenology (The Crisis)*, Husserl attempted to carry out a similar program, and in the course of so doing he laid bare the motives which led Galileo to constitute modern natural science naturalistically, that is, to construe natural science in such a way that it had to understand itself as the only possible type of science. Husserl's analysis is remarkable and compelling, and is a great masterpiece of philosophical reconstruction. Nevertheless, today, in psychoanalytic work (despite numerous disclaimers) and in culture generally, the naturalistic or positivist conception of science still prevails. This suggests that in some important respect Husserl's reconstruction of Galileo's path of thinking was incomplete. (My supposition here is that if Husserl had definitively solved the problem of constituting a nonpositivist science then his solution would have been widely disseminated and incorporated into all subsequent work, just as, for example, Einstein's Theory of Relativity has been incorporated into physics, after it became widely known and widely understood.) As we shall see, this incompleteness can be rectified through augmentation of Husserlian phenomenology with aspects of contemporary feminist philosophy of science.

If, however, neither model of psychoanalysis is compatible with Husserlian phenomenology, how can phenomenology contribute to a resolution of the conflict between them, and thus of the contemporary theoretical impasse in psychoanalysis? The following considerations will answer this question.

In *The Crisis*, Husserl spoke of psychology as "the decisive field" of phenomenological investigation.[42] It has been shown that the science of psychology that Husserl had in mind was not only experimental psychology of perception, but psychoanalysis as well.[43] In addition, Husserl conceptualized an intimate, mutually fulfilling relationship between phenomenology and psychology. Indeed, *The Crisis* as a whole is an explication of a way into phenomenology through psychology. Within the framework of the phenomenological standpoint toward psychology elaborated by Husserl, and given the current crisis within psychoanalysis, one can anticipate the concrete possibility that, as a means of resolving its theoretical impasse, motives towards a phenomenological conception of psychoanalysis as a science might emerge from within psychoanalysis itself. That is, since neither the hermeneutic nor the natural science model has gained complete ascendancy, and since there are, as we shall see, compelling reasons for rejecting both of these, a third model, one which construes the *Lebenswelt*, the psychic field, as a self-sufficient whole and thus as the proper domain of investigation for a scientific psychoanalysis, might emerge. A critical examination of Wallace's book will show that incipient motives toward phenomenology have already emerged, and this despite the fact that Wallace espouses the natural science interpretation of psychoanalysis. The way in which a phenomenological model of psychoanalysis emerges from the collapse of the positivist and hermeneutic models, and the relation between this and the feminist critique of Freud and positivism will be explicated in the course of the following analysis of Wallace's work.

If the analysis to be presented here is correct, and it is found that significant motives toward phenomenology are emergent in Wallace's work, we must ask: why has Wallace not discovered phenomenology, either on his own or through his research in philosophy? The analysis here suggests that Wallace either will never accept phenomenology as the proper philosophical foundation for psychoanalysis, or, he will accept it if and only if he gains two fundamental insights. First, he must see that, contrary to his claim, his analysis of psychoanalysis does not transcend positivism, it does not, that is, move beyond the standpoint that only the natural world as conceived within the attitude of natural science, the naturalistic or positivist attitude, can be an object of scientific investigation, and second, he must discover that despite significant theoretical gains expressible as motives toward phenomenology, his analysis will not transcend positivism until he reconceptualizes the problem as the presence in psychoanalysis of a positivist, misogynist core.

Here another problem comes to the fore: it may seem that this lengthy section discussing Wallace's views amounts merely to an effort to persuade Wallace himself that phenomenology is the way to go for psychoanalysis.

Though it is obvious how this impression might be generated, it is an inadequate view of the intent embodied in this section. Analysis of the dynamics of Wallace's deployment of his various concepts and arguments shows that the movement of his thought, poised on the threshold of a breakthrough into phenomenology, is obstructed by conflictual material that is unthematized by him. Wallace's effort to refute the hermeneutic interpretation and reconceive psychoanalysis as a nonpositivist natural science is obstructed by his failure to grasp the positivist-misogynist nexus in psychoanalysis. Furthermore, the deployment of argument in Wallace's book is defensive. His conclusions can be precisely located as substitutes for other conclusions that would emerge if he had confronted the positivist–misogynist link within the Freudian model of psychoanalysis. It can further be said, though not herein substantiated through the appropriate research and comparative analysis, that Wallace's thinking is paradigmatic for the humanistic disciplines at their present stage of development.

5. THE PROMISE OF PHENOMENOLOGY IN CONTEMPORARY PSYCHOANALYSIS

On first reading, Wallace's book seems unpromising as the locus of an incipient directedness toward phenomenology. Phenomenological investigation begins with a conscious act of suspension of all ontological commitments, all beliefs regarding the ultimate ontology of the world, that it can be known whether or not the world exists independent of subjectivity. This act of suspension of ontology precipitates the phenomenological attitude in and through which the world can be investigated in its primordial evidentiality— just as it gives itself to a consciousness shorn of metaphysical presuppositions. Wallace, however, endorses and defends the natural science model and reiterates that his ontological stance is that of monistic materialism: matter exists independent of consciousness and is what actually is, true being.[44] The claim that natural science—which takes matter so conceived as its object of investigation—is the only possible type of science is entailed by this stance. This notion of naturalism is the standpoint phenomenology aims to correct.

From his perspective, Wallace attempts to refute the hermeneutic model as developed by Schafer. Since Schafer finds ontological commitments to be problematic,[45] in line, at least in part, with the phenomenological standpoint, it would seem that his hermeneutic stance is a more promising locus for motives toward phenomenology. Such, however, is not the case, and not only because Schafer rejects science in toto, that is, rejects the possibility of obtaining scientific, and, equivalently for him, natural science knowledge of universals and of regularities in the psychic field.[46] Schafer's stance is also unpromising because, in the absence of any regard for the viability of a science of psychology, one must call into question the meaning of his skepticism regarding ontological commitments. Skepticism, as Husserl pointed out, is not at all the same as the phenomenological attitude, which is not skepticism, a sustained state of doubt regarding whether the world can be known to exist independent of subjectivity. Rather, the phenomenological attitude is an act of *suspension of judgment* regarding the ultimate ontology of the world, for, the ultimate ontology of the world is in principle unknowable. Performing the suspension of judgment opens up a new world of being, of investigation—the lifeworld, the world just as it gives itself to subjectivity, before any abstractive acts or ontological judgments.

The suspension of ontological commitments does not entail the rejection of scientificity. The phenomenological attitude does not, and in principle cannot, mean denial that there is being. That being is cannot be denied. Suspension of ontological commitments would entail the rejection of scientificity for the subjective sphere as such only if either the being of subjectivity were implicitly held to be identical to matter, or if subjectivity were said to have no being at all. In the former case, subjectivity would be denied any self-sufficiency, any being-status in and of itself, and could not as such be viewed as an object of scientific investigation. The principal reason why theorists fall into the reduction of subjectivity to materiality, in the form of the claim that subjectivity is an epiphenomenon of materiality or in the form of mind-brain identity, is that the terms 'subjective' and 'subjectivity' are taken to mean something idiosyncratic—that is, that subjectivity is held to be relative to the individual person, or to culture, or to a historical period. The category mistake here is to equate subjectivity with its contingent contents, which are relative, rather than to see that insofar as all persons are subjects there are universal aspects of subjectivity as such, as a self-closed, in the sense of irreducible to any other mode of being or existence, i.e., unique field of investigation.

However, reduction of subjectivity to materiality does not apply to Schafer: he claims that subjectivity is immaterial.[47] Since Schafer claims that subjectivity has an immaterial mode of existence yet denies it the being status of an object of scientific investigation, we must ask, if subjectivity exists, why can it not be scientifically, that is, systematically and methodically, investigated as a self-sufficient sphere? The only circumstance that would preclude such an investigation in principle would be that subjectivity has no being at all, and, as noted above, this is impossible.

Wallace's stance is more phenomenologically promising than Schafer's both because he seeks knowledge in the scientific sense and because his monistic materialism is deployed defensively: it is, I will show, a substitute for an attitude that might emerge and is resisted. This latter attitude is one in which subjectivity is grasped as a self-sufficient sphere and thus as a proper object of scientific investigation: the phenomenological attitude.

In attempting to understand Wallace's book and the motivation underlying his views, it is important to realize that he is committed to the consensus regarding the clinical setting outlined earlier in this chapter. Moreover, it is clear from Wallace's approach that he aims to do full justice to the traditional components of humanism within the framework of the psychoanalytic tradition after Freud, as is especially evident in Wallace's numerous presentations of case histories. Empathic responsiveness to persons, commitment to easing human suffering, concern for the transmission and actualization of values—all of these are on his agenda as motivated and modulated through the analytic perspective. One could argue that these were also on Freud's agenda. However, Wallace differs from Freud in that he wants to eschew the kind of discourse in which Freud engaged, a discourse that the psychoanalytic community has collectively termed the "mixed" discourse of purposiveness and natural science causality and has emphatically, and, because of its pervasiveness in Freud's texts, not without severe trauma, repudiated.

There is no question that any serious student of Freud is confronted with a perplexing dilemma, one that finally has emerged within psychoanalysis as an embarrassment, if not a positively humiliating state of affairs. Freud spoke the language of purpose, that is, of meaning, and he spoke the language of natural science, despite that that these two discourses imply incompatible ontological or metaphysical assumptions, the former that subjectivity is a self-sufficient sphere of investigation, and the latter that only that which exists independent of subjectivity exists, that is, the physicists' "matter." Indeed, one can even find in Freud's corpus statements which demonstrate his awareness that these two realms of discourse require mediation;[48] yet, Freud did not attempt systematically to resolve this problem in his discourse. Apparently he wanted it all three ways: psychophysical determinism, purposiveness, and compatibility between them.[49] Moreover, and most important, Freud did not address directly the most serious problem that resulted from his use of the mixed discourse of purpose (psychology as such) and mechanism (natural scientific reduction): that this mixed discourse represented, and generated in students of psychoanalysis, an equivocal conception of the nature of reality. This is reflected in the uses of the term "reality" in psychoanalytic discourse: there is "psychic reality" and "external reality" and some relation between them, whatever it may be! For this reason, despite Freud's explicit claims to have been operating with an unequivocal, materialist conception of reality (although he also claimed to be a Kantian), he has been extensively criticized for having, rather, a dualistic conception of reality, and one entirely ungrounded in the philosophical sense.[50] In this respect, Wallace is a post-Freudian: on one hand, like Freud, he is tempted to live in three worlds of discourse, that is, purpose, mechanism, and compatibility; on the other hand, he is powerfully motivated to develop a unitary discourse, especially and above all in the face of the crisis in psychoanalytic theory and practice. In the face of this crisis, attempting to live in three worlds spells suicide: psychoanalysis can no longer afford the luxury of its mixed discourse and the equivocal conception of reality associated with that discourse, not in the face of the onslaught it faces today. Above all, psychoanalysis must find a discourse that will honor precisely its own uniqueness, precisely that which, in the absence of its own language, has forced its practitioners and theoreticians to speak of "our science"—psychoanalytic science, which has as its object of investigation the field of psychic reality (especially the unconscious) as it discloses itself within the therapeutic field. The therapeutic field is the field of the radical empiricism of psychoanalysis, the field which, if naturalistically reduced, disappears, as does psychoanalysis itself. However, in order to develop a univocal discourse, it is necessary for the field of investigation of psychoanalysis to be conceived unequivocally.

Owing to the nature of its origin, psychoanalysis has always had as one of its central preoccupations the effort to characterize its uniqueness, that owing to which it is the unique discipline which all analysts take it to be, and that which, they believe, is virtually impossible for nonanalysts and nonanalysands to grasp. Traditionally, the uniqueness of psychoanalysis has been held to lie in its concept of psychic determinism. Those who, like Schafer, espouse the hermeneutic interpretation of psychoanalysis, claim that the concept of psychic determinism is part and parcel of the metapsychological, and therefore reductionist, program of Freud. According to Schafer, the distinguishing feature of psychoanalysis is, rather, its all pervasive emphasis on the person as agent, as the one who, in order to find relief, must acknowledge her or his role in creating and sustaining her or his inner conflicts.[51] Wallace is fully aware of this significant aspect of the psychoanalytic view. He deals with the issue of agency under the rubric of "self-determination," which he regards as compatible with psychic determinism as such: "From our consideration of 'free will' and determinism it follows that the analysand is always self-determining, hence 'free' in Spinoza's sense of the word: 'That thing is called free which exists from the necessity of its nature alone, and is determined to action by itself alone.'"[52] In response to Schafer's claim that agency should displace psychic determinism as the key concept of psychoanalysis, Wallace claims that Schafer has an incoherent concept of human freedom as unmotivated, that is, undetermined by anything at all.[53] Wallace claims, moreover, that Schafer views all psychic occurrences as contemporaneous and thus ignores that human beings have histories inscribed in memories and that the present is determined by the past, that is, consciousness, present experience, is determined by the unconscious, the repository of past experience.[54, 55] Thus Wallace, in contrast to Schafer, retains the classical view that the distinguishing feature of psychoanalysis is its concept of psychic determinism. Here, I will neither discuss this point nor enter into the free will-determinism debate because my primary interest is the way Wallace plays off over and against Schafer. Suffice it to say that within the phenomenological framework, the free will-determinism duality is suspended, as are all binary oppositions. My point is, rather, that despite that they each propose what they take to be mutually exclusive formulations of the uniqueness of psychoanalysis, determinism and indeterminism, and despite his naturalistic conception of science, Wallace, no less than Schafer, views the psychic as given within the analytic therapeutic field as a uniquely existing, and thus unequivocally self-sufficient, sphere. It is not just that for Wallace psychic determinism characterizes the psychoanalytic field; most important, psychic determinism is that which enables the psychoanalyst to have privileged access to the psychic field as such, that access which psychoanalysis alone potentiates since only in the therapeutic field constituted by psychoanalyst and patient does the psychic stand forth purely as it gives itself, as purely psychological.

Wallace is well aware that the move into hermeneutics was and is motivated in part by the flight from reductionism, and that it is a means of attempting to conceptualize and identify unambiguously, over and against reductionism, that which makes psychoanalysis uniquely psychoanalysis. He sees that because the hermeneutic approach is relativistic and thus militates against uniquely determining anything at all, that it also poses the threat of the dissolution of psychoanalysis. However, while resisting hermeneutics, Wallace cannot adopt the same kind of mixed discourse as Freud. He sees that mixed discourse must be abandoned, for it cannot overcome the flight into hermeneutics; indeed, mixed discourse has led to the move into hermeneutics. On the other hand, because he grasps the integrity of the psychological field, and because he wants to be able to demonstrate determinism in the psychological field as conceptualized by psychoanalysis, that is, as purely psychological, he cannot speak the reductionist language of natural science. Wallace's solution to this dilemma is to claim that determinism, which he takes to be the sine qua non of science, is not itself univocally determined. Following Bunge,[56] Wallace maintains that there are several modalities of determinism: efficient causality in the natural science sense, determinism by purpose, as in psychoanalysis, dialectic determinism, etc. Wallace maintains, therefore, that psychoanalysis need not be condemned to a mixed discourse nor need it be either reductionist or hermeneutic; instead, psychoanalytic theory can univocally describe and explain the psychic field through a determinism of purpose, a telic determinism. According to Wallace, telic determinism is determinism nonetheless, and in no way conflicts with monistic materialism and natural science causality, that is, with the notion that matter is the only thing that exists.[57] Thus, Wallace maintains that psychoanalysis as a science is both deterministic and non-reductionist, that is, non-positivist.

But we must ask, how is it that Wallace believes that the psychic field can exhibit a determinism of purpose whereas only matter exists and is causally determined in the natural science sense? If the psychic field is in actuality material, as Wallace's views suggest it must be, why then is it not causally determined? Wallace insists that his viewpoint is that of a monism of matter; yet, he finds mechanistic reductionism intolerable because he wants to be able to demonstrate psychic determinism within the psychic field purely as it gives itself in the therapeutic setting. And well might he wish to, for there is no doubt that the Freudian thrust is just so to claim, and to claim to be able to demonstrate, that there is psychic determinism in the very unfolding of an analysis on the phenomenological level, as it were, of the therapeutic field. Wallace claims that even though psychoanalysis will deal with only one type, the telic (purposive), there are, nevertheless, two compatible types of psychic determinism—natural science-causal and telic. Thus, he indicates that he has grasped that if reductionism is true then determinism on the therapeutic level is not demonstrable because the psychic components of the determined event—the psychically determining components—cannot be known to be truly, that is, causally, determining and determined prior to the reduction to material entities. It may be that, when reduced, the two entities, for example an idea and the defensive reaction following upon it, are not at all causally related and even may not be spatially and temporally contiguous. Indeed, Wallace indicates his awareness not only that such a reduction has never been carried out, but that there are reasons to believe that it never can be achieved.[58] Thus, even though he eschews describing the psychic field in terms of natural science causality, Wallace's claim that there are two types of psychic determinism indicates his failure to achieve an unequivocal conception of the psyche and thus a univocal discourse. A univocal discourse made possible by an unequivocal conception of the psyche is precisely that which Schafer claims to have achieved with his "new language for psychoanalysis" (see 77n28)—action language. Wallace's own mixed discourse undermines his attempt both to demonstrate the inadequacy of hermeneutics on one hand and the viability of a scientific model on the other.

The overall thrust of my exegesis is this: Wallace believes that the meaning of science is that it is a framework wherein determinism, universals, and regularities are shown, and knowledge can be conceptualized and obtained.[59]

Moreover, he is aware that natural science can lead to knowledge because its object of investigation is construed as a self-sufficient, self-closed sphere—that is, it is construed monistically. At the same time, he is confronted with an interpretation of psychoanalysis—hermeneutics—with much of which he is in strong agreement as over and against Freud, especially insofar as it repudiates mechanistic reductionism. However, at the same time as it problematizes the ontology of the psyche, psychoanalytic hermeneutics, represented by Schafer, repudiates altogether the idea of science and views the psychic field in terms of an indeterminist concept of freedom. It seems as though in order to have science and knowledge, one must have an ontological commitment. Wallace, confronted with this dilemma, paradoxically announces that his ontological commitment is to matter, while at the same time he gives clear evidence of awareness that the integrity and irreducibility of the psychic field render such a commitment gratuitous and incoherent: "This vignette also provides support for my . . . speculation . . . that aspects of symbolically mediated behaviors may forever defy reduction to physiological models."[60] Thus, Wallace's insistence on monistic materialism is deployed strategically, that is, defensively, as I have described. But why is it not surrendered in favor of the phenomenological reduction, the deliberate, systematic suspension of all ontological commitments, which, as Husserl showed, discloses subjectivity—the psychic field—as a self-sufficient sphere, and thus as a proper object of scientific investigation?

In a framework in which both positivist reduction and hermeneutic relativism are rejected, and in which the psychic sphere is conceptualized as able to be investigated purely as such, it seems astonishing that a monism of matter is affirmed. Yet, if a monism of matter is not affirmed, what would be the source of the scientificity of psychoanalysis, of its potential to discover universals and regularities? Wallace's assertion of a materialistic monism serves the purpose of doing justice to the Freudian emphasis on the bodily aspect of psychosexual development and it serves the purpose of providing a totalizing framework for the self-continuous, self-sufficient domain presupposed by all science.[61] Wallace also deploys his materialistic monism to indicate the falsity of any subject-object split.[62] But monistic materialism is sharply at variance with Wallace's grasp of the irreducible, determinate uniqueness of the psychic field: if ultimately only matter exists, why is the psychic field not naturalistically reducible? And if it is so reducible, why are not psychopharmacology and neurology more important, that is, more true, than psychoanalysis? It is precisely in his grasp of the irreducible and determinate nature of the psychic field and the need for a method that will yield knowledge of universals and regularities with respect to that field that Wallace approaches the phenomenological conception of the psychic as the locus of a constitutive, universal *a priori*.

At a crucial point in his discussion of determinism, Wallace comes remarkably close to achieving a constitutive analysis, in the Husserlian sense, of the meaning of determinism. He raises the issue as to what accounts for psychic determinism, that is, for the passage from meaning to meaning. He criticizes those who seem to have an indeterminist conception of the psyche, "who wish to avoid deterministic propositions while preserving the ordering and connecting principles that only determinism can supply."[63] On the next page, he writes, "If psychoanalysis abandons . . . determinism, must it not also relinquish its claims to be a . . . science demonstrating . . . universalities . . . and . . . regularities between antecedent conditions and subsequent behaviors?"[64] Wallace seems quite close here to grasping that the structure of all postulated determinisms, including that of the natural world, is in fact the structure of meaning formation as such, that is, that causality presupposes meaning (motivation)[65] rather than vice versa.

Incipient motives toward phenomenology are, then, clearly evident in Wallace's thought. However, at this point one may object: in what sense are these motives referred to as "incipient"? In response, I argue that Wallace's belief in a materialist ontology is deployed defensively. In his book, this ontology is invoked often, yet it is given no consistent philosophical grounding. On the contrary, Wallace expresses certain ideas, for example the possibility that reduction of the psychic to the physical is in principle impossible, which would call his materialist ontology into question. As a belief, an attitude—the naturalistic attitude—ontological materialism loses some of its motivational weight and is thus deployed not substantively but substitutively, in the absence of a more well-motivated belief. A more well-motivated belief, a belief with a greater motivational "weight,"[66] would enable the same conceptual structure while eliminating interference from inherently, though not obviously, contradictory beliefs. Nevertheless, there is little in this analysis of the motivation of Wallace's beliefs to generate the presumption that the defensively held belief will be surrendered in favor of the phenomenological attitude. The crucial question is, what is necessary in order for this surrender to occur?

The sense of the path of thinking developed in this chapter is that, despite the fact that it is incipient in his thinking, Wallace will not be able to adopt the phenomenological perspective that there can be a non-naturalistic science of the subjective until he becomes aware of, and through self-investigation is able to abandon, the misogynistic aspects of Freud's theory of psychosexual development. In that theory, Freud associated femininity with subjectivity, with an inability to grasp the subject-object split. From this perspective, maleness is identified with maintaining the subject-object split so that the male can be conceived as able to be truly objective by having the ability to separate himself from his subjectivity (when he overcomes his need for love of father, what, according to Freud, females cannot achieve). It is important to point out that the "subjectivity" to which females were relegated by Freud is not subjectivity in the phenomenological sense—subjectivity as both the history of a given psyche and as the universal *a priori* of consciousness in general. The subjectivity in which, in Freud's view, females are trapped, is, rather, what is sometimes termed "vicious subjectivity," and what Husserl termed the "subjective relative"—subjectivity as the mere repository of irrational prejudices.[67] From the perspective of the critique made here, it is more accurate to say that Freud confused or conflated what he viewed as the *discovery* of the subject-object split, and the consequent rejection of the subjective field as a proper object of scientific investigation, with the constitution or *formation* of the subject-object split. As is now the consensus in psychoanalytic theory, the subject-object split is an erroneous view of the nature of reality. In the language of phenomenology, further investigation shows that the constitution of the subject-object split through the intentionality of consciousness was a "blind intention." A blind intention is one for which there was no adequate evidence, no experiential givenness.

I am not claiming here that commitment to these masculinist aspects of psychoanalytic theory is a feature of Wallace's personal history, his course of psychosexual development. I am suggesting, however, at the very least, that the association of femininity with subjectivity and the delegitimation and disparagement of both are built into, that is, to use Husserl's term, "sedimented"[68] in Western culture in general and in Freud's theory of psychosexual development in particular.

There is no explicit evidence that Husserlian phenomenology was constituted with feminist motives. Since, however, Husserlian phenomenology is par excellence the philosophical viewpoint that has as its core the notion that subjectivity is a self-sufficient domain of scientific investigation, it follows, if phenomenology is correct, that it decisively transcends positivism and with it the misogyny that, I have maintained, is positivism's necessary accompaniment. However, in the absence of any evidence, how can these feminist motives be shown to be potentiated within phenomenology? In order to answer this question, it is necessary to do what Husserl always recommended and which he designated as the essence of the phenomenological method of philosophical reconstruction: examine the origins. In the next section, then, in order to show the compatibility of Husserl's analysis with feminist philosophy of science, I will examine some aspects of his explication of the origin of the naturalistic worldview. However, it is important first to point out that the phenomenological quest for origins is not an instance of the "originological fallacy" often attributed to Freud.[69] Rather, the Husserlian regression to origins is a complex back and forth movement for the purpose of grasping a motivational nexus: "Thus we have no other choice than to proceed forward and backward in a zigzag pattern; the one must help the other in an interplay."[70] The purpose of the regressive analysis is to make possible motivational change. In this respect, phenomenology is akin to psychoanalysis.

6. THE PHENOMENOLOGICAL CRITIQUE
OF NATURALISM (POSITIVISM)

A careful reading of Husserl's explication of Galileo's path of thinking[71] leaves no doubt that, for Husserl, the motives operative for Galileo were potent and led straight to naturalism. In a great masterpiece of philosophical reconstruction, Husserl exposes, explores, and builds motive upon motive with breathtaking clarity. Since my aim in this presentation is to focus on certain explicit, determinate interstices in Husserl's analysis, I will allude only briefly to some of these motives.

According to Husserl, naturalism, ontological materialism, came into existence when Galileo hypothesized that the sensuous plenum, the world as immediately, sensuously experienced by everyone, is an illusion, and is merely relative to the experiencing subject, and that only that which is directly or indirectly measurable actually exists as true being.[72] (This indicates the often overlooked inner alliance between naturalism and relativism. From this point of view, Wallace's natural science view and Schafer's hermeneutic view are two aspects of the same perspective: that natural science is the only possible type of science.) It follows that for Galileo only the investigation of the natural world, the measurable world, is science and can yield real knowledge of true being. Husserl shows that this hypothesis was motivated by a path of remembering bound up with a path of forgetting. Remembered were the mathematics, astronomy, and science of his, Galileo's time, conjoined with the Renaissance's remembering of Greek philosophy and mathematics. This conjunction motivated the hypothesis of a science of measurement and of measurables which would encompass all: the infinities of both geometric space and the sensory manifold. Forgotten was the origin of science, mathematics, and philosophy in the pre-scientific lifeworld which has its own aims and purposes.[73] Forgotten also, due to the traditionalization of geometry, was the intrinsically human capacity for reactivation of sense: "Reactivation is the human capacity or ability to reawaken the primordial sense that sedimented (traditional) sense covers over. . . . As finite and mediate, the ability to reactive sense can be lost, a plight that Husserl felt gave rise to the crisis in philosophy which characterized modem times." [74]

Thus, the capacity for reactivation is the capacity for insight into the primal institution of any meant, that is, the origin of any meaning, in order to grasp its actual sense as it gives itself. For example, rather than accepting it unquestioningly from the tradition, one could reactivate the sense of any geometric axiom or proof and see it firsthand in order to disclose in and for oneself its intrinsic sense or nonsense. Galileo failed to reactivate the meaning-intention that geometry bears within itself: the meaning of its origin in an abstractive intention, an abstraction from the lifeworld as a whole, and that this abstractive act was performed for the purpose of helping to solve human problems, problems which are nonetheless subordinate to the overall struggle of humanity for a strictly rational, truly happy life. In thus forgetting the prescientific lifeworld, Galileo threw a "garb of ideas"[75] over it, a garb which covered over the obvious fact that the lifeworld as it gives itself, the world as immediately experienced, including, but not restricted to, the sensuous plenum, has its own overall causal style, its own inner and outer regularities, its subjective and intersubjective invariant senses, that can be investigated as such. Galileo, a "discovering and a concealing genius,"[76] obscured the fact that the lifeworld including the sensuous plenum, has its own invariances that can be methodically examined and discovered and made the basis of a science of the whole of human experience. For example, Galileo ignored the invariant style of the lifeworld which always and necessarily gives itself immediately to consciousness in the form of objects, whether in perception, fantasy, or memory. In short, in forgetting the lifeworld as the necessary meaning-fundament of all sense, and in forgetting the very capacity to reactivate the meaning-fundament of all sense, Galileo forgot his humanity.

Immediately after his exposition of the origin of naturalism in the Galilean worldview, Husserl proceeds to show how the dualistic worldview of Descartes, the radical subject-object, that is, mind-matter, split arose as its direct consequence. In this process, authentic subjectivity was forgotten, and replaced with a concept of "mind" as objectively correlated with the world, a world now denuded of all subjective predicates.[77] On the basis of the foregoing, it is now necessary to examine the following quotations from *The Crisis*:

A. In order to clarify the formation of Galileo's thought we must accordingly reconstruct not only what consciously motivated him. It will also be instructive to bring to light what was implicitly included in his guiding model of mathematics, even though, because of the direction of his interest, it was kept from his view: as a hidden, presupposed meaning, it naturally had to enter into his physics along with everything else.[78]

B. It did not enter the mind of a Galileo that it would ever become relevant, indeed of fundamental importance, to geometry, as a branch of a universal knowledge of what is (philosophy), to make geometrical self-evidence—the "how" of its origin—into a problem. For us, proceeding beyond Galileo, in our historical reflections, it will be of considerable interest to see how a shift of focus became urgent and how the "origin" of knowledge had to become a major problem.[79]

C. But does not this manner of objectivity, to be practiced on one abstract aspect of the world, give rise to the following thought and the conjectural question: Must not something similar be possible for the concrete world as such? If one is already firmly convinced, moreover, like Galileo—thanks to the Renaissance's return to ancient philosophy of the possibility of philosophy as episteme achieving an objective science of the world, and if it had just been revealed that pure mathematics, applied to nature, consummately fulfills the postulate of episteme in its sphere of shapes: did not this also have to suggest to Galileo the idea of a nature which is constructively determinable in the same manner in all its other aspects?[80] (33)

In statement A, Husserl points out that philosophical reconstruction necessitates investigation of hidden, presupposed, nonconscious meanings. In statement B, he indicates that philosophical reflection also involves a historical perspective. Statement C is the one which now must be scrutinized carefully. In this statement, Husserl, referring to all of the motives which he reconstructed, asks, "did not this also have to suggest to Galileo" the idea which Husserl calls naturalism: the relegation of the lifeworld to the merely subjective-relative? The question relevant to our concerns here is the following: what is the force of Husserl's remark, "did not this also have to suggest to Galileo"? Did Husserl believe that he had exhaustively uncovered Galileo's motives? My response to this question is the following: the sense of phenomenology is that nothing prevents us from bringing to bear on Husserl's reconstruction additional motives gained from historical perspective and from further research. Most important, the phenomenological standpoint motivates one never to accept any reconstruction as complete in a falsely absolutized manner;[81] rather, as phenomenologists we must emphasize uncovering directionalities of sense, mindful always that phenomenological investigation is an infinite task. In addition, reflection upon *The Crisis* itself in its unfolding will persuade us that Husserl's reconstruction of Galileo's motives was incomplete. The direction Husserl took in *The Crisis* from Galileo to Descartes, Locke, and Kant charted a motivational path which led to dualism and psychologism (naturalization of the psyche). After exposing the incoherencies in this path, Husserl then constructed a way into phenomenology itself through psychology, which he designated as "the decisive field" of phenomenological research. In the last part of *The Crisis,* Husserl indicated his acute awareness of the depth dimension of human affectivity as part of the flowing motivational streams constitutive of egological life in its sociality and historicity.[82] Thus, everything moves us to reflect backward with our psychological insight to continue to lay bare the presuppositions sedimented in Galileo's thinking and, mutatis mutandis, in the thinking of all those who remain in the naturalistic attitude.

7. FEMINISM AND THE PHENOMENOLOGICAL CRITIQUE OF POSITIVISM (NATURALISM)

At this point, Evelyn Fox Keller's work, noted above, can be used to augment Husserl's phenomenological explication of the origin of naturalism. At one point, Keller discusses the two major interpretations of quantum mechanics in terms of a cognitive impasse. This impasse, she maintains, is the result of the inability of physicists to abandon the two basic tenets of classical physics, identified by Schrödinger as (1) the objectivity of nature, that is, its existence independent of the observer, and (2) the knowability of nature in the sense of a one to one correlation between attributes of correct theories and the states of nature itself. [83] It can readily be seen that these two tenets express the naturalistic attitude as described by Husserl.

The two major interpretations of quantum mechanics are the statistical and the Copenhagen interpretations. Keller explains that the statistical interpretation denies the second tenet by claiming that nature exists independent of the observer but is not knowable as such. The theoretically constituted wave functions do not correspond to the states of nature as such; the collapse of the wave function when direct observations are made indicates that what actually exists is particles, not waves. Here knowability is denied whereas objectivity is affirmed. The Copenhagen interpretation denies the first tenet, arguing that theoretical wave functions do correlate directly with the states of the system. The collapse of the wave function when observations are made is taken to indicate that the system does not exist independent of the observer. Thus, on the Copenhagen interpretation, nature is knowable, but not objective, that is, not objective in the naturalistic sense of existing independent of the observer. (Keller, who is a theoretical physicist, rejects as implausible both the many worlds interpretation of quantum mechanics and Wigner's claim that the act of knowing as such exerts force on the system, thus producing observations).[84]

Keller questioned how it is that in spite of fifty years (now seventy-five years) of experimental confirmation of quantum mechanics this impasse has not been resolved. She relates this issue to Piagetian cognitive psychology, explaining that Piaget drew a parallel between the historical development of science and the cognitive development of individuals. She argues that a new cognitive structure is necessary to interpret quantum mechanics correctly.

Quantum mechanics involves new knowledge that does not correlate with the classical schema as described by Schrödinger: a schema in which knowledge and objectivity are construed on the basis of a radical subject-object (mind-matter) split in and by which the knowability-objectivity criteria of the classical paradigm are generated. Furthermore, Keller follows Piaget in claiming that the absence of the appropriate cognitive structure results in repression of the new knowledge. In this case, the repressed new knowledge is that the relation between subject and object cannot be such as it is represented in the classical paradigm. However, Keller sharply criticizes Piaget for ignoring the insights of psychoanalysis into the affective aspects of psychological development, especially as they are interwoven with cognitive development.[85]

The point of greatest interest here is Keller's explanation of the reasons for the impasse in quantum theory. In presenting her explanation, it will be helpful to recapitulate some aspects of her ideas already discussed. Modem natural science, she explains, was constituted on the basis of motives that compromised its capacity for an authentically objective conception and investigation of nature. She shows that, owing to the vicissitudes of psychosexual development in bourgeois Western societies, the exclusion of women from science was merely symptomatic of the genderization of science itself. For Keller, the basic tenets of natural science, "knowability" and "objectivity" in the naturalistic sense described above, presuppose a model of maleness built into Western culture. According to this model, maleness means a point of view such that mind and nature are radically split off from one another, and mind can observe and investigate nature free from any prejudices. Keller shows, however, that natural science as so conceived was not and is not free from subjective and historically motivated prejudices, especially the desire for domination and control of nature that flows from the operative model of maleness. The thrust of Keller's book is to show that in order to overcome its current impasse, and in order to progress more fruitfully in the future and realize its full emancipatory potential, natural science must be reconceptualized so that it may develop a human, rather than male, attitude toward the natural world.[86]

Unlike some other scholars working toward a feminist reevaluation of science,[87] Keller insists upon the objectivity and scientificity of natural science. Her claim is that when natural science is reconceptualized and an authentically human standpoint is attained, the goal of science will still be objectivity in the sense of the quest for truth: Keller does not envision a reformed science as a hermeneutic discipline. She does not think that a non-naturalistic science loses its scientificity. On the contrary, she rejects all relativism.[88] Keller is, of course, fully aware of the fact that the historical claims by scientists to have discovered the certain truth were part and parcel of the maleness of gendered science. She believes, rather, that science is only meaningful as science when conceived as a search for truth, where truth itself involves the interrelationship between subject and object, observer and nature:

> I define objectivity as the pursuit of a maximally authentic, and hence maximally reliable, understanding of the world around oneself. Such a pursuit is dynamic to the extent that it actively draws on the commonality between mind and nature as a resource for understanding. Dynamic objectivity aims at a form of knowledge that grants to the world around us its independent integrity but does so in a way that remains cognizant of, indeed relies on, our connectivity with that world.[89]

Thus, Keller's definition indicates that authentic scientific objectivity necessarily includes awareness that the relation between, that is, the commonality and connectivity of mind and nature are such that this relation is a constitutive feature of the scientific attitude and the scientific investigation of nature. The overall aim of Keller's book is to show that the genderization of natural science has been an obstacle that has hindered its progress and that natural science will fulfill its emancipatory promise when it becomes human rather than male. What, then, is the relevance of Keller's work to my aim of showing how phenomenology can assist psychoanalysis in resolving its own theoretical impasse?

Above, I indicated that Husserl's interpretation of the origin of naturalism is at the same time an interpretation of the origin of the inability of the practitioners of the humanistic disciplines to conceive their object of investigation as itself a proper object of scientific investigation. Consequently, naturalism means not only that the natural world is misunderstood, that true nature is both revealed and concealed; naturalism means also that the psychic is designated, and denigrated, as the "subjective-relative" and declared not amenable to specifically scientific investigation which would obtain knowledge of regularities and universals. The naturalistic misconception of the nature of science and the delegitimation of the scientificity of the psychic are thus simultaneously co-constituted. Following this, I argued that it is consistent with the spirit of Husserl's analysis and with phenomenology itself to augment Husserl's own analysis by uncovering additional motives leading to the constitution of naturalism. Finally, then, my aim in introducing Keller's work is to show that in order to conceive natural science non-naturalistically, it is necessary to uncover not only the lifeworld (in Husserl's sense) and the motives that led to its concealment; it is also necessary to uncover additional motives which prevent the emergence of a more rational conception of the nature of science as a whole.

Earlier, a passage from *The Crisis* was quoted in which Husserl claimed that naturalism came into existence when, seeing that all shapes could be represented, and their motions explained, mathematically, Galileo inferred, necessarily yet incorrectly, that all aspects of the sensory plenum, the world as given in immediate experience, are, directly or indirectly, mathematizable. In *The Crisis*, Husserl did not phenomenologically explicate the motives in and through which Galileo's mistaken inference was necessitated. It has been argued in this chapter that those motives can be explicated if phenomenology is augmented by feminism. Given Keller's analysis, *one can infer that masculinist motives led Galileo to regard the indirect mathematizability of the sensory plenum as warrant to relegate subjectivity, experience itself qua experience, to the inferior status of mere illusion, unreality, that which in principle cannot be an object of scientific investigation.*

However, is not Husserl himself vulnerable to the same critique? Why is it that he himself did not suggest the possibility that Galileo was motivated by masculinist motives to reject the possibility that the world as it gives itself to subjectivity can itself be as such an object of investigation, in and with its irreducible sensory fullness? Certainly, it is possible, even plausible, to suggest that Husserl, too, was not able to identify masculinism as ideological distortion that thwarts science. However, at least one can say that Husserlian phenomenology bears within it as an essential component the motive, or motif, of self critique through self investigation:

> The psychologist . . . is in search of nothing other than a method of positive scientific character for passing beyond everyday self-knowledge and knowledge of human beings. But in finding himself compelled to develop the method of phenomenological reduction, he makes the discovery that in fact no one actually arrives in his [ordinary] self-knowledge at his true and actual self, the being which is his own as ego-subject and as the subject of all his self-knowledge and mundane accomplishments, that all this shows itself only through the reduction, and that pure psychology is nothing other than the infinitely toilsome way of genuine and pure self-knowledge . . .[90]

Masculine prejudice arises out of a complex of social, cultural, and psychosexual-developmental factors. This complex of factors is expressed as misogyny, as the implicit or explicit belief that females are inferior: subjective rather than objective where "objectivity" is more highly valorized, and thus lacking scientific ability. As we have seen, Keller shows that the tendency to exclude that which is psychologically and culturally identified as female has influenced the conceptual foundations of science itself and must be overcome if science is to progress.

However, as was pointed out earlier, Keller cannot ground non-naturalistic science because she does not think within the phenomenological attitude; that is, she does not bracket or suspend all ontological commitments. Since the

Lebenswelt only comes into view as such within the phenomenological attitude, Keller cannot conceptualize the *Lebenswelt* as the object of investigation of the humanistic disciplines in general and of psychology in particular. Moreover, then, she cannot conceive natural science as it is conceived within the phenomenological perspective: as just one, not the only, type of science. Yet this reconception of natural science is the precondition for the possibility of the type of progress she hopes for from natural science.

CONCLUSION

Psychoanalysts today face challenges that forced on them a dichotomy that they have not yet grasped as false: a dichotomy between naturalistic and hermeneutic interpretations of the nature of psychoanalysis. Wallace's naturalistic conception of science as coextensive with natural science is precisely what prevents him from reconceiving psychoanalysis as a nonnatural science, a science of the psychic purely as psychic—a science of meaning. Wallace's views indicate that, while on one hand he perceives the significance, for the survival of psychoanalysis as such, of grasping the uniqueness and irreducible integrity of the psychic field, on the other hand, because he conceives natural science as the only possible type of science (naturalism), he defensively clings to it in order to salvage the scientificity of psychoanalysis. It seems that, for Wallace, the only alternative to psychopharmacology is a self-sufficient psychic sphere, whereas the only alternative to hermeneutic relativism is naturalism, which rejects the self-sufficiency of the psychic sphere. Despite this impasse, Wallace has reached a standpoint that should enable him to abandon naturalism in favor of a conceptualization of psychoanalysis as a phenomenological discipline. If we ask why Wallace clings to the idea that natural science is the only possible type of science, the answer provided in this paper is that he does so because he perceives, perhaps unconsciously, that to abandon this belief is simultaneously to abandon masculinist ideology, a step he is not yet prepared to take.

An attempt has been made here to show that phenomenology demonstrates that naturalism is an error, a misinterpretation of the nature of the physical world. According to Husserl, the motives which led to naturalism were the forgottenness of the lifeworld, the world presupposed by all science, and the forgottenness of the intrinsically human capacity for the reactivation of the origin of meaning in intentional acts of the constituting psyche. In addition, I have introduced the work of Evelyn Fox Keller to show that, though this was not in Husserl's purview, in significant part the motives leading to naturalism flow from masculine prejudice and the genderization of science. Once naturalism is grasped as an error and its motives are laid bare, one sees that there can be a legitimate science of psychology, of the psychic as such. Once science is understood nonnaturalistically, the subjective is no longer construed as the merely subjective-relative and is thus no longer delegitimated as a proper object of scientific investigation.

We must now look toward the formation of a phenomenological psychoanalysis. I would argue that this is finally the meaning of *The Crisis* itself: that to be introduced to phenomenology, to become a phenomenologist, is to work toward the constitution of an authentic psychoanalytic science of subjectivity. An authentic psychoanalytic science of subjectivity would be one in which psychoanalysis both recognizes, and is encompassed within, the theory and praxis of phenomenological self-investigation as a necessary prerequisite for investigation of intersubjectivity—the interpersonal field of psychoanalysis.

One of the necessary accompaniments of such a phenomenological psychoanalysis will have to be the development of a feminist version of psychoanalysis, one which embodies the insight that Freud's theory of psychosexual development was constituted by him in its specificity on the basis of irrational motives that were intimately bound to an unacknowledged misogyny, and therefore prevented him from experiencing women and men as equally, and thus fully, human. A feminist model of psychoanalysis can emerge in the framework of the phenomenological conception of psychology as a science of meaning, the phenomenological discipline in and through which the link between naturalism and misogyny is laid bare and broken, dissolving both. Thus, phenomenological reconceptualization preserves psychoanalysis's integrity as a human science of meaning and allows it to move beyond the natural science-hermeneutic deadlock.

Finally, another link between feminism and phenomenology can advance the claim that it is only through phenomenology that psychoanalysis can rid itself of its naturalistic-misogynist core. In the analysis of Wallace's views, it was pointed out that he adheres to the notion that the distinctive feature of the psychoanalytic standpoint, that which makes psychoanalysis what it is, is its concept of psychic determinism. In attempting to refute the hermeneutic interpretation by constituting psychoanalysis as a historical science, Wallace touches upon another crucial aspect of the specificity of psychoanalysis: that psychic determinism is correlated to the capacity of human beings to trace back to the origin of their own psychic states. In this respect, psychoanalysis is profoundly homologous with phenomenology. Husserl explicated how Galileo inherited from the tradition of geometry the forgottenness of the characteristically human capacity to reactivate meanings sedimented in subjectivity so as to explicate their sense or nonsense. What is the relevance of feminism to this forgottenness of reactivation? What does the phenomenological, psychoanalytic notion of reactivation have to do with the relation between science and feminism?

For this we can turn to Husserl:

> In the eidetics of space, or material nature, of mind, etc., we engage in dogmatic science under the title "ontology." We judge about spatial formations as such, psyches and psychic properties as such, about human beings as such. We judge about what belongs to objectivities like these "as such" in truth, and that implies here: belongs to them in unconditioned universality. Phenomenology in our sense is the science of "origins," of the "mothers" of all cognition: and it is the maternal-ground of all philosophical method: to this ground and to the work in it, everything leads back.[91]

The repudiation of both the natural science and hermeneutic models of psychoanalysis, made possible by phenomenology informed by feminism, can motivate the emergence of an authentic science of the subjective: phenomenological psychoanalysis. Psychoanalysis can then finally bring to light what has for so long been hidden in its depths: its vocation as agent and field for the liberation of humanity.

NOTES

1. In this chapter I do not discuss the work of the leading feminist psychoanalyst-theorist, Jessica Benjamin. This is due to neither disagreement nor oversight. In this chapter I am focused on the natural science-hermeneutics theoretical bifurcation and Benjamin does not deal with this issue in any explicit manner.

2. An excellent overview of the natural science versus hermeneutic debate can be obtained from the papers in Merton Gill and Phillip Holzman, *Psychology versus Metapsychology* (New York: International Universities Press, 1976). For a more recent treatment of the continuing, conflictual bifurcation of psychoanalytic theory, including clinical theory, see Irwin Z. Hoffman, *Ritual and Spontaneity in the Psychoanalytic Process: A Dialectical-Constructivist View* (Hillsdale, NJ: The Analytic Press, 1998). Hoffman's book is an excellent discussion of the permutations in the conflict between positivism, or "objectivism," and hermeneutics in psychoanalytic theory since Gill and Holzman's book was published. Hoffman refers to his own perspective as "dialectical constructivism," and he, like others, believes that any claim that psychoanalysis can be a science is ipso facto positivist. Though Hoffman is a profound thinker and a gifted writer, he does not resolve the issue. In his book he discusses relativism in several contexts and claims that his view obviates what he refers to as "radical relativism," yet, he offers no philosophical stance that grounds his claims. He maintains that his dialectical constructivism leaves room for "an independent reality" but does not explain what exactly this means—independent in what sense, and, if not "wholly independent of ourselves," how is this independence to be conceived? (Hoffman, *Ritual,* 21–22).

3. Sigmund Freud, *New Introductory Lectures on Psychoanalysis*, Standard Edition, v. 22 (London: Hogarth Press, 1933), 160.

4. Sigmund Freud, *Psychoanalysis and Telepathy*, Standard Edition, v. 22 (London: Hogarth Press, 1922/1955), 179.

5. Peter Gay, *Freud: A Life for Our Time* (New York: Norton, 1988), 34–35.

6. Freud, *New*, 170.

7. Donald P. Spence, *Narrative Truth and Historical Truth* (New York: Norton, 1982).

8. In a recent article, Sidney J. Blatt attempts to resolve the problem by advocating "methodological pluralism." However it is hard to understand how two standpoints that are radically opposed in both their ontology and their epistemology, as are positivism and hermeneutics, can be encompassed in a methodological pluralism. See Sidney J. Blatt, "Minding the Gap between Positivism and Hermeneutics in Psychoanalytic Research," *Journal of the American Psychoanalytic Association*, 54, no. 2 (2006), 571–610.

9. The psychoanalysts Robert Stolorow and George Atwood have given the name "psychoanalytic phenomenology" to their theoretical orientation as presented in their two co-authored books, *Faces in a Cloud* (New York: Jason Aronson, 1979) and *Structures of Subjectivity* (Hillsdale, NJ: The Analytic Press, 1984). These authors devote a great deal of attention to differentiating their standpoint from that of Husserlian phenomenology. In my 1984 review of their work, I show that, despite their explicit rejection of it, their standpoint is compatible with that of Husserlian phenomenology. See Marilyn Nissim-Sabat, "Psychoanalysis and Phenomenology: A New Synthesis," *The Psychoanalytic Review*, 73, no. 3 (1986), 273–99.

10. Judith Van Herik, *Freud on Femininity and Faith* (Berkeley: University of California Press, 1982), 196. For some of my insights into, and formulations of, Freud's views, I am indebted to Van Herik's magisterial book. Van Herik's book is unusually richly documented, and some of my references to it rely on her profuse references to Freud. What I aim to do for the relation between misogyny and positivism in Freud, Van Herik has done for the relation between his misogyny and his views on religion. See also Chapter 2 of this volume for an analysis of Van Herik in which I use her insights for a critique of Freud's moral theory.

11. Sigmund Freud, *Civilization and Its Discontents*, Standard Edition, v. 2 (London: Hogarth Press, 1930/1961), 72.

12. Charles Bernheimer and Claire B. Kahane, eds., *In Dora's Case: Freud-Hysteria-Feminism* (New York: Columbia University Press, 1985).

13. Van Herik, *Freud*, 134.

14. Van Herik, *Freud*, 100–104.

15. Van Herik, *Freud*, 23, 130.

16. Evelyn Fox Keller, *Reflections on Gender and Science* (New Haven, CT: Yale University Press, 1985).

17. Keller, *Reflections*, 62.

18. Keller, *Reflections*, 87.

19. Sigmund Freud, *The Claims of Psycho-Analysis to Scientific Interest*, Standard Edition, v. 1 (London: Hogarth Press, 1913), 186.

20. Van Herik, *Freud*, 134.

21. Van Herik, *Freud*, 130.

22. Edmund Husserl, *The Crisis of European Sciences and Transcendental Phenomenology* (Evanston, IL: Northwestern University Press, 1970), 9.

23. Sigmund Freud, *Project for a Scientific Psychology*, Standard Edition, v. 1 (London: Hogarth Press, 1895).

24. Sigmund Freud, *The Interpretation of Dreams*, Standard Edition v. 4–5 (London: Hogarth Press, 1900).

25. Merton Gill, "Metapsychology Is Not Psychology," in Merton Gill and Philip S. Holzman, *Psychology versus Metapsychology* (New York: International Universities Press, 1976), 71–105.

26. John E. Gedo, *Beyond Inter*pretation (New York: International Universities Press, 1979), 235–39.

27. Stephen J. Ellman and Michael Moskowitz, "An Examination of Some Recent Criticisms of 'Metapsychology,'" *Psychoanalytic Quarterly*, 49 (1980), 641–46.

28. Roy Schafer, *A New Language for Psychoanalysis* (New Haven, CT: Yale University Press, 1976), 192.

29. Edwin R. Wallace, *Historiography and Causation in Psychoanalysis* (Hillsdale, NJ: Analytic Press, 1985).

30. Schafer, *New*; Roy Schafer, *The Analytic Attitude* (New York: Basic Books, 1983).

31. Schafer, *The Analytic*, 255.

32. Robert E. Palmer, *Hermeneutics* (Evanston, IL: Northwestern University Press, 1969).

33. An excellent discussion of the issue of hermeneutic relativism can be found in Joel Weinsheimer, *Gadamer's Hermeneutics* (New Haven, CT: Yale University Press, 1985), esp. 40–41, and n. 35, p. 40.

34. Schafer, *The Analytic*, 190.

35. Schafer, *The Analytic*, 255.

36. Wallace, *Historiography*, 82.

37. Wallace, *Historiography*, 214.

38. Gill and Holzman, *Psychology*.

39. In order to present the theoretical situation in contemporary psychoanalysis, the natural science and hermeneutic standpoints are treated as if they are irreconcilable, for this is how they are conceived in psychoanalytic theory. The standpoint implicit in this chapter is that the relationship between the natural science and hermeneutic standpoints can be mediated within the framework of phenomenology.

40. Husserl, *Crisis*.

41. Husserl, *Crisis*, 272–73.

42. Husserl, *Crisis*, 202.

43. Herbert Spiegelberg, *Phenomenology in Psychology and Psychiatry: A Historical Introduction* (Evanston, IL: Northwestern University Press, 1972), 135–36; Marilyn Nissim-Sabat, "Psychoanalysis, Phenomenology, and Feminism" (Unpublished paper presented at the meeting of the Husserl Circle, 1988).

44. Wallace, *Historiography*, 45, 165, 190.

45. Schafer, *New*, 7; Schafer, *The Analytic*, 234–35.

46. Schafer, *New*, 192.

47. Schafer, *New*, 5.

48. Schafer, *New*, 1–9.

49. One might argue that Freud did not experience purpose and mechanism as incompatible because, in his mind, purpose is just a mode of mechanism. On the other hand, some interpreters of this phenomenon maintain that Freud did not, or would not have reduced purpose to mechanism.

50. Melvin Feffer, *The Structure of Freudian Thought* (New York: International Universities Press, 1982); Marilyn Nissim-Sabat, "Review of The Structure of Freudian Thought by Melvin Feffer," *Review of Psychoanalytic Books*, 2, no. 3 (1983), 429–39.

51. Schafer, *New*.

52. Wallace, *Historiography*, 246.

53. Wallace, *Historiography*, 209.

54. Wallace, *Historiography*, 151.

55. I have explored the relation between Freud's positivism, his misogyny, and his conception of the relation between consciousness and the unconscious in Marilyn Nissim-Sabat, "The Role of the unconscious in Critical Social Theory" (Unpublished paper presented at the meeting of the Society for Phenomenology and the Human Sciences, 1989). In this paper I concluded that the relation between consciousness and the unconscious in Freudianism is homologous with the subject-object split of positivism.

56. Mario Bunge, *Causality and Modern Science* (New York: Dover, 1979).

57. Wallace, *Historiography*, 165.

58. Wallace, *Historiography*, n., 195.

59. Wallace, *Historiography*, 214.

60. Wallace, *Historiography*, n., 195.

61. According to Wallace (Wallace, *Historiography*, 228), a consistent acceptance of natural scientific determinism rules out any transcendental position, and thus any mind-body, ontological dualism. As we have seen, Wallace claims that his position is nonreductionist, that it does full justice to subjectivity. Space limitations forbid an extensive discussion of this point; however, it should be noted that Husserlian phenomenology shows, on the contrary, that only a transcendental position can disclose the psychophysical unity of the human person without reducing subjectivity to objectivity or vice versa.

62. Wallace, *Historiography*, 59.

63. Wallace, *Historiography*, 213.

64. Wallace, *Historiography*, 214.

65. The relation between causality and motivation in Husserlian phenomenology was the theme of my doctoral dissertation: Marilyn Nissim-Sabat, "Edmund Husserl's Theory of Motivation," Ph.D. diss. De Paul University, 1977.

66. Edmund Husserl, *Ideas Pertaining to a Pure Phenomenology and to a Phenomenological Philosophy, First Book* (The Hague, The Netherlands: Nijhoff, 1982), 332.

67. Husserl, *Crisis*, 126.

68. Husserl, *Crisis*.

69. Wallace, *Historiography*, 41.

70. Husserl, *Crisis*, 58.

71. Husserl, *Crisis*, 21–57.

72. Husserl, *Crisis*, 21–57.

73. See Galileo Galilei, The Assayer, in *The Essential Galileo*, ed. and trans. by Maurice A. Finocchiaro (Indianapolis: Hackett, 2008), 185–89. In interpreting this material, it is important to bear in mind that Galileo was an advocate of atomism, according to which, in the view of Democritus, only atoms and the void exist.

74. John P. Leavey, "Preface: Undecidables and Old Names," in Jacques Derrida, *Edmund Husserl's The Origin of Geometry:* An Introduction (New York: Nicholas Hays, 1978), 12.

75. Husserl, *Crisis*, 51.

76. Husserl, *Crisis*, 52.

77. Husserl, *Crisis*, 60–64.

78. Husserl, *Crisis*, 24–25.

79. Husserl, *Crisis*, 29.

80. Husserl, *Crisis*, 33.

81. Edmund Husserl, *Formal and Transcendental Logic*, trans. Dorian Cairns (The Hague, The Netherlands: Nijhoff, 1969), 279.

82. Husserl, *Crisis*, 235–40.

83. Keller, *Reflections*, 141.

84. Keller, *Reflections*, 144–49.

85. Keller, *Reflections*, 147–49.

86. Keller, *Reflections*, 178.

87. Liz Stanley and Sue Wise, *Feminist Consciousness and Feminist Research* (London: Routledge and Kegan Paul, 1983); Sandra Harding, *The Science Question in Feminism* (Ithaca, NY: Cornell University Press, 1986).

88. Keller, *Reflections*, 178.

89. Keller, *Reflections,* 116–17.

90. Husserl, *Crisis*, 260–61.

91. Edmund Husserl, *Ideas Pertaining to a Pure Phenomenology and to a Phenomenological Philosophy, Third Book* (The Hague, The Netherlands: Nijhoff, 1980), 69. The references to "mothers" and "maternal ground" in this quotation from Husserl are most likely allusions to the "realm of the mothers" in Part II of Goethe's *Faust*.

Chapter Four

Addictions, *Akrasia*, and Self Psychology:[1] A Socratic and Psychoanalytic View of *Akrasia* as Victim Blaming

INTRODUCTION

The aim of this chapter is to show, not only that *akrasia*, or weakness of will, fails, as many have contended, to account for human actions that appear to be contrary to what the actors believe is in their own best interest; in addition, the aim is to show that the attribution of *akrasia* to human actors is a form of victim blaming and thus ought not to be made.

In pursuing these aims, I claim that when people with addictive disorders, e.g., cocaine and alcohol dependence and abuse, use mood altering substances, they act consonantly with their actual beliefs as to what is in their own best interest; that is, they act rationally. I contend, moreover, that, all things considered, given their internal and external constraints, given the options available to them, when using mood altering substances addicted persons do act in their own true or actual best interest. However, experience of addicted persons' behavior and their expressed beliefs regarding their behavior invites the opposite conclusion.

Addicted persons strike observers as paradigmatic cases, not at all of rationality, but precisely of that form of irrationality referred to in the literature of philosophy and classical scholarship as incontinence, weakness of will, or *akrasia*, the term used by ancient Greek philosophers that means, etymologically, lack of self-control. Indeed, people with addictive disorders themselves frequently and very emphatically maintain that they believe that their addictive behavior is contrary to their own judgment as to what is in their own best interest and is, therefore, irrational. That is, they view themselves as akratics, people afflicted with akrasia. When asked why, then, do they persist in their addictive behavior, they are likely to reply that it is just because they are addicted persons, or because they can't control themselves, or because they are weak, or bad. They may say that they use addictive drugs and abuse alcohol because they "just like to get high." At the same time, they will insist that they know that "using" is bad for them and that they shouldn't be getting high. Thus, not only others, but the addicted persons themselves as reporters of their own behavior and inner states, view and describe themselves as akratics, as people who intentionally and deliberately, that is, knowingly,[2] act against their own best interest. Such individuals often elicit in family members and care givers extreme frustration and demands that they control themselves.[3] Interestingly, addicted people rarely blame others for their plight, for example those who psychologically, physically, or sexually abused them in childhood.[4] On the contrary, they often say, at least in cases of psychological or physical abuse, that it didn't harm them, or that they needed it, or that it was a long time ago, and so forth. In addition, addicted persons frequently say that their plight as addicts is due to their own shortcomings, lack of will power, stupidity, self-destructiveness, etc. Victims of sexual abuse are notorious for blaming themselves and for suffering from guilt because they "enjoyed" the experience. Thus, addicted people who are in actuality victims of abuse blame themselves for their suffering, and, in so doing, deny that they are victims of anyone except themselves. Denying that they are victims, they see themselves as akratics, as being afflicted with weakness of will. As I will show, this self blaming stance is a form of victim blaming; that is, in discounting the abuse they suffered at the hands of others, their abusers, and thus discounting their own history of victimization, in blaming themselves they blame victims, themselves, who are not to blame.

What is the basis for my claim that despite their own disclaimers addicted persons are acting consonantly with their *actual* beliefs as to what is in their own best interest?

The basis for this is another claim: that addicted persons have mistaken beliefs regarding their own actual beliefs. If this is correct, the consequence is that addicted persons may very well be acting consonantly with their *actual* beliefs as to what is in their own best interest, but deny this because they have mistaken beliefs as to what are their actual beliefs. How this comes about is germane to my argument and will be discussed at length below in the context of a discussion of the relation between pleasure and the good. First, however, I will present a rationale for the claim that addicted persons have mistaken beliefs regarding their actual beliefs as to what is in their own best interest. This rationale will be developed in the context of a discussion of aspects of Plato's *Protagoras,*[5] the dialogue that contains Socrates' most extensive discussion of *akrasia*. This path will be pursued in order to show that *akrasia* does not and cannot exist, and, further, that attributing it to victims is a form of victim blaming.

SOCRATES, PROTAGORAS, AND *AKRASIA*

When in *Protagoras* Socrates maintains that there is no such condition as weakness of will, he argues with hypothetical putative akratics whom he creates imaginatively for dialogic purposes and whom he represents as maintaining that they acted against their own best interest because their beliefs regarding what is best for them were "overcome"[6] by strong feelings, pleasure in particular. For Socrates, all putative akratics are in the same case—they believe their better judgment was defeated by a strong feeling, whether of fear, or love, or temptation to pleasure, and so forth; however, whatever the initial feeling, the behavior in response to it results, the putative akratic believes, in a reduction in pain or an increase in pleasure or both.

In developing his argument, Socrates points out that what actually occurs is that, at the time of acting, self-described putative akratics act on the basis of their *actual* beliefs as to *which actions will afford them the greatest pleasure.* The putative akratics do not deny this; they affirm that they acted as they did out of desire for the greatest pleasure; but, they maintain, in addition, that they were wrong to do so because the action resulting in the greatest pleasure is just the action they judge to be wrong and therefore contrary to their own best interest. What Socrates shows is that their actual belief is that the action they perform yielding, they believe, the greater pleasure is the action they *actually* believe to be in their own best interest, despite their claim to believe the opposite. Socrates rejects the akratics' claim to believe that the actions that they perform, the ones allegedly bringing about the greater pleasure, are *actually* believed by them to be wrong, that is, contrary to their own best interest. He maintains, on the contrary, that an action that actually yields the greatest pleasure attainable is in the actors best interest and therefore cannot be wrong. That is, the putative akratics may be mistaken in their belief regarding which action will yield the greater pleasure, but they are not wrong in their actual belief that the action that yields the greater pleasure is in their own best interest. Socrates maintains that no one ever has or can establish a standard or criterion for judging the goodness or badness of an action other than the yield of pleasure or pain concomitant with or consequent upon that action,[7] and that all actions deemed to be good, that is, to yield the greatest pleasure attainable, are ipso facto in the actors' best interest.

To explain this point, we can use the following example (not used by Socrates): assuming that adultery is morally wrong, the adulterer, if found out, might say, akratically, that he "knew that the act of adultery is wrong, but did it despite this knowledge because his knowledge was overcome by the pleasure of the moment." In view of Socrates' claim that pleasure is the good and pain is the evil (bad, wrong), and therefore that, to be clear, one should speak either of pleasure and pain, or of good and evil,[8] Socrates would gloss the putative akratic's statement as follows: substituting for 'wrong,' that is, evil, the term 'painful,' the adulterer's statement becomes, "I knew it was painful" (i.e., that the painful consequences would exceed the pleasurable consequences), "but did it nevertheless because I was overcome by the pleasure of the moment." This justifies the inference that when the putative akratic states that he knew that the painful consequences would exceed the pleasurable consequences, that is, that he knew that the act of adultery is wrong, that he actually did not know any such thing. Had he known or actually believed this rather than just believed that he believed it, he would not have been motivated to perform the action, for, Socrates maintains, no one can knowingly choose pain over pleasure, or evil over good. Thus, the putative akratic's claim that he was overcome by pleasure means, for Socrates, that he was ignorant, that is, that despite his disclaimer, he actually believed incorrectly that the pleasure would exceed the pain, and that this error, this ignorance, was what led to the action.[9] In other words, *the putative akratic was mistaken as to what his actual belief was: he believed he believed that the action was wrong, that the painful consequences would exceed the pleasurable ones, but, in actuality, he believed the opposite and acted on that opposite belief.*[10] (In assuming that adultery is indeed morally wrong, we see that this putative akratic's actual belief—that the pleasure of adultery exceeded either the lesser pleasure or the pain of faithfulness—was incorrect; that is, that in fact he chose the lesser pleasure of adultery over the greater pleasure of faithfulness, or of honesty, and that thus his action was indeed wrong, as he incorrectly believed he believed.) Socrates' view is that all actions are either right or wrong, good or evil, and actions cannot be neither right nor wrong nor both right and wrong. The *Protagoras* advances this view, and is a sustained attack on Protagoras' sophistic relativism.

Thus, Socrates' view is that, despite claims to the contrary, no one can do what they believe is not in their own best interest, that is, choose pain over pleasure, though one certainly can be mistaken as to what is in one's own best interest. Therefore, self-described, putative akratics who mistake bad for good and out of ignorance choose the action that yields the lesser pleasure or the greater pain, are not aware of what their own actual beliefs are. All putative akratics perform that action that they, mistakenly or not, believe will yield them the greater pleasure, and, in so doing, actually believe that they are acting rightly, acting in their own best interest. Thus, despite their own claim to have acted wrongly out of weakness of will, they are not, nor can anyone be, akratic. Given Socrates' claim that pleasure is the standard for the judgment that an action is good, that action performed by the putative akratic to yield the greater pleasure is ipso facto the action that the putative akratic judges to be good, despite any beliefs to the contrary. This shows, then, that Socrates' claim is that despite the putative akratics' claims to have done so, no one can do what they believe is not in their own best interest where another action is attainable, since right action or action that yields either the greater pleasure or the lesser pain is what is in everyone's best interest. Thus, the putative akratic, in maintaining that she acted against her own best interest, is not aware of what her actual beliefs are regarding what is or was in her own best interest. The putative akratic actually believes quite correctly that obtaining the greatest pleasure available is what is in her own best interest, for, on Socrates' account, it is impossible not to believe this, and everyone actually does believe it; but, she believes that she believes that such actions are not in her own best interest and are therefore wrong.

If, however, it is argued that the attribution of weakness of will concerns only the persons' beliefs as to what they themselves believe, regardless of whether those persons believe they believe what in fact they do or do not believe, then this is trivial; for, it is undeniable that persons can act contrary to what they believe they believe where they are mistaken as to what they actually believe. They can do so precisely because they are mistaken as to what they believe, and are in fact acting consonantly with what they actually believe. But this is not at all what is meant by *akrasia*. If it is further alleged, as proponents of *akrasia* do allege, that people can act contrary to what in fact they actually do believe, regardless of the correctness of their beliefs regarding what they actually do believe, that is, even if they are correct regarding what they believe their beliefs to be, then Socrates denies this. Socrates' strong claim in *Protagoras* is that in all cases in which it appears that people are acting contrary to what they believe is in their best interest, in fact such putative akratics are ignorant in the sense that they are mistaken in their belief as to what they in fact do believe, and, in addition, they may be mistaken in their beliefs regarding what is in their own best interest, that is, what will afford the greater pleasure. An adulterer, for example, may believe that the act of adultery will afford him the greater pleasure, and thus the greater good, but may very well be mistaken. But in this case the adulterer is not mistaken regarding his beliefs as to what he actually believes; rather, he is mistaken regarding *reality*, regarding what actions in fact will yield for him the greater pleasure. Thus, the Socratic perspective, unsurprisingly, rules out ethical and moral relativism, and implies, on the contrary, that it is possible to discern that which is intrinsically, actually in one's, and everyone's, best interest.

Given the above, in order to obviate the charge that my formulations are question begging, it important to make clear what are some of the constraints on addicted persons that affect their judgments about, and consequent beliefs regarding, what is available to them in terms of alternative behaviors. For, it is reasonable to ask what the reasons are that explain addicted persons' erroneous judgments as to what array of possible actions, that is, of sources of happiness, is available to them. Why is it that such persons very infrequently, if at all, admit that they think that what they are doing is in their own best interest, as I, following Socrates, have maintained? In response, Socrates would maintain that, like almost everyone else, *addicted persons believe that pleasure and the good are separate and different.* Socrates' refutation of weakness of will in *Protagoras* depends on his claim that, on the contrary, pleasure not only is good, but that it is the good itself.

Many, including the late great Plato scholar Gregory Vlastos, who were and are aware of the far-reaching implications of this claim, have maintained that Socrates did not say or believe that pleasure is the good, and that even if he did, he didn't. Vlastos could not accept that Socrates believed that pleasure is the good becauset he thought that this would warrant the conclusion that Socrates was a hedonist, for Vlastos an unacceptable conclusion, one he deemed contrary to the entire Socratic-Platonic ethos.[11] However, in an essay written in 2002, classical scholar C.J. Rowe maintained that, "Recently . . . resistance to the idea of Socrates and/or Plato as a hedonist (or as taking hedonism seriously in one form or another) appears to have weakened considerably."[12] This statement is followed by extensive citations of the relevant more recent literature. Rowe quotes also from a much earlier book by J. and A.M. Adam in which the authors focus on a point made above. Responding to (and quoting) a famous statement by Schleiermacher that hedonism is "utterly unsocratic," Adam and Adam wrote that,

> There is nothing degrading in the theory as it is worked out by Socrates, since it is not the balance of pleasure in each individual species of pleasure which we are recommended to choose, but the balance of pleasure generally and in the long run: it would be quite open to Socrates to maintain that the lower pleasures are never to be chosen, because they are always followed by more pain. . . .[13]

Here Adam and Adam imply a view of Socratic hedonism that I believe is indeed present in the *Protagoras*, and that is the view that the greatest pleasure a human being can experience is in acts of virtue (not the "lower pleasures," but the higher ones). This seems evident when, after showing that the putative akratics are suffering not from *akrasia*, which for Socrates is impossible, but rather from ignorance, Socrates says,

> Well then, my friends, I say to them, seeing that the salvation of human life has been found to consist in the right choice of pleasures and pains, in the choice of the more and the fewer, and the greater and the less, and the nearer and remoter, must not this measuring be a consideration of their excess and defect and equality in relation to each other?[14]

For Socrates, the salvation of human life is not separable from virtue; it is, in fact, virtue that is the salvation of human life.[15] On this account, virtue is knowledge of the right choice of pleasures and pains. This implies, for example, that when Antigone went to her death for burying her brother against the law of Creon, the pleasure she experienced (in that she correctly judged what was in her best interest, and consequently correctly chose the lesser of two evils) was greater than the pain of her sorrow, losses, and death. If she had not believed this, she would not have acted as she did; if her action was indeed virtuous, then her pleasure was the greatest attainable at that time, and from the Socratic point of view, I believe, this is to be understood as literally true. Socrates own life and death, as presented by him in the *Apology,* exemplified his belief that virtue should not be sacrificed to physical survival. Of course, Socrates' argument in *Protagoras* implies that to know the good is to do the good for we cannot knowingly choose pain over pleasure, that is, evil over good.

Thus, it is not enough to specify against *akrasia* that people cannot act against what they believe they believe to be in their own best interest; it is not enough because people can and in fact do so if their belief regarding what they believe is in their own best interest is erroneous. But this is not what is meant by weakness of will. What is meant by weakness of will is that people act contrary to what they actually do believe, on some evaluation, is in their best interest. It is thus necessary to show, in all instances in which people appear to be acting against what they believe is in their best interest, that in fact they are merely acting against what they erroneously believe to be their beliefs as to what is in their own best interest. In short, it is necessary to show that the good, happiness itself (possession of the good), is pleasure. Although I believe that reflection on what is meant by the concept of the good would demonstrate that good means and is the greatest pleasure or *eudaimonia,* that is, happiness, I cannot demonstrate this here. Therefore, in the hope of stimulating further work along these lines, I merely take on the lesser task of showing that addiction is just such an instance of people acting not against what they believe is in their own best interest, but against what they erroneously believe they believe. If I can show this, then the burden of proof is on the supporter of *akrasia* to provide a genuine instance of someone acting against what she actually believes, rather than erroneously believes, are her beliefs regarding what is in her own best interest. The literature shows that this already has been to a large extent the terms of the debate. And the reason this has already been the terms of the debate is that the notion of weakness of will is itself paradoxical and counterintuitive. That is to say, it is the task of the supporter of *akrasia* to show why a person would *not* act in accordance with what she actually believes is in her own best interest. I do not know how this can be shown, since the notion of one's best interest is just the notion of what is conducive to one's happiness.

Refutation of A. Mele's Defense of *Akrasia*

However, a vigorous attempt has been made to turn the tables and place the burden of proof on those who reject *akrasia*. According to Alfred Mele, rejection of *akrasia* rests upon proving that there exists a species of best judgment that he calls a "nonartificial, *Akrasia*-proof variety of best judgment."[16] By "nonartificial" Mele means that it is not just that there was no other contrary motivation external to the judgment present when the judgment was made, but also that the judgment is "*Akrasia*-proof" on grounds purely internal to the phenomenon of judgment itself. Moreover, included within the scope of factors external to the judgment is Aristotle's notion of what Mele refers to as "*eudaimonia*-based best judgments"; that is, Mele claims that the intention of attaining happiness is external to the judging itself. According to Mele, "even for Aristotle, not all best judgments are explicitly based on considerations of *eudaimonia*."[17] This then is a significant difference from the Socratic-Platonic stance. For Socrates, in *Protagoras, all* judgments are based on the desire for happiness. This is precisely why Socrates rejects *akrasia*, namely because it is the claim that there are judgments regarding what action is best where "best" does not mean best in relation to good where happiness is the highest good. That is, for Socrates, the goal of *eudaimonia* is in principle characteristic of, *and thus internal to,* all judgments as to what is in one's best interest. This is implicit in the view that pleasure is the good and that attainment of the good is *eudaimonia* itself. Therefore, it seems to me that it is incumbent on Mele to explain how such an *Akrasia*-proof judgment is even *conceivable,* for it would mean that a person could knowingly choose what is believed to be a source of unhappiness where it is believed that happiness is attainable. I submit that it is not conceivable, and that, therefore, such judgments cannot be the standard for an *akrasia*-proof judgment. The point is that it is precisely because pleasure is the good, and because it is in everyone's best interest to seek to attain the greatest pleasure, whether in the short or long run, and therefore the greatest good, that *akrasia* is ruled out. Indeed, *akrasia* is ruled out in that people can, and indeed do have mistaken beliefs about their actual belief that pleasure is the good. Thus, in order to prove that *akrasia* is possible, it is necessary to prove that a person's judgment as to what is in her best interest can be either indifferent or contrary to her desire for happiness. The burden of proof then is on those, like Mele, who support *akrasia*.

The purpose of this chapter is to show that addictive behavior is a paradigmatic case of people acting against, not what they believe to be in their own best interest but against what they erroneously believe they believe to be in their own best interest. It is necessary to specify that, given their internal and/or external constraints, they are acting as they should to promote what is in fact in their own best interest. To make my point perfectly clear, despite their own claims regarding what they believe themselves to believe, addicted persons not only believe that their use of mood altering substances is their best alternative; in fact, given their constraints, it *is* their best alternative and they not only believe they are, but in actuality they are acting in their own best interest, that is, rationally. That is, they are in fact pursuing the greatest pleasure attainable by them, *all things considered,* that is, given their internal and external constraints, and this is what rationality is for Socrates. Contrary to Mele,[18] the 'all things considered' stipulation does not rule out the refutation of *akrasia* because this stipulation is omnipresent in all human judgment and action. Perfect happiness, and thus the highest possible pleasure, is an ideal, and, as such, that toward which we strive. We attain happiness imperfectly; that is, 'all things considered,' but only in the light of the ideal.

TREATING ADDICTION: ADDICTS AS VICTIMS

Clinical work with addicted persons has emphasized their characteristic difficulty with regulation of affect and their acute hypersensitivity to painful affect.[19] As a client of mine in the halfway house for recovering addicted persons in which I worked stated, "I hate mental pain and discomfort, I just can't stand it." In attempting to show the relevance of both Self Psychology[20] and the Socratic rejection of weakness of will to the understanding and treatment of addictive disorders, the impaired affect regulation capacity of the addicted person will be emphasized. Affect regulation problems are symptomatic for many psychological problems. As my client's remarks suggest, for addictions, an etiological factor may be a narcissistic disturbance that may cause the addicted person to experience negative affect as a narcissistic blow.[21] Due to space limitations, the possible etiology of this problem will only be suggested, though my own psychodynamic orientation suggests that a full etiological profile is available.[22] For the sake of the present discussion, then, I will assume that, in addition to narcissistic disturbances, people with addictions have an acute and pervasive difficulty in that they are relatively unable to experience psychic pleasure. Because they are unable to balance psychic pain with memories of past, or expectation of future gratification, addicted persons find feelings of psychic pain or discomfort intolerable. In addition, as many who have worked in this field have seen, addicted persons find it virtually impossible to manifest healthy self-assertion, that is, they are unable to interact with others in such a way that their own normal emotional needs will be at least satisfactorily met, and they are afflicted with an all-pervasive fear of rejection. Moreover, addicted persons commonly have a very poorly developed sense of self. Thus, substance use provides a single solution to two inseparable problems: 1) it induces a feeling of psychic pleasure; and 2) it enables addicted people to believe that they have control over their affective states, thus relieving excruciatingly painful feelings of shame and "near zero self-esteem"[23] due, in part, to perception of inner passivity and helplessness. More often than not, this passivity is a consequence of having been abused physically, psychologically, or sexually. For example, it frequently occurs that people with substance abuse disorders were psychologically abused in that they were forced at a very young age, e.g., 8 years old, to care for and be responsible for younger siblings; in this way they were robbed of their own childhood.

People with addictive disorders, then, are people who see themselves as having but one option regarding their ability to experience well-being—the use of mood altering substances to induce such a feeling. Human beings cannot tolerate a situation in which they do not ever experience the pleasurable sensation of well-being. This helps to understand additional characteristics of addicted persons' thought patterns and behaviors. Most addicted persons manifest a curious ostensible lack of moral disquietude regarding their actions; they talk about their pervasive dishonesty, their thefts, deceptions, lies, conniving, sale of drugs, and illegal and immoral behavior of all kinds, including violence, with an apparent lack of conscience.[24] It is my contention in this chapter that addicted persons are people who actually believe that their actions are ethically and morally correct. They actually believe, contrary to what they believe they believe, that pleasure is the good and in this they are correct. They believe, moreover, that in choosing the pleasure of drug use, they are justified in all of their behaviors, in all of the actions they take to obtain those drugs, for they believe that the pleasure they attain is greater, in excess of any pain they suffer from using *or pain they inflict on others in obtaining and using their drugs.*[25] This belief is incorrect; however, the constraints within which addicted persons function internally and externally do not allow them to grasp that they are choosing the lesser pleasure over the greater. It is for this reason that I stated above that addicted persons are in fact pursuing the *greatest pleasure available to them, all things considered.* The actual or really greater pleasure would be recovery through resolution of their psychic disorders; however, considering their internal and external constraints, they are, all things considered, and for a variety of reasons, e.g., lack of experience of psychic pleasure through empathic nurturance, unable to grasp that this will yield a pleasure greater than that of substance abuse. I do not mean to say that the addicted persons are inherently unable to grasp that they chose the lesser pleasure; I only mean that at the time of choosing they are unable to do so.

Thus, addicted persons, despite appearances, are no more akratic than any other persons who claim to, or are evaluated as, acting contrary to their own judgment as to what is in their own best interest. From the vantage point of the outside observer, the addicted person has other options, other alternatives; the addicted person can stop using, or seek help, etc. From the addicted persons' perspective, they have no other options. The reason for this belief is that, by and large, they are people who have not experienced feelings of well-being or psychic pleasure in any sustained experience in any other way than through the use of mood altering substances. They are people who are unable to nurture themselves and who have not been nurtured by others. They suffer from chronic profound low self-esteem and grossly immature personality development which renders them unwilling to control their impulses, despite their belief that they are willing to do so and would if they could. They are unwilling to control their impulses because, as we have seen, they actually do not believe that it is in their best interest to do so. These characteristics are quite consistent with an evaluation that addicted persons are people who lack psychological structure, that is, their psychic life is not governed and organized by a cohesive self.[26]

In a group therapy session, the following discussion occurred. A halfway house client had been rotated to a higher level of care—that is, he was moved from the halfway house to a residential treatment program. The difference is that in the residential program the client will be under much closer scrutiny and a much greater degree of external control. This client's former halfway house peers went to visit him in the residential facility. Back at the halfway house in the group therapy session, the halfway house clients reported that the client in the residential facility looked terrific, was doing very well, was happy and glad to be there, was making great progress, etc. These people believed that this apparent change for the better in their former peer showed that he was definitely, finally on the road to recovery. The therapist, myself in this instance, pointed out to this group of recovering people that most likely their former peer's appearance of marked improvement was due to the fact that now, in the highly structured residential program, he is relieved of the intense anxiety he experiences when he is free to do as he pleases, that is, the marked anxiety that is a concomitant of lack of internal controls due to lack of internal personality structure and that leads him to use cocaine. During the course of this discussion, the group therapy clients reported that they had now begun to see at long last what is meant by the phrases "internal controls" and "internal structure." Indeed, given their own lack of internal personality structure or self-development, it is not surprising that the concept of internal personality structure would be difficult for the addicted persons to grasp conceptually or experientially.

Addicted persons are quite capable of stating that they see that the long-range consequences of their actions will result in terrible losses for themselves, that is, that they will lose their jobs, their friends and family, their homes, their health, and so forth. Yet at the same time, they do not associate with these aspects of their lives the sense of well-being they derive from use of mood altering substances; they do not experience their jobs, friends, family, homes, health, and so forth, as related to the inner pleasure that is usually described as a sense of well-being or contentment or deep satisfaction or feelings of self-worth and self-esteem. Their inner lives are such that, despite appearances, they are unable to derive such pleasures from these aspects of their lives. Moreover, the addicted persons are often in relationships with spouses, lovers, jobs, friends, etc. that enable them to function well enough to maintain a steady supply of drugs without providing interpersonal experiences that might stimulate the development of inner personality structure. Owing to their chronic dysphoric state and relative lack of inner self and personality structure and development, addicted persons do not at all manifest weakness of will. On the contrary, given these parameters of their existence, their behavior is rational in the sense that their actions are consonant with their actual beliefs as to what is in their own best interest—the pursuit of pleasure or happiness.

At this point then we can begin to see why I maintain that psychotherapy using the psychoanalytic self psychological theoretical standpoint and treatment model is most appropriate for people with addictive disorders. Self Psychology is a treatment modality that is designed to facilitate the development of internal personality and self-structure. Self Psychology delineates stages and levels of self development that are paralleled by stages and levels of relatedness to others. Mature, that is, satisfying, relations with others presuppose the internal representation of a beneficent and loving agency, the "selfobject," that mediates the transferential aspects of human interrelatedness. The self psychologist views the field within which therapy takes place as an empathic field wherein the therapist provides a corrective emotional experience for the client by interacting with the client differently from those in the client's past. Specifically, the self-psychologist recognizes the reality of the client's inner life, feelings, and need for mirroring and twinship modes of relationship, that is, the slow and careful building within the client of empathic bridges both to herself and between herself and others.[27]

In psychoanalysis today, there is an ongoing intense debate regarding the role of therapist induced pleasurable experiences in clients. Those who adhere to the so-called conflict model of psychopathology have indicted self-psychology as no more than a means of providing emotional gratification for clients. This would suggest that any apparent benefits from the therapy represent a mere flight into health rather than actual inner growth. There is no doubt that the experience of empathy is intensely pleasurable inasmuch as it satisfies the human need for recognition, understanding, and acceptance. However, empathy in the context of Self Psychology does not at all connote sympathy; rather, empathy is a method of experiencing and understanding the patient's inner life. Yet the terms of the debate regarding Self Psychology suggest that psychoanalysis today is afflicted with the same puritanical fear of pleasure that afflicted its founder, Freud, for whom, in the words of Philip Rieff, "sexuality remains bound by its original instinctual character"[28] and for whom "[P]pleasure is defined after the manner of Schopenhauer, as a negative phenomenon, the struggle to release oneself from unpleasure, or tension."[29] Moreover, American society today is dominated by the same puritanical condemnation of pleasure, as expressed, for example, in the fact that contraceptives are so much more difficult to obtain here than in European countries, suggesting the conclusion that our social goal is not to prevent, for example, teenage pregnancy, but rather to prevent sexual behavior itself.

CONCLUSION

Thus, the separation and differentiation between pleasure and the good on both the individual and cultural levels contributes significantly to the perpetuation of behavior such that large numbers of people, and I believe everyone from time to time, believe that we act deliberately and intentionally, that is, akratically, against full awareness of what is actually in our own best interest. Because we believe that 'good guys finish last,' that is, that doing good results in suffering, we are prevented from comprehending and experiencing virtue, ethically and morally correct behavior, as the ideal of human welfare and personal happiness. Until we do comprehend this, we will continue to wonder whether or not a human being can intentionally act against what is in her own best interest, as if she could knowingly choose pain over pleasure, misery over happiness, or as if there is a special category of people, spectacularly deficient, who choose pain over pleasure.[30] It is in this sense, in the sense that it implies the existence of just such a category of people that I maintain that the notion of *akrasia* is a form of victim blaming.

NOTES

1. Self Psychology is one of the most prominent and important theoretical orientations in psychoanalysis today, both nationally and internationally. Further information is provided below in the text and endnotes.

2. I assume here that the notion of knowledge relevant to the discussion of *akrasia*, particularly in relation to the subsequent discussion of *Protagoras*, is knowledge construed as active, as knowledge in full possession of the knower. For a discussion of the relevance of active knowledge to Aristotle's discussion of *akrasia* in the *Nicomachean Ethics*, see: Filip Grgic, "Aristotle on the Akratic's Knowledge," in *Phronesis*, XLII, 4 (2002), 336–358.

3. The discussion in this paper of the behavior and self-description of persons who are addicted to controlled substances is based on my own experience as a Certified Addictions Counselor and Clinical Supervisor in a halfway house for recovering addicts (The Gateway Foundation) in Chicago, 1993–2001.

4. For documentation and discussion of the connection between substance abuse and parental abuse see, *Trauma and Substance Abuse: Causes, Consequences, and Treatment of Comorbid Disorders*, edited by Paige Ouimette and Pamela Brown (Washington, DC: American Psychological Association, 2002).

5. Plato, *Protagoras*, edited with an Introduction by Gregory Vlastos (Indianapolis, IN: Bobbs-Merrill, 1956). Though *Protagoras* is a middle dialogue and thus not in the group of early dialogues considered to be authentically Socratic without admixture of Plato's views, I will refer to the leader of the discussion and his views as Socrates since this is his name in the dialogue.

6. Plato, *Protagoras*, 58.

7. The view that pleasure is the good is usually known as hedonism. While it is uncontroversial that Socrates' hypothetical interlocutors, the "many" in *Protagoras,* accept the principle of hedonism, whether or not Socrates accepted it is controversial. This point will be discussed below.

8. Plato, *Protagoras*, 60.

9. Plato, *Protagoras*, 63.

10. Socrates discusses the claim that the pleasure of the moment, or pain of the moment, pleasure and pain experienced in the here and now in contradistinction to future pains and pleasures, is greater than future pains and pleasures. Socrates explains through dialogue that if immediate pleasure can be experienced without any attendant consequences of greater pain in the future they would be good. For example: overeating which is pleasurable but leads to pain that outweighs the pleasure. While Socrates does not discuss directly what today in ethical theory is called "moral imagination," implicitly this is what he is recommending—that people imagine future pains and pleasures consequent on their present actions before they act. His strong point is, though, that whether future pleasures and pains are considered or not, the standard of right and wrong, good and evil, is and can only be, pain or pleasure. See, Plato, *Protagoras*, 58–62.

11. Plato, *Protagoras*, xxxix–xlv.

12. Christopher J. Rowe, "Hedonism in the *Protagoras* Again," in *Plato's Protagoras: Proceedings of the Third Symposium Platonicum Pragense*, edited by Ales Havlicek and Filip Karfik (Prague, Czech Republic: OIKOYMENH, 2003), 135. This book is an excellent collection of articles by noted scholars regarding the most discussed and controversial aspects of Plato's *Protagoras*.

13. Quoted in Rowe, "Hedonism," 134, n. 5.

14. Plato, *Protagoras*, 63.

15. Virtue includes of course concern for the well-being of other persons and thus for the consequences of one's actions for other persons. In this chapter, I assume that both Socrates' and Plato's ethical views encompassed this dimension of virtue. For Socrates, harming others, i.e., acting in a non-virtuous manner, caused immediate harm to one's own soul.

16. Mele, Alfred, *Autonomous Agents: From Self-Control to Autonomy* (Oxford: Oxford University Press, 1995), 25.

17. Mele, *Autonomous,* 24.

18. Mele, *Autonomous,* 21.

19. R.J. Pandina, V. Johnson, and E.W. Labouvie. "Affectivity: Central Mechanism in the Development of Drug Dependence," in: M.D. Glantz, and R.W Pickens, eds., *Vulnerability to Drug Abuse* (Washington, DC: American Psychological Association Press, 1992), 179–210.

20. For information regarding Self Psychology, see notes 21 and 27 below.

21. Jerome D. Levin, *Treatment of Alcoholism and Other Addictions: A Self-Psychology Approach* (Northvale, NJ: Jason Aronson, 1991), 2: "Kohut viewed addictive behavior as an attempt to deal with narcissistic disturbance." Heinz Kohut (1913–81), of the Chicago Institute for Psychoanalysis, was the originator of Self Psychology, a version of psychoanalysis which places great emphasis on the development of a mature self in contrast to the Freudian emphasis on resolution of inner conflict. Levin's book is an excellent introduction to Self Psychology, including its history and development to 1991. For additional resources on Self Psychology, see the website of the International Association for the Study of Psychoanalytic Self Psychology, http://www.psychologyoftheself.com/.

22. There is no general agreement in the fields of psychiatry and psychotherapy as to the etiology of addictive disorders or even regarding whether or not there is more than one cause of these disorders. Several models have been proposed including various biogenic and various psychogenic models, and models that combine both domains. Though in this chapter I refer to addictions as mental disorders, my own view, in consonance with psychoanalytic Self Psychology is that addictions are, rather, *symptoms* of mental disorders and should be treated as such.

23. Levin, *Treatment,* 174.

24. The personality profile of the addicted person presented here is based on my own training as a psychiatric social worker, eight years' experience as an addictions counselor, as well as on literature by prominent experts, for example the book by Levin cited above. Nevertheless, there is no conclusive evidence that would identify a dominant personality type among addicted persons. Furthermore, some of the traits mentioned, for example chronic dishonesty, are a consequence rather then a cause of the disorder. When such persons are sober, they are horrified by their actions when under the influence.

25. Socrates believed that all evil (immoral acts) is done in ignorance. This includes, of course, pain and suffering inflicted on others. Socrates' view was that, to use contemporary parlance, "what goes around, comes around"; that is, if we harm others, we make our community bad, and thus harm ourselves. Socrates also believed that in harming others, we harm ourselves directly and immediately, in our souls.

26. Levin, *Treatment,* passim.

27. Heinz Kohut, *The Analysis of the Self: A Systematic Approach to the Treatment of Narcissistic Personality Disorders* (New York: International Universities Press, 1971); Heinz Kohut, *How Does Analysis Cure?,* edited by Arnold Goldberg and Paul Stepansky

(Chicago: University of Chicago Press, 1984); Marilyn Nissim-Sabat, "Kohut and Husserl: The Empathic Bond," in Douglas Detrick and Susan Detrick, editors, *Self Psychology: Comparisons and Contrasts* (Hillsdale, NJ: Analytic Press, 1989),151–174.

28. Philip Rieff, *Freud: The Mind of the Moralist* (Chicago: University of Chicago Press, 1979) 153.

29. Rieff, *Freud*, 155.

30. The case of the masochist seeking physical pain (whether associated with sex or not) is often raised (especially by students in my philosophy classes, usually with a snicker or two) as a counterexample. In my view, this move fails to defeat my (and Socrates') argument. This is so because one can plausibly maintain that despite the appearance of a preference for unnecessary pain, the masochist chooses physical pain as a form of punishment to alleviate, albeit temporarily, the greater pain of intolerable feelings of guilt. It is a sophistic mode of thinking to claim, as students sometimes do, that the masochist literally, in a one-to-one correlation, experiences pain as pleasure. This is not credible because pain is pain and pleasure is pleasure and neither can be both painful and pleasurable. Usually, when students are asked why they think it is possible for someone to experience pain as pleasure directly they respond: "I don't know—I'm not one of them!!"

Fanon, Phenomenology, and the Decentering of Philosophy: Lewis R. Gordon's *Her Majesty's Other Children: Sketches of Racism from a Neocolonial Age*[1]

This chapter is both an appreciation of the work of Lewis R. Gordon and an exploration of some of his major themes. In particular, in order to underscore its significance to Gordon's project—the development of a liberatory existential phenomenology and sociology—I enlarge upon his discussion of the decentering of philosophy.

In chapter five of *Her Majesty's Other Children*, "Uses and Abuses of Blackness: Postmodernism, Conservatism, Ideology," Gordon writes,

> For I am not so much antimodern as I am anti-Eurocentrism. There are elements of modernity that I avow and elements that I reject. To reject Eurocentrism is not identical to rejecting European civilization *in toto* or rejecting modernity, and it is a seriously racist form of reasoning that would make white people the only bearers of a modern consciousness. One would have to conclude, in effect, that black people are incapable of being modern or developing their own forms of modernity or alternatives *beyond* premodernity, modernity, and postmodernity (102). (Quotations are from *Her Majesty's Other Children*, unless otherwise noted.)

Gordon's statement that he is "not so much antimodern" as he is "anti-Eurocentrism" and does not reject European civilization in toto is but one instance of the critique of postmodernism that permeates many of the essays in his book.[2] Here, he points out that rejecting Eurocentrism does not entail rejecting modernism. I begin my discussion with this provocative passage because it exemplifies a dimension of what seems to me to be most valuable in Gordon's work. His claim that rejecting Euro-civilization in toto "is a seriously racist form of reasoning that would make white people the only bearers of a modern consciousness" is quite startling, inasmuch as many of those postmodernists who urge rejecting Euro-civilization and modernism in toto often do so in the name of anti-racism, reflecting the belief that modernism has at the very least perpetuated forms of oppression, if not brought them into existence. Gordon's methodology of rejecting the postmodernist rejection of modernism in toto bears directly on his advocacy of the development of an existential sociology as a corrective to this and other forms of racism, and also on the way in which he grounds existential sociology in the constitutive phenomenology of Edmund Husserl. Thus, importantly, Gordon's critique of postmodernism is neither gratuitous nor tangential to his main themes, nor is it an otiose turning of the tables. Rather, it is integral to his project of recreating radical theory so as to avoid the pitfalls of the past that failed to generate an adequate praxis against racism and sexism and, not coincidentally, led to the abandonment of liberatory theory.

In order to develop these themes, first I will show how Gordon motivates his claim that rejection of Euro-civilization in toto is racist. Next, I will elaborate on the theme of decentering philosophy that is central to Gordon's work and can focus his critique of postmodernism. Following this, I will discuss Gordon's advocacy of constitutive, that is, Husserlian, phenomenology and existential sociology as a corrective for postmodern and misreadings.

PITFALLS OF THE POSTMODERN CRITIQUE OF EUROCENTRISM

As just noted, Gordon claims that rejecting European culture and modernism in toto is a "seriously racist form of reasoning" in that it would "make of white people the only bearers of modern consciousness." The racism evident in such a rejection in toto is evident in how it shamelessly abstracts from the situatedness of black people in their historical and contemporary existence in both Africa and the African diaspora. Rejection of modernism in toto is abstract and ahistorical; as such it reduplicates the ahistoricality that Eurocentrist racism falsely attributed and attributes to Africana culture and black people, for example as found in Hegel.[3]

In contrast, there is the example of Frantz Fanon, Africana psychiatrist, philosopher, and revolutionary, whose description and analysis of the existential situation of Africana peoples is unsurpassed today, and gives the lie to the conflation of Eurocentrism with European civilization and modernism. In creating his unique amalgam of revolutionary theory and activism, sociogenic psychoanalysis, and existential phenomenology, Fanon drew on the work not only of Africana thinkers, for example, Cesaire, Senghor, and others, but also on that of Marx, Freud, Merleau-Ponty, and Sartre. The example of Fanon shows that restricting the meaning of modernism and European culture to a culture of domination is a form of essentialism in the most ideological sense. Extirpating those sources of revolutionary, liberatory theory and praxis that arose within modernism, not just in the West, but, globally as well, means what Eurocentrism has always meant: denial that black people have any reflective consciousness or capacity for reasoning at all or for knowing the sources of their oppression, and consequent denial that they can create and have created liberatory theory and praxis. It is in this sense that Gordon maintains that rejection of European culture and modernism in toto is a seriously racist form of reasoning.

Gordon sees his own project of developing a liberatory theory and praxis as a continuation and enlargement of the project of Fanon, whose work is an ever-present source of inspiration to him. In *Her Majesty's Other Children*, chapter 2, "Fanon, Philosophy, and Racism," Gordon describes Fanon's project in this way:

> . . . Fanon's normative position is a form of existential humanism. His call for the "restoration of humanity" makes his existential humanism a form of *revolutionary* existential humanism. Restoration is here full of irony, for Fanon would have nothing to do with what humanity may have been but what humanity ought to be and possibly could become. It is a restoration of what has never been. It is to struggle toward a new kind of future. For him, the Rousseauean remark of humanity in chains is a lived reality and the demand for a freedom achieved by greater *humanization* is a lived obligation of every individual. (30)

There is abundant evidence that today the need for "greater *humanization*" is exigent. We live in an environment in which, for example, large numbers of white people, indoctrinated and aided and abetted by the denial of human historical situatedness that characterizes contemporary Western culture with its capitalist engineered pandemic of denial (witness the presidency of George W. Bush in the USA), believe that they have been subjected to systemic institutional discrimination which goes by the name of "reverse discrimination." Moreover, many white Americans have a paranoid fear of blacks, whereas daily individual and institutional horrendous violence against blacks is tolerated as the norm.[4] This situation is a seriously racist form of living in denial of reality with a consequent reversal of responsibility and of the parameters of victimization. As Gordon often points out, Du Bois encapsulated this reversal when he wrote that, instead of being people with problems, blacks in America became a problem people—they became the problem (64). Is not this attitude—that black people are the problem—an enabling factor in the persistence in the USA of police killings of unarmed black people?

To see this existential situation for what it is reveals that it is a dangerous distortion to maintain that the contemporary world, with its racism, colonialism, neocolonialism, misogyny, and heterosexism is the consequence or fulfillment of the 'humanist' project of modernity. As Gordon points out, a salient and significant aspect of that modernist project, which was not hegemonic and closed, was and is the quest for a liberatory theory and praxis. Denial of historical and contemporary existential reality is the *modus operandi* of the culture of dehumanization. Fanon's and Gordon's view is that that project of humanization has never yet been fulfilled. That man was born free but is everywhere in chains describes the human situation today at least as well as it described Rousseau's Europe, and humanity is in need, not of a rejection of European civilization in toto, but of a humanizing revolution, that is to say a revolution that will bring forth, as Fanon hoped, a new humanity.

DECENTERING PHILOSOPHY

In the concluding lines of chapter 4, "Sex, Race, and the Matrices of Desire," Gordon writes that "the obvious methodological consideration is that theorizing sex, gender, and race in an antiblack world calls for understanding of ideal typifications of lived realities. It calls for an existential sociology" (85). The book itself begins the process of developing an existential sociology. In the light of what has already been said, in order to provide a concrete sense of what Gordon means by existential sociology, we will turn to the concluding remark of chapter two: "Like Fanon, philosophy must decenter itself in the hope of radical theory and become, in its embodiment, a critically self-questioning practice" (45). One of the implications of this remark, developed in several of the essays in the book, is that poststructuralism, postmodernism, deconstruction, etc., despite claims made by some of the practitioners of these persuasions, *do not* decenter either Eurocentrism, modernism, or philosophy.

The term "decenter" and some of its cognates, "decentration" for example, is one of Gordon's 'operative concepts' (to use a phrase that has been used to categorize some of Husserl's relatively unthematized but nonetheless pregnant concepts). I would like to explore this term and some of its actual and possible meanings as a guiding thread to open up for study some of the important theoretical innovations in Gordon's work, for example, as mentioned above, his attempt to develop an existential sociology grounded in constitutive phenomenology as a corrective for forms of bad faith, including racism, sexism, and aspects of postmodernism.

The term "decenter" has been used in at least two different ways; therefore, it is important to be clear as to how Gordon uses it and how it is being used here. Germane to the present context, to decenter might mean either (a) to step back from a center so as to get a better view in order to change it, if necessary; or, (b) it might be taken to mean to gain awareness of the illusory, that is ideologically constructed or interpellated nature of centers and to deny that they have or can have any other mode of existence (see note 5). Postmodernist thinkers frequently use the term decenter in the sense expressed in (b): to designate their view that all centers or sources, for example, subjects, egos, universals, are illusory and thus, like modernity, are to be discarded in toto.[5] For example, philosopher Steven M. Rosen wrote that ". . . decentering, taken by itself, does not actually bring us AFTER postmodernism, since said decentering of modernist universality is what postmodernism ACCOMPLISHES" (Rosen's emphasis).[6] The sense of this communiqué is that going beyond or coming after postmodernism is not a matter of undoing the alleged postmodernist decentration of modernist universality. Indeed, the view is widespread that the positive aspect of postmodernism is that it decenters, or, so to speak, takes the ground out from under, or 'deconstructs' constructs, for example, 'universals.' Thus, Rosen's remark presupposes that "decentering" means, not just critiquing modernist universality, but exposing it as illusory and thus discarding it with the expectation or hope that philosophers at least will no longer appeal in certain ways to such concepts or constructs as "universals." So, for Rosen, to philosophize after postmodernism is to take as one's point of departure the postmodern "decentration," that is, extirpation of "modernist universality."

Since we have already seen that the project of Fanon and Gordon is a project of humanization, it is clear that when Gordon says that "Like Fanon, philosophy must decenter itself in the hope of radical theory," he is using the term decenter in sense very different than the way Rosen and the postmodernists use it. Gordon is using it, rather, in sense (a): as a call to step back from our centers as individuals and our collective centers as societies in order to get a better view so that changes can be made, where necessary, in order to humanize ourselves and our societies. This point can be illustrated in the context of a discussion of universals. In the following quotation, Gordon discusses the problem of universals and universality in the context of Fanon's critique of antiblack racism:

> Fanon argued that the European practice of science was such that to achieve objectivity it often denied the existence of the black in its construction of the human being. Universality was, therefore, a door available only through the exclusion of blacks. The obvious problem, however, is that the exclusion of blacks signified de facto failure of universality; it signaled an artificial structuring of one branch of humanity into a species above another. (144)

Thus, the "de facto failure of universality" of which Gordon speaks is the failure of antiblack racism to constitute universality as such—that is, failure to constitute the category, or eidos, 'human being' as a universal, that is, so that in principle no human being is excluded. This constitutive failure is noted by Gordon when he remarks that the "failure of universality. . . signaled an artificial structuring of one branch of humanity into a species above another."

The difference between this Fanonian critique of the modus operandi of universals in antiblack racist thought on one hand, and postmodern thought's discarding of universals on the other hand, is clear. Gordon's statement that the "European practice of science . . . denied the existence of the black in its construction of the human being" is a critique of the failure of Eurocentrism in its exclusion of the black from the universal: "human being." Just so, the critique is not of the universal 'human being' qua universal, but of the attempt to pass off a particular, the white human being, as the universal. From this point of view, discarding universality in toto does not advance the critique of antiblack racism; on the contrary, it obstructs that critique: "Philosophy that fails to account for existence is, therefore, trapped in a bad-faith claim to universality. In Fanon's critique, then, there is a perspective beyond particularity and universality, a perspective that sees multiple worlds" (44). The bad faith universality of which Gordon speaks is that of the racist; however, it applies just as well to the postmodern perspective. First, those who discard universality believe that just invoking it entails bad faith—therefore, from this perspective, all uses of universality are in bad faith, and are equally complicit. In other words, neither the racist nor the postmodern critic of the racist acknowledge that the category 'human being' encompasses all human beings, past, present, and future, and therefore that racism artificially limits its scope to some. So, how then can the racist be held accountable as a racist? What then would be a notion of universality that is not complicit in one form or another of oppression? It seems to me that when Gordon refers to Fanon's critique as a "perspective beyond particularity and universality" that "sees multiple worlds" he suggests something akin to, or better an existential recasting of, Hegel's concrete universal or individuality as the unity of the universal and particular.[7] Such a notion is also expressed by Alice Cherki in her recent biography of Fanon:

> Difference, in the hands of the culturalists [e.g., Gardiner, Mead] is posited as a challenge to the universalism that informs the great systems of Western knowledge. Fanon, on the other hand, views culture as a point of temporal and spatial reference that is also a conduit to the universal; moreover, his insistence on the way one culture can radically alter another clearly sets him apart from the culturalists.[8]

He [Fanon] believed that human beings, provided that they were in possession of language and of their own history as subjects, could progress from difference to the universal.[9]

As noted above in the statement by Rosen, the postmodern sense of decentering universals means, on the contrary, that the categorical character of universals is to be discarded as illusory. Gordon's stance is, rather, that philosophy must decenter itself so that bad-faith versions of universals can be critiqued and discarded. Since he does not urge rejection of the categorical character of universals, for example, 'human being,' a corollary of Gordon's usage of decentration is, it seems to me, that in order to decenter, there must be a preexisting center, and, if that center were to disappear or come to an end, there could be no decentration. That is, the telos of decentering in this sense is to reconstitute the center, not eliminate it. The sense of this stance is that centering is inherent in our being as humans.

The eminent psychoanalyst and victimologist Robert K. Lifton expresses this meaning of decentration with perspicacious and penetrating clarity in his book, *The Protean Self* ('protean' is Lifton's term for self-actualization):

I must separate myself . . . from those observers, postmodern or otherwise, who equate multiplicity and fluidity with disappearance of the self, with a complete absence of coherence among its various elements. I would claim the opposite: proteanism involves a quest for authenticity and meaning, a form-seeking assertion of self. (8–9) . . . So absorbed in its own struggle to hold together, the fragmenting self is unable to be concerned with others, and tends to be unable to mobilize the cohesiveness to perform the empathic act. For that act, one needs to be capable of decentering, of stepping back from one's own involvements sufficiently to enter into the mind of another. And for that decentering, one requires prior centering, a prior capacity for ordering of experience along various dimensions—temporal, spatial, and emotional. . . . The fragmented self is neither centered nor decentered, but uncentered in the sense of lacking precisely these forms of self-ordering.[10]

Thus, decentration, so far from being the end of the illusion of any center or origin, is precisely, in Gordon's and Lifton's usage, the ground for the possibility of a radical reconstitution of one's own center or that of one's culture. As the term itself implies, and as Lifton points out, in order to decenter, one must always already be centered; thus, decentering is very different from uncentering. Rather than a process of uncentering, or fragmentation, the dialectic of centering and decentering means that one steps back from one's compulsions, one's false consciousness, one's modes of bad faith, and, in line with Fanon's concept of sociogenesis, from those modes of bad faith instantiated as ideal typifications in societies and internalized as such. Moreover, one does so, one decenters one's own self, and one decenters philosophy in order to recognize one's capacity, and our capacity to reconstitute that center, radically, from the ground up, from the root, on the ground of one's intersubjectively constituted, shared lifeworld with others, with all other centers, all other persons.

In and through such a decentering we can recognize, as Gordon frequently points out, that contingency is not the same as accident; that is, that we are as humans centers or agents of change. In Gordon's words,

> We find, then, in the advancement of bad faith as an index of human possibilities, a principle of positive contingency and agency: That although the human world may be contingently constituted (neither by necessity nor fate nor destiny), it is never accidental. It is a world of responsibility and the irony of limited choices. By limited choice, I mean decisions based on options available. Options are what are available *in* the world; choices are what we make on the basis of those options, including how we may interpret the options themselves. (75)

In other words, the postmodern avatars of what they call decentering succeed only in throwing out the baby (agency, freedom) with the bathwater (reified universals). They do this because they *believe* that the villain in the story is the illusion of centering itself, rather than the reification of a structure, ". . . a prior capacity for ordering of experience along various dimensions, temporal, spatial, emotional," (Lifton) that inheres in us as human beings.

Decentering and Language

How can racism be understood or critiqued if it is not understood *sub specie aeternitatis*, so to speak? We can say, for example, "Joe is a racist, he is prejudiced against black people. In speaking with an African American, he referred to him using the 'n' word." This is descriptive and perhaps expresses disapproval. But, does it offer any sense of the meaning of "racist" other than by defining (dictionary style in terms of usage) racist as one who is prejudiced against black people? Must we not infer that Joe's notion of the universal "human being" is compromised by an "artificial exclusion" (Gordon) of some human beings from the category of which they are, existentially and evidentially, members? And, infer also that this artificial exclusion is correlated with a belief—that black people are not human beings and are members of an inferior species? Isn't this what is meant in this context by "prejudiced"? But, can thinking these thoughts occur without the mediation of universals, categories? That is to say, can thinking occur without mediation of universals, for example, the universal "human being," that are posited or intended as idealities? Postmodern thought hypostatizes categories, sets them up as straw existents so they can be knocked down. I say this because use of categories, even with the belief that they are *sub specie aeternitatis*, does not necessarily posit them as having a determinate content in such a way as to be incompatible with freedom of act or with freedom of thought. For example, in Husserlian phenomenology, the category or eidos 'human being' is the index of an infinitude of *a priori* possibilities of being human. But, being human, is nevertheless determinate, it is not nothing at all, not an empty significance.

Why does the racist artificially exclude blacks from the category human? Why does he posit a bad faith universality? Why does the racist fail to acknowledge existence? How can these questions be answered, or even asked, unless we acknowledge that there is a difference between the free instantiation of universals on one hand, and bad faith artificial limitations on 'universality' on the other hand? Isn't the racist's bad faith constituted by the lie to himself—denial that blacks are given to him existentially, evidentially, as human beings, as he is so given? Or, if universals, for example, 'human being' are suspect—suspected of imposing a deadly reiteration of the same—is language to be reduced to a Carnap-like "object" language (that Carnap failed to constitute), a positivist reduction of language to its ostensive function? Or to a vacuous nominalism?

This analysis suggests that some postmodern, structuralist, and poststructuralist thinkers perpetrate the fallacy of equivocation in their formulations. They claim that language is a self-referential system, but they also maintain that they are *not* proposing that words—terms like "justice" or "love," i.e., universals, be used while at the same time alleging or believing that they have no referent *"hors de language"*—outside of language. This is an equivocation, a case of desiring to have your cake and eat it, too. But, you can't have it both ways: you can't speak of 'justice' yet at the same time deny its reference to an eidos, an ideality that is in some sense outside of language, or, at the very least, not constituted in toto by language. You can't invoke language's referential capacity by using terms that have references *hors de language*, yet deny the existence of such referentiality. Is it not the case, rather, that the self-referential structure of language exhibits language's dependence on an *a priori* infinitude of possibilities to say what we mean and mean what we say—to intend and fulfill, evidentially, or fail to fulfill, our intentional meanings? Intentionality brings us to phenomenology.

PHENOMENOLOGY AND EXISTENTIAL SOCIOLOGY

Phenomenology

What is the center? Given the above, it is important to see that the meaning of 'center' (subject, universals) for Gordon, Lifton, and Fanon is an open prior capacity for ordering experience, rather than a closed, absolutized, yet illusory phenomenon. In an important paper in a volume on phenomenology and politics, Gordon refers to "the poststructuralist critique of identity and phenomenology" as "anti-essentialism without intentionality," and he points out that "the rejection of intentionality erases an account of agency . . ." and is therefore a form of bad faith. What we need then is a theory of,

> radical constructivity . . .wherein even social constructions are shown to be redundant by virtue of the constructedness or achievement of sociality itself. . . . The constitutive dimension of phenomenological investigation raises an important limitation to all essentialist claims. Eidos is, after all, presentationally complete and thus existentially incomplete. Phenomenology points to the human field of political presentation.[11]

Gordon's discussion of the relevance of constitutive phenomenology to agency, and through that to the rigorous methodology of avoiding the fall into bad faith can be augmented by reference to Husserl himself. In an unpublished manuscript, Husserl wrote that " 'Subject' is just another word for the centering [*Zentrierung*] that all life has as egological life and, hence, as living to experience something, to be conscious of something."[12] Considered phenomenologically, centering is then nothing less than the intentionality of consciousness and the ego as it constitutes itself, as Husserl wrote in *Cartesian Meditations*, "in the unity of a history,"[13] that is, the ego in its situated historicity. We can now see that abandoning constitutive, transcendental phenomenology, which was one of the inaugural acts in the constitution of postmodernism, means abandoning the centering that is the locus of our freedom, our humanity. In phenomenological terms, the center is, as Gordon pointed out, the intentionality of consciousness, the locus of our freedom, as, he might have added, the creators and bestowers of meaning. Abandoning phenomenology also means positing a binary pair, an either/or: either essentialism or centerlessness, that is, uncenteredness, fragmentation. Phenomenology and existential sociology reject this binary as we struggle to reconstitute radical theory and praxis for a human future. In the framework of existential phenomenology, decentration means, in Gordon's words, "room for a critical philosophy premised on the recognition of the constant threat of bad faith."[14]

Existential Sociology

Gordon's call for an existential sociology is a call for a phenomenological/existential investigation into the typical modes in which bad faith is deployed. For an example of such a topos of bad faith we can return to Gordon's discussion with which I began this paper: the discussion of the bad faith, racist aspects of the rejection of European culture and modernism.

In the claim to reject Eurocentrism by rejecting Euro-civilization in toto, there is the reduplication of Eurocentrism inasmuch as, since Eurocentrism cannot be equated with Euro-civilization in toto, the rejection of Euro-civilization in toto devolves into an essentialist reduction of Euro-civilization to Eurocentrism. This in turn reveals the bad faith reversal: the desire to impose another essence (that precedes existence): that is, anti-essentialism, for, postmodernism is constituted as just such a negation of what its avatars construe to be essentialism, and is thereby a form of essentialism itself. It is not surprising then that such a standpoint ends up negating the historical actualities of liberation struggles and the project of humanization. As Gordon points out in chapter nine, "Tragic Intellectuals on the Neocolonial-Postcolonial Divide":

> . . .deconstructionists suggest they may not be able to distinguish between right and justice. . . .The problem is in the bad-faith presentation of ideological commitment to begin with—signaled by. . . [an]. . . avowal against deciding rightness and justice itself. . . . Nothing can be said, that is, to a Third and Fourth World people's violent response to First World opulence and the ongoing violence unleashed for the sake of its profit and at times preservation. (174)

A similar analysis can be made of the phenomenon of the claim of reverse discrimination—that it rests on a bad faith claim of whites to be victims of discrimination whereas it is precisely discrimination that the alleged victims seek to maintain: that is, they claim to be victims in order to maintain their unacknowledged desire to continue to be victimizers, that is, to maintain their dominance. Thus, the secret of the claim of being a victim of reverse discrimination is the desire for power and domination, both of which are usually unavailable to victims of discrimination.[15]

Such reversals are one of the sociological *topoi* or commonplaces of bad faith that would be thoroughly investigated in an existential sociology. Their phenomenological deconstruction reveals why phenomenology with both its existential and hermeneutic momenta is essential for any liberatory theory and praxis.

CONCLUDING REMARKS

Her Majesty's Other Children is a collection of essays that exemplify how existential phenomenology negotiates its rigorous critique of bad faith through existential sociological analyses of various cultural formations, for example, the ways in which sex and race are socially coded so as to converge upward and downward in the status hierarchy. Along the way, Gordon discusses and critiques Kwame Anthony Appiah, Henry Louis Gates, and Cornel West, and offers moving tributes to Lorraine Hansberry and Edward Said, among others; he writes about black intellectuals and academic activism, he explores the aesthetics of black music, Jazz in particular; as a musician he presents an informed, aesthetico-political critique of rap. In chapter nine, "Tragic Intellectuals on the Neocolonial-Postcolonial Divide," he presents a theory of tragedy, of Sophocles' *Antigone* in particular, along with a critique of postmodernism in which he emphasizes the role of the audience, a human, existential factor all too absent from postmodernist ruminations and tracings of traces. With his lucid and generous style and luminous and humane intelligence, Lewis R. Gordon helps us to become engaged phenomenologists, to suspend our disbelief in our capacity to tolerate awareness of our state of ontological exigence, to use Marcel's phrase, so that we can see what is existentially, evidentially there to be seen, and, as Gordon urges us, act in the spirit of an eleventh thesis written long ago.

NOTES

1. Lewis R. Gordon, *Her Majesty's Other Children: Sketches of Racism from a Neocolonial Age* (Lanham, MD: Rowman & Littlefield, 1997).

2. Lewis Gordon does not reject all aspects of postmodern thought; rather, he rejects postmodernism as an ideology and believes that one can be postmodern without being postmodernist.

3. Gordon has elaborated extensively on these themes in two of his recent books: *Disciplinary Decadence: Living Thought in Trying Times* (Boulder, CO: Paradigm Publishers, 2006) and *Introduction to Africana Philosophy* (Cambridge, UK: Cambridge University Press, 2008).

4. The election, in 2008, of a black man, Barack Obama, to the presidency of the United States, given Obama's political stance, his ethnic background, the mass rejection of the Bush presidency, and the collapse of the Republican Party, does not necessarily suggest that the normativity of antiblack racism in the USA has ended.

5. According to R. Radhakrishnan, "Poststructuralist Politics: Towards a Theory of Coalition," in Doug Kellner, ed. *Postmodernism/Jameson/Critique* (Washington, DC : Maisonneuve Press, 1989),

> The critique of the center as organizing principle brings together a number of poststructuralist thinkers who in many ways are dissimilar: Althusser with his notion of 'excentration,' Derrida's interrogation of the center, the Deleuzian 'meaning event' in search of a decentralized historiography, and Foucault's whole-hearted endorsement of Deleuze. The opposition to this center is often specific as in the repudiations of phallo-centrism, photo-centrism, gyno-centrism, ethno-centrism, logo-centrism, andro-centrism, etc. Often the contestation is indeterminate and algebraic as in the quarrel with centrism as such. The underlying conviction is that the duree of the center is politically and theoretically bankrupt. The center is neither real nor authoritative. As Derrida shows us, the trope of

the center effects its reality as a reality of power and control. Reality seems centered only because a certain system of thoughts has made it mandatory that we think in centrist terms. Quite literally, we have been mystified into believing that "if the center will not hold, mere anarchy will be loosed upon the world." Unlike a centered critique that acquiesces in the normativity of the center, a decentered critique empowers critical reflexivity to 'deconstruct' that which it reflects upon. (318)

Noted contemporary political theorist Chantal Mouffe expresses the postmodern view of decentering in this way in her book, *The Return of the Political* (London: Verso, 1993, reprinted 2005):

To be capable of thinking politics today, and understanding the nature of these new struggles and the diversity of social relations that the democratic revolution has yet to encompass, it is indispensable to develop a theory of the subject as a decentred, detotalized agent, a subject constructed at the point of intersection of a multiplicity of subject positions between which there exists no a priori or necessary relation and whose articulation is the result of hegemonic practices. (12)

6. Posted by Steven M. Rosen, November 16, 1997, to the After Postmodernism Conference listserv. The archives of the listserv of this conference are no longer available for consultation. The After Postmodernism Conference papers can be found at http://www.focusing.org/apm.htm.

7. *Her Majesty's Other Children* includes several discussions by Gordon of his and Fanon's critique of Hegel's racist dismissal of Africa as unworthy to be considered in his schema of world history. However, for Gordon, I am quite sure, this does not warrant dismissal of Hegel's philosophy in toto.

8. Alice Cherki, *Frantz Fanon: A Portrait*. Translated by Nadia Benabid (Ithaca, NY: Cornell University Press, 2006), 34.

9. Cherki, *Fanon*, 35.

10. Robert Jay Lifton, *The Protean Self* (New York: Basic Books, 1993), 208.

11. Lewis R. Gordon, "Identity and Liberation: A Phenomenological Approach," in *Phenomenology of the Political*, ed. by Kevin Thompson and Lester Embree. (Dordrecht, the Natherlands: Kluwer Academic Publishers, 2000), 204.

12. E. Husserl, *Ms 3 III*, 26a. Cited and translated by James Mensch in "Freedom and Selfhood" in *Husserl Studies*, 14, 56, note 24.

13. E. Husserl, *Cartesian Meditations*. Trans. by Dorian Cairns (The Hague, the Netherlands: Nijhoff, 1969), 75.

14. Gordon, Lewis, *Fanon and the Crisis of European Man: An Essay on Philosophy and the Human Sciences* (New York and London: Routledge, 1995),19.

15. This analysis of the bad faith aspect of claims to be victims of reverse discrimination does not rule out the possibility that such a claim can be made without bad faith. However, all too often in such claims the distinction between racism against an oppressed minority (African Americans) and discrimination against a member of the majority group (whites) is either suppressed or trivialized. Yet, prima facie, whites have more options available to them than do blacks. Nevertheless, the rights and well being of individuals in their particularized existential situations should, of course, always be considered.

Chapter Six

Race and Culture: Victim Blaming in Psychology, Psychiatry, and Psychoanalysis

INTRODUCTION

Aims and Outline

The aim of this paper is to explore the problem of victim blaming in psychiatry. In the first part of this Introduction, the problem is framed and discussed and evidence for victim blaming in psychiatry, with emphasis on antiblack racism, is presented. This is followed, in the next part, with a discussion of the work of select philosophers who have engaged deeply and critically with psychology, psychiatry, and psychoanalysis and the interrelation of these with issues of race and culture. Some of the relevant work of these pivotal and highly influential philosophers, namely Michel Foucault and Frantz Fanon, will be engaged regarding their critiques of these disciplines as they have been constituted in Western culture. The pertinent question in engaging these philosophers is whether or not their respective stances provide an approach, or a corrective, that can eliminate victim blaming from psychiatry. In addition, the tradition of Freudian Marxism (Erich Fromm, Wilhelm Reich, and Herbert Marcuse) will be critiqued through an analysis of E.V. Wolfenstein's, *Psychoanalytic Marxism*, a seminal contribution to the project of synthesizing the two bodies of thought. The analysis of the crucial issue of victim blaming in psychiatry will finally then be fully engaged through a critique of Wolfenstein. This will be followed by a conclusion in which it is suggested that in order to eliminate victim blaming from psychiatry it is necessary to bring to bear the resources of Husserlian phenomenology.

The Problem

That "race" is a cultural construct is widely acknowledged, not only in critical race theory[1] but in medicine as well.[2] As such, "race" is not the same phenomenon as biological diversity within the species; therefore, it is not an aspect of the biological substrate of human cultures. Rather, race exists by virtue of "raciation,"[3] a process of cultural production. Moreover, raciation is *racism*: cultures constitute groups (either within or outside the dominant culture itself) as raced others, and thereby as deficient in some alleged essential characteristics of humanness. Thus, race and culture are linked in and through the historical and material character of race as a cultural construct.

Given this, why, in this essay, is race not subsumed within culture as one of many culturally constituted phenomena? Why race *and* culture? The separation entails an assumption: while it may be that human existence is necessarily encultured, it is not inevitable that human cultures engender raciation. Thus, we are here concerned with culture insofar as racialized oppression, racism, exists within it, and insofar as it may be possible to reconstitute some institutions—psychiatry for example—as nonracist.

An organizing thread for this essay can now be formed as a question: how can the psychosocial situatedness of persons who are victims of oppression yet inherently free be understood and changed? This question pertains to the etiology, diagnosis, and treatment of mental disorders in that such disorders are manifestations, on one hand of inner, i.e., psychic compulsions (modes of self-oppression), for example, defenses, dissociated phenomena, and so on, and, on the other hand, they can be consequences of or responses to oppression originating outside, both in the family and in broader cultural institutions and practices. The values in play here are mental health and empowerment of patients and practitioners. Actualizing these values requires a critical examination of the relation between inner (psychic) and outer (cultural) oppression in the etiology of mental disorders. The question posed above can be further concretized in this way: why would individuals freely adopt modes of crippling inner oppression as a consequence of outer oppression? This brings to the fore the issue of victim status.

One of the most pervasive ways in which collusion with oppression is enacted is through victim blaming. Even when oppression is acknowledged, victim blaming (by victims themselves, perpetrators, or society) denies any relation between, on one hand, oppression originating in society, such as racism, and, on the other hand, inner oppression, such as self-blame or other psychic compulsions. Consequently, reflecting such denial, the victim blaming stance posits either a decontextualized, abstract, and thus dehumanized notion of human freedom—agency as atomized willing: "Just say no!," or an insuperable determinism as denial of human freedom.[4] Neither of these positions is satisfactory.

In psychiatry, some racialized victim blaming has taken the form of belief in putative biological racial characteristics that increase susceptibility to certain mental disorders, as well as the belief that some racial characteristics preclude mature agency. These claims suggest biological or genetic determinism. On the other hand, individuals and institutions that blame victims by alleging that they are "free" to change the conditions of their existence but choose not to do so fail to acknowledge the existence of forces that originate externally in cultural institutions that may induce inner, psychic self-oppression. Collusion on the part of victims, in the form, for example, of identification with the oppressor/aggressor and consequent self blame, might be instituted to ward off psychic collapse or to avoid actions against oppression that could result in physical or psychic death. Collusion in this sense is both a free act and a response to oppressive forces where no other option is, or is believed to be, available. What is necessary is to develop a perspective on freedom and agency in relation to oppression that obviates victim blaming of both types and thus enhances forces of resistance and change.

RACIATION IN PSYCHIATRY

Two examples of racist practices in psychiatry are (1) the racialized attempt to exterminate the Jews of Europe by the Nazis and their collaborators, including psychiatrists,[5] and (2) the continued institutionalization and practice of antiblack racism in psychiatry in the United States, Great Britain, and other European and non-European countries and cultures. The focus here is on antiblack racism. Raciation generates social attitudes that institutionalize the victim blaming stance, which holds that black people are the problem rather than what is actually the case: that the problem is racism against blacks.[6]

Collusion of Psychiatry with Raciation

An important contribution is Thomas and Sillen's *Racism and Psychiatry*.[7] Written to document how racism was institutionalized under the rubric of "scientific" psychiatry, the authors cite numerous works written by psychiatrists and social scientists. Myths of the inferiority of the brains of black people, myths of phylogenetic traits that allegedly reveal racial inferiority, and falsification and misuse of statistics "proving" much higher incidence of mental illness in blacks are all documented. For example, "a well-known physician. . . had a psychiatric explanation for runaway slaves . . . *drapetomania,* literally the flight-from-home madness."[8] These 'diagnoses' coincided with the "view that psychological characteristics. . . are determined by an inherited constitutional structure."[9] A more recent treatment is *Forensic Psychiatry, Race and Culture* by S. Fernando et al. The authors cite evidence to show that, "today in the UK, and very likely in most European countries . . .the forensic thrust within general psychiatry confuse[s] questions of crime and illness, and. . . allow[s] racism to become intimately involved in this amalgam."[10] Of particular interest is the discussion of racism in relation to schizophrenia:

> Schizophrenia was associated at its birth. . . with ideas of racial degeneration. . . at a time when the dogma of skin-colour racism was being incorporated into European thinking. . . . Europe. . . has become multiracial. . . . As stresses. . . arising from. . . racial interaction affect Europe, . . . schizophrenia is again being implicated. . . . And [it] . . . is the diagnosis. . . used to medicalise black protest, despair and anger.[11]

Cross Cultural Psychiatry, an edited volume, contains articles on psychopharmacology and ethnicity. For example, W. B. Lawson states that

> African Americans. . . are more likely. . . to be involuntarily committed and to be placed in seclusion or restraints. . . . African Americans. . . are overdiagnosed with schizophrenia and consequently are more likely to receive antipsychotics when they are not needed. . . . African American patients with clear cut bipolar affective disorder. . . were often initially diagnosed with schizophrenia.[12]

Finally, in *Fair Sex, Savage Dreams: Race, Psychoanalysis, Sexual Difference*, Jean Walton discusses, for example, Joan Riviere's influential essay, "Womanliness as Masquerade." Riviere analyzes a woman's dream and ignores the fact that the threatening male in the dream is black.[13] Walton shows that psychoanalysis has colluded with racism from its inception.

In these ways, victim blaming, the stance of holding victims of oppression responsible, through alleged genetic or biological defects, or through prejudice that renders victims invisible to the racist, or in other ways, for example, as we shall see further below, by refusing to address issues of race and racism with patients, show that victim blaming is endemic to psychiatry, psychology, and psychoanalysis.

Impact of Raciation on Victims

A classic treatment is Grier and Cobbs's *Black Rage*. The authors, both psychiatrists, present case histories that illustrate the inseparability of racism and mental disorder in victims. They discuss, for example, a black woman who "thought it a fundamental truth that black women. . . were ugly. . . she was ugly."[14] A recent treatment is C. J. P. Harrell's *Manichean Psychology: Racism and the Minds of People of African Descent*. Harrell details the devastating physiological, cognitive, developmental, and emotional consequences of racism, which he encapsulates as "Manichean psychology":

The Manicheans conceived of blackness... as evil. Whiteness... became associated with good. ... People of African descent become associated with evil and inferiority. We come to see Caucasians as superior and inherently good... [thus, racism] influences... beliefs about the efficacy and competence of human beings as a function of their race [and] racist information influences standards of beauty and body image.[15]

These works document the racism in psychiatry and its devastating consequences and provide rich resources for further study.

Causes of Raciation in Psychiatry

What are the causes of racism in psychiatry? Certainly, they are the same as the causes of racism in culture at large. However, there is no generally accepted explanation of the causes of racism. There is a consensus that racism is a form of dehumanization, of denial of the humanity of a group of persons who are different in ways that are held to be "inferior"—that is, nonhuman or inhuman. Denial of the role of external cultural or societal oppression in the formation of mental disorders is an enactment of dehumanization in that it is equivalently denial of sociality, of interdependency as a constitutive character of the human.[16] It is, then, pertinent to inquire whether there are aspects of psychiatry that collude with dehumanization. An aspect of psychiatry that is often held to be dehumanizing is the "medical" or "biomedical" model, a form of physicalism or physicalist reductionism.

The medical model entails a disease concept that somatizes symptoms and abstracts from socially constituted stressors. It abstracts from history, culture, and the person as subject; consequently, cultural and individual differences and their effect on etiology, diagnosis, and treatment are discounted. Moreover, the medical model is associated with the positing, and imposing, of ethnocentric cultural "universals" of normality that derive from a biomedical conceptualization of the person. Finally, the medical model incorrectly purports to be a value-free perspective on health and illness.[17] According to the authors of a recent (2008) article in *Current Opinion in Psychiatry*,

The physicalist perspective entails a series of correlated [unquestioned] assumptions in psychopathology. The biological, genetic, neuronal, synaptic . . . levels and their physical constituents are believed to be endowed with the status of ultimate reality, whereas behavior and experience tend to be seen as epiphenomenal, causally ineffective, and basically uninteresting, reducible to the underlying dysfunctional modules. Psychiatric symptoms have therefore no meaning or role to play in the economy of the patient's subjective life.[18]

Clearly, within the physicalist perspective as explained by these authors in relation to the mental sciences, consideration of the role of oppression or any other forms of victim blaming is strictly ruled out. These authors, as will be discussed below, are part of a growing trend to improve patient care by discrediting the medical model as dehumanizing in both theory and practice, and to do so by utilizing an antidote: the perspective of philosophical phenomenology.

No claim is made here that the medical model is the only factor that sustains racism in psychiatry. Nevertheless, as shown earlier and as is shown in the discussion that follows, those who have studied this issue extensively focus on the medical model as a central factor in and through which racism has been instituted and perpetuated in psychiatry.

THREE PERSPECTIVES ON RACIATION IN PSYCHIATRY

Michel Foucault

Michel Foucault, French philosopher and cultural historian (1925–84), was influenced by Kant and Nietzsche. In his essay on the Enlightenment, Foucault points out, Kant, for the first time, questioned the meaning of humanity in a particular historical situatedness.[19] But Foucault also saw the philosophical tradition as having failed to free itself from the binary of reason and unreason, sanity and madness, two sides of the way in which state power, by creating internal warfare, institutes and sustains oppressive practices. The influence of Nietzsche is shown in Foucault's appropriation of Nietzsche's genealogical method, which allows for historical analysis without presupposing either an origin or ultimate foundation for the phenomena in question.[20]

Foucault's early work is an indictment of the medicalization of psychiatry as a process that has served not merely to rationalize existing forms of domination but to create them. For Foucault, the new form of political power that began developing in the seventeenth century, the state form, necessitated the development of techniques to control society and, as well, to regulate individuals. Consequently, psychiatry became a medical specialty whose discourse generated the socially operative concepts of normality and abnormality. These then led to practices of exclusion of the abnormal, the mad, from society.[21]

Foucault named this historically evolved form of state power "biopower." This means that the state assumed power not merely, as in previous periods, over life in that the sovereign power could let live or kill; now the bourgeois state assumed control over the conditions and qualities of human life. Once the bourgeoisie gained power, it became preoccupied with health and the transmission of heredity diseases and "degeneracy." For Foucault, sexuality and race are produced in this process. Given Foucault's nominalist philosophical stance, sexuality and race are social "objects" produced by discourse, with no extradiscursive reference. Thus, psychiatry participated in the creation and deployment of state biopower by providing a scientific rationale for discourses of sexual and racial purity.[22]

Foucault discusses race in several texts. The focus here is on his (1991) article, "Faire vivre et laisser mourir: la naissance du racisme" (as cited, translated, and discussed by Stoler[23]). Foucault wrote that "what inscribes racism in the mechanisms of the state is the emergence of biopower"; [it is a] "means of introducing. . . a fundamental division between those who must live and those who must die."[24] For Stoler, interpreting Foucault, racism "fragments the biological field, it establishes a break. . . inside the biological continuum of human beings by defining a hierarchy of races, as a set of subdivisions in which certain races are classified as 'good,' fit, and superior."[25] And, (quoting Foucault) "racism is the condition that makes it acceptable to put [people] to death in a society of normalization."[26] Thus, "races," for example, Africans, become abnormal by definition, and, as such, expendable.

Of particular interest is Foucault's (1982) view of the formation of the subject as a process of subjectification or subjugation: "This form of power. . . categorizes the individual, marks him by his own individuality, attaches him to his own identity. . . . It. . . makes individuals subjects. . . [i.e.,] subject to someone else by control and dependence. . . . Both meanings suggest a form of power which subjugates and makes subject to."[27]

Thus, Foucault engaged the issue of victim status in recognizing that oppression functions on the intrapsychic level, on the level of the individual, and does so by constructing forms of subjectification that are forms of subjugation. He clarified the ways that oppressive state power, by imposing processes of normalization through the collusion of psychiatry, colonizes the individual who becomes an instrument for the enforcement of existing power relations, including racism.

There are, however, two problematic aspects of Foucault's thought that bear directly on the issue of victim blaming: denial of agency (i.e., Foucault's antihumanist stance) and relativism. Freundlieb shows that Foucault's "virtually complete neglect of human agency and of processes of reasoning does not allow him to account for historical change. . . other than in terms of the 'agency' of a system of anonymous rules and elements."[28]

Freundlieb also shows that "the epistemological role that the theoretical concept of a discourse as a historical *a priori* plays in Foucault. . . leads to a self-destructive relativism."[29] That is, Foucault accords a range of freedom to his own discourse that he denies to all other discourses. To these problems we can add that emphasized by Stoler: Foucault's elision of the phenomenon of colonialism.

The theory of the nature of victim blaming that I am developing in this chapter and in this book presupposes human agency and freedom, and eschews relativism. While Foucault's research and his insights into the functioning of state power have been extremely influential and justly so, his own work as a scholar, writer, and philosopher stand as testimony against his denial of agency and his relativism. How can he explain why his views are to be preferred to any other and how it is that his views are not just another manifestation of the oppressive forces of biopower? This cannot be explained within the constraints of his own theories.

Frantz Fanon

Born in Martinique (1925–61), Frantz Fanon trained as a psychiatrist in France and then took a post in a hospital in Blida, Algeria. In contrast to Foucault, Fanon proclaimed his perspective to be that of a new humanism. From the beginning, Fanon criticized the dehumanizing practices of psychiatry. Fanon was influenced by both Marxism and the existential phenomenology of Jean-Paul Sartre, as well as by psychoanalysis. His work is important because it shows that the Freudian register of psychosexual development in colonial societies must be subsumed within a sociogenesis of mental disorder.[30] Fanon stressed that the oppressor relied on the "epidermal" character of antiblack racism,[31] and he discovered that the psyche of the colonized person is pervaded, consciously and unconsciously, by the belief structure of the colonists: that is, denial of the humanity of the colonized. Thus, Fanon found that the pathology of his psychiatric patients in Algeria was neither ontogenic nor phylogenic; rather, it was sociogenic—brought about by the totalistic oppressive system of the French in Martinique and Algeria.[32, 33] This force of this totalistic oppression was expressed by Fanon as being constituted by the epidermalization of blackness which was simultaneously the ontologization of whiteness.

Summarizing Fanon's work, Lewis R. Gordon writes: "Like Fanon, philosophy must decenter itself in the hope of radical theory and become, in its embodiment, a critically self-questioning practice."[34] Gordon alludes to Fanon's awareness that philosophy was not self-critical regarding race. Kant and Hegel, both of whom made extensive, explicitly racist remarks, are exemplary. Fanon wrote that "ontology, when it is admitted once and for all that it leaves existence by the wayside, does not permit us to understand the being of the black."[35] He indicted Western philosophy for ontologizing the human essence as white so that whiteness became a criterion for humanness. This ontology does not permit us to understand the lived experience of the black, or, therefore, to empathize with the incalculable suffering this ontology has imposed. Fanon's aim in his two masterpieces, *Black Skin/White Masks* and *The Wretched of the Earth* was to initiate a process of black disidentification with whiteness that would free blacks to re-create their own lived reality, the conditions of their actual existence. Thus, beliefs regarding who and what one ontologically is must be bracketed, "left by the wayside." This process of de-centering philosophy as lived in one's sense of one's own being would lead, Fanon hoped, to overcoming any sociogenic identification with the oppressor and to a struggle for liberation in the name of all humanity. It would lead, that is, to freeing the individual person from self-blame, from the self-victimization induced by the totalistic oppression of the French in Algeria.

Fanon did not reject psychiatry as such. Indeed, he included in *The Wretched of the Earth* case histories showing that racism in psychiatry is induced sociogenically by the Eurocentric ontology of whiteness[36] within a medical model that then legitimates it with the imprimatur of science. Fanon believed, however, that there can be a non-Eurocentric psychiatry. His support for revolution in Algeria was a psychiatric prescription for the restoration of mental health, not, as some have argued erroneously, through catharsis but rather through detoxification. Given the almost unimaginable brutality of French oppression in Algeria, Fanon believed that only confrontation with the oppressor offered the oppressed the possibility of detoxification— the possibility, that is, of claiming their lives as human beings.[37]

Foucault praised psychoanalysis as liberating individuals from subjecthood. For Fanon, in sharp contrast to Foucault, it is not subjecthood that is dehumanizing; it is, rather, the denial of subjecthood, of humanness, that leads to pathological defenses like self-blame and identification with the aggressor. True to his Sartrean inspiration, Fanon posited freedom as the being of humanity; his views are thus incompatible with Foucault's denial of agency.

Critique of Fanon is through hindsight. Fanon died in 1961 at the age of 36, near the end of the Algerian revolution. From a Fanonian perspective, did the Algerian revolution succeed? Have Algerians disidentified with whiteness? These questions cannot be answered here. However, European and non-European cultures are still afflicted with racisms, including antiblack racism. Moreover, raciation in psychiatry is barely diminished.

Following Fanon, I propose that psychiatry, including psychoanalysis, must revise itself to incorporate the sociogenic aspect of the etiology of mental disorder, including instances in which sociogenesis is the primary etiological factor. A relevant question is this: Isn't sociogenesis an etiologic factor in all mental disorders? And, if it is, what sort of theory can encompass this etiology? Fanon would not have disagreed regarding the

ubiquity of sociogenesis; however, in hindsight we can see that the sociogenesis of raciation is, as Foucault maintained, a means of maintaining the
status quo by constitution of society as riven by internal wars. Put another
way, Fanon underestimated the systemic depth of the forces that generated colonialism, for example, its relation to capitalism as an exploitative,
dehumanizing *system*.

Alternatively, cannot psychiatry in general, and psychoanalysis in particular, both recognize the ubiquity of sociogenesis and see it as an etiological,
diagnostic, and treatment factor, one that can function as a potential source,
not only of genuinely ameliorative therapy, but of liberatory practice as well,
even in societies not on the brink of revolution? Can genuinely ameliorative
therapy be anything but liberatory practice, if, that is, oppression is an etiological factor in mental illness? These are the questions that psychiatry must
ask if racism within psychiatry is to be addressed.

CRITIQUE OF E. V. WOLFENSTEIN
AND FREUDIAN MARXISM

E. V. Wolfenstein's book, *Psychoanalytic Marxism,*[38] is a remarkable com-
pendium and analysis of the tradition of Freudian Marxism; it is a critique of
the latter and its major figures, and a treatise that develops a unique perspective on Marxism, Hegel's dialectical philosophy, psychoanalysis, and critical
race theory.

As Wolfenstein points out, "classical Freudian-Marxism is primarily the
work of three men: Wilhelm Reich, Erich Fromm, and Herbert Marcuse."[39]
All three saw psychoanalysis as a supplement to Marxism. Reich, originator
of "sexual politics," was a psychoanalyst and social theorist who fled "from
the problematics of social life into sexual romanticism and a reduction of
mind to body"[40] and eventually abandoned social theory. For Wolfenstein,
Fromm's social psychology and effort to integrate psychoanalysis with
"Marx's historical ontology" are valuable contributions; however, his "relational concept of selfhood" elides the individual and results in the "sacrifice
of psychoanalysis at the Marxist altar."[41] Marcuse's contribution was to place
repression (Freud) and alienation (Marx) within the same theoretical frame,
which helps us clarify the relationship between them. However, Marcuse's
Hegelian-Marxism splits the "bad totality of the present" and "a purely Utopian future," leading Marcuse to declare that "the class struggle is over and
we have lost."[42] For Marcuse, Freud's theories entail that the death drive and
pleasure (absence of stimulation) are the same, and this ultimately determines
human experience.

Psychoanalytic-Marxism

In chapter 4 of his book, Wolfenstein discusses how psychoanalytic Marxism (his own perspective) moves beyond Freudian-Marxism. Wolfenstein believes that Kleinian object relations theory's emphasis on the reparative capacity of the psyche is more attuned than is Freudian orthodoxy to the social aspects of human development. In addition, Wolfenstein advocates a renewal of Hegelian Marxism's emphasis on the dialectic of recognition. He further maintains that psychoanalytic Marxism goes beyond Freudian Marxism's focus on individuals and families on one extreme and political-economic structures on the other by recognizing that "the pluralization of emancipatory politics . . . generated other theoretical categories, most notably those of race and gender. Henceforth, psychoanalytic-Marxism must also be a critical theory of patriarchy/phallocentrism and racism."[43]

Wolfenstein engages with the issue of race throughout the book, including a psychoanalytic-Marxist analysis of racism. In that section, he discusses Ralph Ellison's famous novel, *The Invisible Man.*[44] In his analysis, Wolfenstein touches on the issue of the sociogenesis of mental disorders. He provides a Kleinian psychoanalytic diagnosis of the protagonist as attempting a "schizoid solution to the problematics of the paranoid-schizoid position" in his efforts to "heal himself from the wounds of invisibility"[45]—that is, from the effects of a racist society. Citing Foucault and others, Wolfenstein remarks that "the paranoid-schizoid position [Melanie Klein] is a social structure, a placement and deployment of power, a combination of real persecutory forces."[46] If the Invisible Man were not to advance beyond this point (as numerous actual invisible men do not), we would have an example of a person who internalized oppression by adopting or regressing to a self-crippling psychic structure. The Invisible Man is attempting to cope with psychic extinction—the psychic consequences of his invisibility. At this point, his efforts to heal himself were self-defeating. Here Wolfenstein does touch on the phenomena that generate the question that is the organizing thread of this chapter: how could, and why would, a person freely assent to oppression and, in so doing, institute modes of self-oppression? Up to this point, Wolfenstein's analysis is clear. So, on one hand Wolfenstein sees that the pathology of the Invisible Man cannot be understood apart from sociogenic etiological factors. On the other hand, and as we shall see this is highly significant for Wolfenstein, the Invisible Man is not a patient in psychoanalysis.

Wolfenstein's psychoanalytic reading of Ellison's novel notwithstanding, we must raise this question: how is it that in his book Wolfenstein does not deal with racism *within* psychiatry and psychoanalysis? Though he sees psychoanalysis as a liberatory praxis on the level of the *individual,* despite his awareness of sociogenesis as it affects individuals, for example in *The Invisible Man,*

Wolfenstein separates this from liberatory praxis on the *political* level. That is, since he claims that psychoanalysis as therapy suspends all political phenomena, *Wolfenstein does not see sociogenesis as an etiological factor to be dealt with in the consulting room.* Describing the psychoanalytic dyad, he writes:

> Both patient and analyst are members of a given social order. They create a microcosm... in which, to a greater or lesser extent, interests and conflicts of interest of the macrocosm are suspended. Thus, they are able to give their full attention to the project of individual self-liberation—but only to individual self-liberation. The freedom they create extends to but not beyond the point at which social reality has been bracketed.[47]

That is to say, for Wolfenstein analysts and their patients cannot on any level in the process of therapy address the role of sociogenesis in the formation of patients' issues and disorders.

The Invisible Man was attempting to, and in the novel, does, cure himself; but he was not undergoing psychoanalysis as construed by Wolfenstein, that is, he was not a patient in analysis. Moreover, given Wolfenstein's view of psychoanalysis as therapy, psychoanalysts are not racists or, if they are, their racism will be suspended in the practice of psychoanalysis. But, we may ask, whose practice of psychoanalysis? Contemporary psychoanalysis has moved beyond the view that doing psychoanalysis precludes the analyst from acting out prejudices in the treatment. Moreover, contemporary psychoanalysis is much more explicit than was Freud in identifying parental failure as a primary etiological factor in mental disorder.[48]

It is important to ask how it is that Wolfenstein fails to motivate self-investigation within psychoanalysis. The chief factor is his view that psychoanalytic Marxism is not, and should not be, a synthesis of psychoanalysis and Marxism (as both philosophy and emancipatory practice) and that such a synthesis will inevitably fail to do justice to either the individual or the collectivity. Wolfenstein's critique of both Fromm (for abandoning the intrasubjective dimension) and Marcuse (for abandoning the intersubjective dimension) alleges just such failures. What inhibits Wolfenstein from identifying racism within psychiatry itself and calling for psychiatry's self-investigation is, then, his repudiation of the possibility of a coincidence within psychoanalysis of the aims of praxis: that is, a coincidence between liberatory praxis in the consulting room, the freeing of the individual from inner compulsions, defenses, conflicts, etc., on one hand, and, on the other hand, the struggle to overcome oppression originating in society as it affects and impinges on the development of individuals, including individuals in analysis. However, unless such a coincidence of practical aims is established, thus motivating radical self-investigation, victim blaming cannot be transcended. That is, unless all of the most significant sources of victimization—including sociogenesis, that is, racism both in and outside the consulting room, can be identified, how can patients throw off or transcend their own self-blame; how, that is, can they be empowered to become neither victims nor survivors, and thus agents for human liberation?

CONCLUSION

In examining the problematic of the relations among inner and outer oppression and victim status, we find that these phenomena cannot be understood unless the relation between individual and collectivity is encompassed within a perspective that is beyond psychoanalytic Marxism, for the latter construes individual and social praxis as two separate planes of liberatory praxis.[49] The desired philosophical stance would show that intersubjective life is constitutive for the individual subject at the same time that the subjects, as individuals, constitute intersubjective life. This is not unlike the Marxist idea that an authentically human society is one in which "the free development of each is the condition for the free development of all."[50] This means that human life is individual-psychic (intrasubjective) such that each individual is unique and, at the same time, intersubjective or collective. Thus, the relation between individual and society is mediated by processes of co-constitution. Individuals, each with her or his own unique contribution, collectively co-constitute, and are constituted historically and culturally, by society. If sociality were not constitutive for human beings as nevertheless unique individuals, then the relation between inner (self) and outer (social) oppression could not be understood. Why would an individual consciously or unconsciously blame him or herself for circumstances over which that individual either had or believed him or herself to have little or no control? Rather, self-blame and identification with an oppressor, pervasive subjective features of mental disorders, suggest that the subject is threatened with actual, existential loss of intersubjective embeddedness and thus with psychic extinction. As we have seen, Wolfenstein's relegation of the intrapsychic and intersubjective dimensions of experience to separate planes of praxis cannot resolve the problem. These insights move us beyond psychoanalytic Marxism in Wolfenstein's sense (though not necessarily beyond either psychoanalysis or Marxism) to a phenomenological psychoanalysis based on the transcendental phenomenology of Edmund Husserl and to a conception of a psychiatric practice that can dialectically sublate both the existential humanism of Fanon and Marx on one hand and psychoanalysis on the other hand. This would result in the transformation of psychiatry's self-understanding as a natural-medical science into a self-understanding as "the truly decisive field"[51] of the humanistic disciplines.

The characteristics of transcendental phenomenology that render it the philosophical foundation for psychiatry are as follows:

1. Phenomenology begins with adoption of an attitude that is a condition for the possibility of incorporating Fanon's methodological principle: "We must leave ontology by the wayside." The attitude of methodological suspension of all ontological commitments, (and, equivalently, suspension of "the pregivenness of the world," or belief in the world's givenness prior to subjectivity), was called by Husserl the "transcendental reduction."[52]

2. Given the suspension of ontological commitments, phenomenology opens up the possibility of the most radical self-investigation possible for human beings.

3. For Husserl, each ego [self] constitutes itself uniquely within the stream of inner time. In this respect, Husserl speaks of "the primal 'I,' the ego of my epoche [transcendental reduction], which can never lose its uniqueness and personal indeclinability."[53] Moreover, "Only by starting from the ego and the system of its transcendental functions. . . can we . . . exhibit. . . transcendental-communalization, through which. . . the 'world for all' and for each subject *as* world for all is constituted."[54] Thus, transcendental phenomenology, by affirming the uniqueness of the individual in a manner that in no way rules out communal life, motivates the possibility of both psychogenesis and sociogenesis, as well as the interplay between them on all levels of human existence.

4. In this way, the standpoint of transcendental phenomenology instantiates hope: hope that in our freedom we can remake ourselves and our world so that there shall be no more victims. Such a goal for a humanistic psychiatry, a psychiatry premised on a methodology of radical self-examination, would enable psychiatry, perhaps for the first time, to actualize its core values of practitioner and patient empowerment.

NOTES

1. Naomi Zack "Race, Life, Death, Identity, Tragedy and Good Faith," in *Existence in Black,* ed. Lewis R. Gordon (New York: Routledge, 1977), 98–109.

2. "Editorial." Nature/Genetics, 29, no. 3, 2001, 239–40. See also R. S. Schwartz, "Racial Profiling in Medical Research," *New England Journal of Medicine,* 18 (2001): 1392–1393.

3. The term 'raciation' is a less awkward equivalent of 'racialization'; both terms refer to the cultural production of race and are so used by, for example, Jean Walton, *Fair Sex, Savage Dreams: Race, Psychoanalysis, Sexual Difference* (Durham, NC: Duke University Press, 2001), 241.

4. For a thorough analysis of extant modalities of victim blaming in relation to oppression and psychology, see "What Is a Victim?" chapter one, this volume.

5. For extensive discussion and documentation of the role of German psychiatry in the Holocaust, see, City of Hamburg, Germany Website. "Medical Murder." Retrieved 3/15/02 from http://www.ITZ.uni-ham burg.de/rz3a03 5/psychiatry. html, 1-9. This document, published on the official web site of the city of Hamburg, begins with the following statement: "The participation of physicians, especially psychiatrists, in the Holocaust is unprecedented in history. The crimes of German Psychiatry are unique and unprecedented in the history of mankind." These statements are fully grounded in documented evidence.

6. Lewis R. Gordon, *Existentia Africana* (New York: Routledge, 2000), 69–72.

7. A. Thomas and S. Sillen, *Racism and Psychiatry* (New York: Carol Publishing Group, 1972).

8. Thomas and Sillen, *Racism*, 2.

9. Thomas and Sillen, *Racism*, 4.

10. Fernando, et al., *Forensic Psychiatry, Race and Culture* (London: Routledge, 1998), 119

11. Fernando, *Forensic*, 68–69.

12. W. B. Lawson, "The Art and Science of Ethnopharmacotherapy," in *Cross Cultural Psychiatry*, eds. John M. Herrera, et al. (New York: Wiley, 1999), 69.

13. Jean Walton, *Fair Sex, Savage Dreams: Race, Psychoanalysis, Sexual Difference* (Durham, NC: Duke University Press, 2001), 18–24.

14. William H. Grier and Price M. Cobbs, *Black Rage* (New York: Bantam, 1968), 9.

15. C. J. P. Harrell, *Manichean Psychology: Racism and the Minds of People of African Descent* (Washington, DC: Howard University Press, 1999), 15.

16. Gordon, *Existentia*, 60–86. Gordon here critiques psychology as naturalized, as psychologism, not psychology as construed within phenomenology itself. Phenomenology is discussed in the conclusion of this chapter.

17. For a thorough and incisive discussion of the strengths and weaknesses of the medical model in psychiatry, see Michael A. Schwartz and Osborne Wiggins, "Science, Humanism, and the Nature of Medical Practice: A Phenomenological View," *Perspectives in Biology and Medicine* 28, (1985), 231–61.

18. J. Parnass, L. Sass, and D. Zahavi, "Recent developments in philosophy of psychopathology," *Current Opinion in Psychiatry* 21 (2008): 1–7.

19. Michel Foucault, "Afterward," in H. L. Dreyfus and P. Rabinow, *Michel Foucault* (Chicago: University of Chicago Press, 1982), 216.

20. Dreyfus and Rabinow, *Michel*, 108.

21. Michel Foucault, *Mental Illness and Psychology*, trans. by Alan Sheridan (New York: Harper and Row, 1976), 64–75.

22. Michel Foucault, *The History of Sexuality*, v. 1, trans. by R. Hurly (New York: Pantheon, 1978), 131–59.

23. Ann Laura Stoler, *Race and the Education of Desire: Foucault's History of Sexuality and the Colonial Order of Things* (Durham, NC: Duke University Press), 1995.

24. Michel Foucault, quoted in Stoler, *Race*, 84.

25. Stoler, *Race*, 84.

26. Michel Foucault, quoted in Stoler, *Race*, 85.

27. Foucault, "Afterword," 212.

28. Dieter Freundlieb, "Foucault's Theory of Discourse and Human Agency," in *Reassessing Foucault*, eds. Colin Jones and Roy Porter (London: Routledge, 1994), 168.

29. Freundlieb, *Foucault's*, 154.

30. Lewis R. Gordon, *Her Majesty's Other Children* (Lanham, MD: Rowman & Littlefield, 1997), 144.

31. Gordon, *Her*, 38.

32. Frantz Fanon, *Black Skin, White Masks*, trans. Charles Lam Markman (New York: Grove Press, 1967), 11.

33. Frantz Fanon, *The Wretched of the Earth*, trans. Constance Parrington (New York: Grove Press, 1963), 249–310.

34. Gordon, *Her*, 45.

35. Fanon, *Black*, 88.

36. Gordon, *Her*, 144.

37. H. A. Bulhan, *Frantz Fanon and the Psychology of Oppression* (New York: Plenum, 1985), 131–53.

38. E. V. Wolfenstein, *Psychoanalytic Marxism* (London: Free Association Books,1993).

39. Wolfenstein, *Psychoanalytic*, 53.

40. Wolfenstein, *Psychoanalytic*, 90.

41. Wolfenstein, *Psychoanalytic*, 73.

42. Wolfenstein, *Psychoanalytic*, 87.

43. Wolfenstein, *Psychoanalytic*, 169.

44. Ralph Ellison, *The Invisible Man* (New York: Vintage, 1947).

45. Wolfenstein, *Psychoanalytic*, 346.

46. Wolfenstein, *Psychoanalytic*, 348.

47. Wolfenstein, *Psychoanalytic*, 387.

48. S. A. Pizen, *Building Bridges: The Negotiation of Paradox in Psychoanalysis* (Hillsdale, NJ: Analytic Press, 1998).

49. In addition, understanding requires eschewing a stance like Heidegger's, for whom self and other are held to be unseparated [See Michael E. Zimmerman, *Eclipse of the Self: The Development of Heidegger's Concept of Authenticity* (Athens: Ohio University Press, 1982), 25.] The notion of the unmediated "We" that rules out mediation between individual and collectivity (Heidegger) does not enable a stance outside the ambit of potential victim blaming because it fails to motivate the free act of assent to oppression that the self as unique individual takes to be, however incorrectly, in his or her best interest.

50. Karl Marx and Friedrich Engels, *The Communist Manifesto*, ed. S. Bender, trans. by S. Moore (Norton: New York, 1988), 75.

51. E. Husserl, *The Crisis of European Sciences and Transcendental Phenomenology*, trans. by David Carr (Evanston, IL: Northwestern University Press, 1970), 208.

52. Husserl, *Crisis*, 151–152.

53. Husserl, *Crisis*, 185.

54. Husserl, *Crisis*, 185–186.

Chapter Seven

Autonomy, Empathy, and Transcendence in Sophocles' *Antigone*: A Phenomenological Perspective, with an Epilogue: On Lacan's *Antigone*

SYNOPSIS OF *ANTIGONE*

Of the three plays in the Oedipus trilogy, *Oedipus Rex, Oedipus at Colonus,* and *Antigone,* Sophocles created *Antigone* first; although composed first, it was a creation of his maturity, written when he was in his fifties. Despite the circumstance that it was written first, *Antigone* unfolds the final events leading to the fall of the house of Oedipus. The curse on Oedipus' line began with Oedipus' unknowing, yet nonetheless blasphemous, incestuous union with his mother/wife Jocasta, who bore him two sons and two daughters. After Oedipus' exile, his two sons became antagonists, each one seeking to be king of Thebes. One son, Polyneices, left Thebes, went to Argos, raised an army, and attacked Thebes in order to become king, as he believed was his rightful position. The plot of *Antigone* commences on the day after the battle between the Theban forces, led by Oedipus' son, Eteocles, and the attacking Argive forces, led by Polyneices, Eteocles' brother. After the brothers killed one another in battle, Creon, as the next eligible kin, became King of Thebes. As his first act as sovereign, and contrary to the dictates of prevailing religious belief and practice,[1] Creon issued a *kerygma*, an edict, forbidding the burial of Polyneices, whose body lay outside the walls of Thebes. Justifying his edict on the ground that Polyneices was a traitor to his native Thebes, Creon forcefully informs the Chorus, a group of elderly male aristocrats, that the penalty for burying Polyneices is death. Everyone believes that Creon will carry out his threats. Nevertheless, Antigone, one of the dead brothers' two sisters, citing family loyalty, religious conviction, and compassion for her unburied brother whose soul, she believes, will never find peace unless he is buried, attempts to bury him and is captured in the act. The unfolding of the plot reveals Creon's rigid, angry, paranoid character as he debates with those who oppose his edict and seek to persuade him to release Antigone. He debates in turn with Antigone herself; her sister Ismene; Haemon, her betrothed who is also Creon's son; and the blind prophet, Tiresias. Despite Creon's eleventh-hour change of heart resulting from these debates, he was too late to save Antigone. She committed suicide in the tomb into which he had cast her. *Antigone* is also characterized by the great choral odes that universalize the drama, express the painfully conflictual feelings and attitudes of the members of the chorus, and contextualize the events through allusions to the gods and their relation to human existence.

INTRODUCTION

No summary can do even partial justice to the magnificence of *Antigone,* universally held to be one of the supreme creations of the human mind. Yet, despite this recognition of its stature, no consensus has been reached regarding the overall meaning of the play. There is a scholarly consensus that of the two great adversaries, Antigone and Creon, Antigone's stance is the one that is morally justified.[2] However, despite this consensus, scholars' and commentators' views diverge widely regarding the meaning of the play as a whole. For example, some critics argue that despite the moral superiority of Antigone's action in burying Polyneices in obedience to divine law, the conflict between civil and divine law in *Antigone* is not unambiguously decided in favor of divine law.

Due in part to this ambiguity, philosophers especially have found *Antigone* to be fascinating and have attempted to interpret it in light of certain philosophical principles and ideas. Indeed, there is a remarkable history of philosophical interpretations of Antigone from Aristotle in the ancient world to Judith Butler, whose treatise, *Antigone's Claim,*[3] was published in 2000. Among these philosophers are Hegel, and, more recently, Ricoeur. Interestingly, the latter two philosophers diverge from the critical consensus: both Hegel[4] and Ricoeur[5] hold that Creon and Antigone are of equal moral stature. The existence of this disparity and of other significant differences regarding the overall meaning of *Antigone* suggest the possibility that, thus far, attempts to comprehend the overall meaning and ethical import of the play have not been carried out within a philosophical framework adequate to the task. Such a framework must be radical enough to raise our presentiments, our intuitive perceptions of the meaning of *Antigone,* to the level of cognition grounded in evidence; for it is these presentiments that are the source of the universal esteem in which *Antigone* is held.

The significance of the present essay does not lie in its conclusion that the majority view is correct; it lies, rather, in that this conclusion is reached by adopting the perspective of phenomenology, a method of analysis that takes as its point of departure the need to do justice to our presentiments by raising them, without distortion, to the level of evidential cognition. As Husserl, the philosopher who inaugurated post-Hegelian phenomenology, remarked, "presentiment is the felt signpost for all discoveries."[6] My reflections will be aided by another method—psychoanalysis—that has a similar goal. In particular, I will utilize the insights of Heinz Kohut, originator of the contemporary theory of psychoanalysis known as "self psychology." In addition, the ethical issues of *Antigone* will be approached in a context oriented by placing aspects of the Kantian ethical stance within the framework of phenomenology.

SETTING THE STAGE: PHENOMENOLOGY

Phenomenology, the philosophical perspective developed by Edmund Husserl, invokes a changed attitude toward the world. This change in attitude is brought about by performance of the phenomenological reduction, *the voluntary suspension of belief that the world either does or does not exist independent of consciousness,* of psychic life, or subjectivity. After performing the phenomenological reduction, one is in the phenomenological attitude. The subject-object split does not obtain within the phenomenological attitude inasmuch as that split is correlated with belief that the world exists independent of psychic life. Instead, within the phenomenological attitude consciousness is grasped as *intentional.* The intentionality of consciousness ("noesis") means that objects ("noemata") are constituted as its objective correlates;[7] that is, there is no consciousness without an object, and thus no subject-object split as in the philosophies of, for example, Hume and Descartes. The performance of the phenomenological reduction and consequent disclosure of the world as it gives itself to consciousness as a field of meaning are the aspects that render phenomenology the ideal stance for explicating intuitive perceptions on the level of cognition. This is so because, in putting out of play all judgments regarding the independent existence of the world, natural causality is also put out of play, insofar as natural causality, like the subject-object split with which it is aligned, also presupposes the existence of the world independent of consciousness. Consciousness is then free to investigate its own perceptions, its intentional objects, both inner and outer, just as they give themselves to it. According to Ricoeur,

> . . . phenomenology has given to the classical type of discourse about the will a justification and a foundation. Thanks to the phenomenological reduction, all the naturalist statements about things, facts, and laws are bracketed and the

world appears as a field of meaning. This reduction makes the phenomenon of the will possible. The notion of purpose appears as a particular case—and the most striking one—of the intentional character of every psychic life. Purpose has its noetic side in choice itself and its noematic side in purpose as something which must be done by me and which can be fulfilled or not. The relation of purpose to instincts, impulses, and affects is subordinated to the general concept of motivation, which is neatly set off from natural causality by the phenomenological reduction.[8]

Ricoeur points out that phenomenology grounds the will by providing justification for excluding natural causality and for inserting willing into the phenomenological field of meaning. The exclusion of natural causality is consistent with Kant's view that the will is "a kind of causality belonging to living things so far as they are rational. . . ."[9]

The dramatic action in *Antigone* as it unfolds in the dialogues among the characters focuses in large part on the nature of Antigone's motivation, of her will to do the deed, to bury her dead brother. Here, Kant's concepts of heteronomy and autonomy[10] can facilitate conception and exposition. Heteronomy is the dependence of judgment on factors external to the will itself. External factors, according to Kant, include desires, feelings, and inclinations. Autonomy is absolute negative freedom, willing free from all factors external to rational deliberation, or, in a positive sense, "the property of the will to be a law to itself."[11]

Was Antigone's act of burying her brother in defiance of Creon's edict autonomous or heteronymous? Several external factors are cited in the play as motives for her action. These factors include the curse on the house of Oedipus and the allegation that Antigone possessed the *hamartia,* or blindness, of her father—a tendency to rash action. Antigone denies that these external factors were part of her motivation. She herself sounds like a good Kantian. In her famous speech beginning "I dared. . . ,"[12] Antigone provides her own account of her motivation for burying her brother. She says, to use Kantian language, that she acted in the interest of universal principle arrived at through rational deliberation; she acted, that is, out of the conviction that divine laws, "the immortal, unrecorded laws of god,"[13] supersede Creon's edict forbidding the burial of Polyneices. Furthermore, it is clear from remarks she makes throughout the play that Antigone believed that all of the townspeople of Thebes should act as she did; that is, that her act was universally valid, as required by Kant's notion of autonomous, that is, ethical, action (action in accord with the categorical imperative).[14] However, in thus bringing to bear Kantian ethical concepts, I have ignored the fact that autonomy and heteronomy are viewed very differently within the play than they are by Kant.

For Kant, autonomy is entirely honorific; autonomous action is by definition ethical and moral, it is choice of the good. However, when, in the *kommos,* the scene of Antigone's final lamentations, she is spoken of by the Chorus first as *autonomos,*[15] or self-ruled, and subsequently, even more severely, as *autognotos,*[16] or self-willed, these are terms not of approbation, but of derision. Indeed, Creon and the Chorus view autonomy not at all in the positive, Kantian sense, but rather, negatively as a rampant, self-serving individualism that seeks its own satisfaction in express disregard of the needs of the community. This differs from the Kantian view according to which the actions of an autonomous person are universal in scope and, as such, conducive to the good of all. Thus, it is of great importance in any attempt to evaluate the moral claims of Antigone and Creon to explicate carefully the meaning of autonomy.

In this paper, the claim is made indeed that Antigone is an autonomous person, and the term autonomy is used with moral approbation. However, the meaning of autonomy will be elaborated in terms that go beyond Kant's view by relating autonomy to considerations that were not of explicit concern to Kant, but were of explicit concern to Husserl. In particular, I will elaborate the meaning of autonomy in relation to empathy. The latter concept will be used in the Husserlian sense, according to which empathy is the capacity to apprehend the motivational structure of the psychic life and worldview of the other person as other.[17]

For Kant, autonomy is the foundation of an ethic of respect for persons. It is just because persons are autonomous, that is, rational in an inalienable manner, that they are inalienably deserving of respect as persons. Of course, this does not mean, and certainly did not mean to Kant, that everything that people do is deserving of respect or is an expression of their autonomy. The point of practical reason is to determine what to do through rational deliberation, through perception of duty expressed as obedience to the categorical imperative. In the examples in which Kant evaluates various possible actions as to their conformity or lack of conformity to the categorical imperative, Kant does manifest some sensitivity to the need to probe beneath the surface and to the possibility that apparent conformity to duty may conceal inauthenticity of purpose (after all, the whole point is to determine the goodness of the willing as such).[18] However, he does not draw any direct connection or indicate interrelatedness between autonomy and, not just respect for persons, but empathy for them. Moreover, while Kant did not view feeling and inclination as necessarily in conflict with rational deliberation, he excluded these aspects of our humanity from it. Yet, in the very same speech in which Antigone places the religious laws of the community, "the immortal unrecorded laws of god," above the laws of the king when they conflict, she also says that she buried Polyneices out of compassion for his soul's suffering, that is, to end her own suffering caused by her acute perception of his plight: Antigone claims that she desired to bury Polyneices because she wanted to end his suffering and her own. His suffering was an immediate motivating force for her. This is evidence of her capacity to grasp, to empathize with, his suffering as his: "This death of mine is of no importance; but if I had left my brother lying in death unburied, I should have suffered. Now I do not."[19] From Kant's perspective, as we have seen, these motives must not enter into ethical judgment.

Thus, another purpose of this paper is to show, through an analysis of the character of Antigone, that autonomy as a term of moral approbation cannot be understood in the absence of an understanding of its *necessary* interrelatedness with empathy. Antigone, I will maintain, exemplifies par excellence the unity of autonomy and empathy. We will see, moreover, that the tendency to view autonomy, self-rule, in a morally negative light, a tendency that is manifest not only in the *Antigone*, but in contemporary discourse and feminist discourse in particular as well, results from failure to conceive it in its necessary relation to empathy, and an attempt will be made to explain the motivation for this failure. In a preliminary way, we can say that the unity of autonomy and empathy projected by Antigone terrifies Creon and the Chorus, and it does so because it is a manifestation of transcendence, and is, as such, an unequivocal moral demand.

The transcendence manifested by Antigone is a *human* transcendence. This is reflected in her acute, Socratic awareness of her mortality,[20] and in her repeatedly expressed wish for the approval and assistance of her community. Viewed in this way, human life itself achieves transcendence in and through a communally co-intended striving for collective moral excellence, that is, through empathy *and* autonomy. The following examination of Husserl's notion of transcendental intersubjectivity shows that empathy and autonomy are its components.

In his last work, *The Crisis of European Sciences and Transcendental Phenomenology*,[21] Husserl showed that for the psychologist who is interested in the psychic life or "soul" of the person, the phenomenological reduction, the consciously performed suspension of all objective validities and ontological commitments, leads inevitably to the transcendental-phenomenological reduction, or suspension of the objective validity of the world as a *unity,* as a *whole*. In this attitude, the psychologist discovers that the ontic validities (judgments of real existence) that he or she may perform that are related to *himself or herself* include actual and possible "empathies," or perceptions of others, and that these appear among his or her original intentions, or constitutive acts. This transcendental experience, experience within the field of meaning as a self-closed unity (the *"Lebenswelt"* or "lifeworld"), results in awareness of the ego's situation as a pole within transcendental intersubjectivity (the community of "souls"):

What remains, now, is not a multiplicity of separated souls, each reduced to its pure interiority, but rather: just as there is a sole universal nature as a self-enclosed framework of unity, so there is a sole psychic framework, a total framework of all souls, which are united not externally but internally, namely, through the intentional interpenetration which is the communalization of their lives. Each soul, reduced to its pure interiority, has its being-for-itself and its being-in-itself, has its life which is originally its own. And yet it belongs to each soul that it have its particular world-consciousness in a way which is originally its own, namely, through the fact that it has empathy experiences, experiencing consciousness of others as also having a world, the same world, that is, each apperceiving it in his own apperceptions.[22]

The sense of this passage is that the individual-community polarity can be understood only within the framework of the transcendental-phenomenological reduction. Within this framework, individuality (the individual as person, as subject) and community (autonomy and empathy) are grasped as phenomena that require one another necessarily. This necessity is the mediation of individual and community in the phenomenological field, the field of meaning, the *Lebenswelt.*

Thus, just as Ricoeur noted that phenomenology makes the will possible by inserting it in the field of meaning, so too phenomenology grounds human transcendence through its grounding and recognition of the transcendental status of the intersubjective directionality toward a rational, fulfilling life. *That is to say, the unity of autonomy and empathy, exemplified, for example, as I will show, by Antigone's mode of relatedness to others, is the mundane, that is, worldly, correlate of transcendental intersubjectivity.*[23] Transcendental intersubjectivity is, at the same time, the ground for the comprehension that a rational life for the individual does not conflict with the rational life of the community, that is, that there is no inherent conflict between self and other, individual and community.

An important question implicit in the foregoing is the following: if autonomy and empathy, viewed as moral goods, are mutually inclusive, what accounts for the explicit claims on the part of several characters in the play, especially Creon and the Chorus, that Antigone is autonomous in the negative sense of rampant individualism that excludes empathy, that is, recognition of communal values? Creon is at least consistent: for him, autonomy is anarchy, his most extreme pejorative, and Antigone was fomenting anarchy and thus was morally wrong to oppose him. Others, for example George Steiner in his *Antigones,*[24] are less consistent.

Steiner has written astoundingly wise and beautiful passages extolling the moral grandeur of Antigone's deed;[25] on the other hand, he argues, like Creon and the Chorus, that Antigone was autonomous in the negative sense and thus lacked empathy, especially in her conduct toward her sister Ismene. This critical stance is not at all unusual, and Steiner himself refers to and quotes from classical scholars, translators, and other interpreters who share this view of Antigone: morally unexceptionable in her deed, yet cold, self-willed, and most unempathetic.

In order to understand Steiner's view and my disagreement with it, we must bear in mind that when Steiner speaks of the moral grandeur of Antigone's deed, he does not describe Antigone or her deed as autonomous. For him, autonomy has only the negative sense of self-chosen isolation from the community. Nevertheless, without using the word autonomy in the positive, Kantian sense, Steiner describes her deed as if it were autonomous in that sense, and he explicitly claims that Antigone had reached the level of Kantian ethics.[26] However, as Steiner sees, Kantian ethics does not address the relationship between the individual and the community in the framework of empathic interrelatedness or intersubjectivity. Steiner views Antigone both as a Kantian ethical universalist and as comporting herself without empathy for others, that is, as negatively autonomous, and this is the point of disagreement: Steiner's Antigone is Kantian and lacking in empathy, and, there is nothing in Kantian ethics that renders such a view contradictory. I will show here that Antigone goes beyond Kantian ethics in exemplifying that autonomy as a term of moral approbation must, and does, include empathy. It is in this sense that the unity of autonomy and empathy exemplified by Antigone is, as stated above, the mundane correlate of transcendental intersubjectivity in the Husserlian phenomenological sense. These themes will now be further elaborated through a critical explication of Steiner's views.

STEINER'S *ANTIGONE*

In his exhaustive examination of *Antigone* and the history of its interpretation, representation, and translation, George Steiner, a remarkably gifted prose stylist, characterized the play's uniqueness in this way:

> It has, I believe, been given to only one literary text to express all the principal constants of conflict in the condition of man. These constants are fivefold: the confrontation of men and of women; of age and of youth; of society and of the individual; of the living and the dead; of men and of god(s). The conflicts which come of these five orders of confrontation are not negotiable. Men and women, old and young, the individual and the community or state, the quick and the dead, mortals and immortals, define themselves in the conflictual process of defining each other. Self-definition and the agonistic recognition of 'otherness' (of *l'autre*) across the threatened boundaries of self are indissociable. . . . To arrive at

oneself—the primordial journey—is to come up, polemically, against 'the other.' The boundary-conditions of the human person are those set by gender, by age, by community, by the cut between life and death, and by the potentials of accepted or denied encounter between the existential and the transcendent.[27]

Later, we will reflect on the correctness of Steiner's characterization of *Antigone* in terms of the uniqueness he finds in its thematic scope and structure. For now we can say that he conceives the five *agones* (contests, struggles), (if I may render what I take to be his thought metaphorically), to be like the spokes of a wheel. Each spoke has one agonistic end directed outward and the other directed inward to join a smaller wheel at the center: the outer wheel is 'the other' and the inner one is 'the self.' Thus, to vary the metaphor, the *agones* of male and female, mortal and immortal, individual and community, old and young, human and divine, are played out as modulations on the theme of self and other. Steiner places himself in the company of all those who believe, like Freud, that there is an irreconcilable conflict between self and other, individual and community. However, near the end of Steiner's book it becomes clear that, like a world-weary traveler, he has tired of the *agones* of *Antigone,* which for him have seeded the entire history of Western culture. He has also tired of the *agones* of the scholars, translators, and interpreters, whose failure to agree on anything at all he has richly documented.[28] In his final reflections on *Antigone,* Steiner suggests that Sophocles also had wearied of the *agones* and that the play points toward a way out of this endless combat: ". . . subterranean to Sophocles' most demanding play is a meditation on the tragic partiality, on the fatal interestedness, of even the noblest deed."[29]

Steiner maintains that, despite indubitable authorial sanction for Antigone's superior moral stature, a case can nevertheless be made for the moral claims of Creon. He summarizes this notion in this way:

> There is, rather, the very delicate yet insistent possibility that Creon's intelligence is of a kind which might lead him to apprehend the necessary claims of Antigone's stance; that Antigone is possessed of a force of empathy which might lead her to perceive the rationale of Creon's position. . . . The behavior of the protagonists, and this is true also of Haemon, does seem almost extravagantly wasteful of the opportunities for reciprocal intelligibility offered by the dramatic discourse.[30]

This is not the only instance in his book where Steiner suggests that Antigone is capable of "empathy." However, for him, that empathy has no bearing whatsoever on the negatively construed autonomy that he attributes to her.

Steiner believes, as just noted, that the characters as delineated in the play bear within themselves the resources which, if appropriately deployed, could have forestalled the tragedy by inducing the protagonists to think before taking action. In so doing, they would have been able to enter into dialogue leading to mutual understanding. (Steiner makes clear his view that in the great debates of, respectively, Antigone, Haemon, and Tiresias with Creon, no communication takes place. For him, therefore, these debates were not dialogues.) Steiner, however, and this is most significant, does not speculate as to what was the inhibiting factor, what *prevented* thought from delaying action.

Steiner avers, as we have seen, that Antigone has a certain "empathic force" that, enabling her to see Creon's point of view, would forestall precipitous action, "even the noblest deed," and thus abrogate the tragedy. If, then, empathy leads to dialogue, it links up with the community pole of the individual-community *agon.* We are then led to infer that it was Antigone's individuality, her "tragic partiality," that won the *agon* over and against empathy-community. This is precisely Steiner's interpretation: Antigone's autonomy, that is, individuality in counterposition to community and empathy, caused the tragedy. As we shall see, Steiner brings these points home unequivocally in his interpretation of the famous *kommos,* Antigone's lamentations just before she is led away to her entombment.

One can empathize with Steiner's yearning for a means of palliating the suffering induced by the tragic denouement of the *Antigone.* He finds in the play a message of hope: forgo the deed; think, dialogue. However, as we have seen, he pointedly forbears to interpret or explain otherwise the failure of the protagonists to desist from precipitous, tragic action. How, we may ask at this point, are we to gain control of our ability to desist unless we seek understanding of the causes of our failure to deploy that ability? Steiner implies that asking for reasons for the failure of the protagonists to communicate is the wrong question and is not applicable to the play. He claims that *Antigone* represents a move beyond tragic drama, that is, that Sophocles intimates that the tragic mode can only perpetuate the *agones,* the struggle to the death of the "tragic partialities." For Steiner, the meaning of the play is that through it "Sophocles is educating our feelings"[31] as to the evils of partiality so as to induce us to abandon our own partialities. This implies that partiality is Antigone's (and Creon's) problem. In the case of Antigone, Steiner asserts that her partiality was a function of her "autonomy," her isolating pride, which prevented her from deploying her "empathic force."

Steiner does not discuss Creon in relation to autonomy; rather, he implies that Creon's dedication to civic virtue should be read as an effort to preserve communal values, which Steiner equates with the state, against the incursion of individuality viewed as necessarily destructive. Nevertheless, he does not attribute to Creon either "empathic force" or autonomy in the negative sense of individualism. Fundamentally, despite what he takes to be Creon's crippling psychic infirmities, Steiner sees him as a legitimate representative of the values of the community, especially its will to survive. For Steiner, Creon's tragic partiality is just his apparent inability to understand Antigone's point of view.

Thus, Steiner's various efforts to align Creon and Antigone along the individual-community, that is, autonomy-empathy axis are characterized by his consistent tendency to disallow the mutual inclusivity of autonomy and empathy in Antigone, and his failure to acknowledge the absence of both in Creon. In what follows, my aim will be to show that the tragedy in this most tragic of plays is due, not as Steiner maintains, to a failure of empathy on the part of Antigone and consequent failure of the characters to communicate, but rather to a failure on the part of Creon and the Chorus to be open to the empathy Antigone offers. In particular, I will discuss Creon's character in psychological terms, terms strongly resisted by Steiner.

STEINER'S CREON:
A PHENOMENOLOGICAL-PSYCHOLOGICAL CRITIQUE

In the first part of this essay, the discussion of *Antigone* was placed in the phenomenological framework. Phenomenology, grounds the will (pointed out by Ricoeur above) of the autonomous individual and the empathetic inwardness of autonomous individuals within transcendental intersubjectivity. However, initially nothing was said regarding the phenomenological standpoint vis-à-vis psychology. This is an important omission, especially in view of the fact that in the *Crisis* Husserl "no longer looks on psychology as in a specific relation with transcendental phenomenology but finally identifies them."[32] On this basis, we can draw additional inferences from Husserl's remark, quoted above, that, "it belongs to each soul that it have its particular world-consciousness in a way which is originally its own, namely, through the fact that it has empathy experiences."

In the *Crisis,* Husserl emphasized that psychology, as transcendental phenomenology, is a matter of *self-investigation,* "that pure psychology is nothing other than the infinitely toilsome way of genuine and pure self-knowledge. . . of human beings, as knowledge of their true being and life as egos or as souls. . . ."[33]

The method of attaining phenomenological-psychological knowledge is called by Husserl "eidetic variation" and its goal is,

the invariant, the indissolubly identical in the different and ever-again different, the essence common to all, the universal essence by which all "imaginable" variants of the example and all variants of any such variant, are restricted. This invariant is the ontic essential form *(a priori* form), the eidos, corresponding to the example, in place of which any variant of the example could have served equally well."[34]

Eidetic variation is performed by imaginatively varying a phenomenon until the point at which any further variation would result in a new phenomenon. In the following discussion of the work of the late psychoanalyst Heinz Kohut, the assumption made here is that his work on "narcissistic rage" is in effect the description of a phenomenological-psychological essence disclosed through eidetic variation. This claim is supported by the fact that Kohut viewed empathy as defining the psychoanalytic field; thus, his work contains an implicit reduction to the *Lebenswelt,* the phenomenological field of meaning.[35] What follows is a phenomenological-psychological critique of Steiner's conception of the character of Creon based on Kohut's concept of narcissistic rage.

In his final reflections, Steiner writes that,

> An untapped stillness of understanding is present in Antigone, in the aura of that secrecy which has drawn to her poets, artists, philosophers, political thinkers. But there may be hints of such a stillness, of a perceptive weariness also in Sophocles' Creon. As I move nearer the play, leaving behind aspects emphasized in this study, it is the laying waste of stillness, of understanding heard but not listened to that is beginning to feel central.[36]

Steiner's insight is acute—there is in Antigone a stillness of understanding; he also finds hints of such a stillness in Creon, and he describes it as a "perceptive weariness." Steiner does not explain further the meaning of this stillness, but an explanation is not far off. As stated earlier, Steiner characterizes the uniqueness of *Antigone* in terms of five *agones:* male-female; youth-age; life-death; individual-community; human-divine. Moreover, both his interpretation of the play as a whole and his interpretation of the character of Antigone are cast entirely in terms of relatedness to the *agones.* He sees Antigone as having chosen extreme, individualistic isolation over community. He also views her as attempting to bring about an impossible incursion of the transcendent into the temporal order[37] and as having chosen death over life.[38] Nevertheless, despite the fact that Steiner attributes to Creon neither "autonomy" (extreme individualism) nor empathy, there is no doubt that in his view it is Creon who lives out the *agones* in pathological, debased forms. In the next section we will see that Steiner is incorrect in maintaining that Antigone choose individuality over community and death over life, and that she sought an impossible transcendence. My point here is, then, that the stillness within Antigone is the *absence* of the *agones* within her, and the stillness within Creon is the absence within him of *anything but* the *agones.*

Steiner's description of Creon's character is shockingly accurate. He says that Creon confronts Antigone and Haemon with "homicidal abstractions."[39] These abstractions are those of the five *agones*. It is Creon whose "persuasions are woodenly patriarchal,"[40] who appeals to his age as justification for his attack on youth;[41] it is Creon who "is afraid of being thought or made 'womanly'";[42] it is Creon who "has not committed some local, limited crime, however savage," but has "inverted the cosmology of life and death."[43] Moreover, Creon's conception of the human-divine relationship is perverse: it is "one of utilitarian reciprocity, of invocations and honors proffered in the expectation of condign reward,"[44] and it is "persistently strategic and opportunistic."[45] Finally, with regard to the individual-community *agon*, Steiner tells us that the play demands of us that we "think through or, rather. . . bring to full life in our moral imagining the enigma whereby the 'cursed' deed of Antigone seems to embody the ethical aspirations of humanity whereas the civic legalism of Creon brings devastation."[46] Thus, Steiner describes Creon's character as dynamically constituted and motivated by debased versions of the five *agones* of *Antigone*. However, Steiner does not provide any integrated conception of Creon's character; it is just this absence of any conceptualization of Creon's character as a whole that enables Steiner to maintain that, despite the presence in Creon of crippling prejudices and monumentally destructive rage, Creon's moral stature approaches that of Antigone.

In Steiner's effort to make a case for the moral stature of Creon, he emphasizes a crucial statement by Creon and a crucial line of that statement. Creon's speech occurs during his dialogue with Tiresias just after Tiresias has received a sign from heaven telling him that Creon is the cause of the new pestilence afflicting Thebes. Tiresias exhorts Creon to consider that he has made a mistake and to turn back. This sends Creon into an extremity of rage. He heaps abuse on Tiresias, calling him a "fortune teller."[47] Then, he says:

> You'll never bury that body in the grave,
> not even if Zeus' eagles rip the corpse
> and wing their rotten pickings off to the throne of god!
> Never, not even in fear of such defilement will I tolerate his burial, that traitor.
> Well I know, we can't defile the gods —
> no mortal has the power.[48]

The crucial line is the last in which Creon remarks that we mortals do not have the power to defile the gods. Steiner's astonishing comments on this line are as follows:

> Has Creon discovered, in the bleak clairvoyance of his rage, the abyss of 'non-relation' between mortal and divine? . . . For if no human pollution can defile

the gods, then the non-burial of Polyneices is a trivially immanent [worldly, mortal] act. And Antigone's agonistic reflex becomes simultaneously excessive and reducible to a wholly private, sentimental impulse. The tragedy need not have been . . . the grandeur of the statement does stand. It echoes forward to attitudes as philosophically and morally consequent as are the ethics of *caritas* and compassion announced by Antigone.[49]

Steiner's reference to the "abyss of non-relation between mortal and divine" means something very different than Antigone's "I am only mortal."[50] Steiner believes that Antigone does *not* appreciate the " 'non-relation' between mortal and divine." He maintains, rather, that Antigone aimed to do what is not only impossible, but in fact immoral: to mediate between the mortal and the divine, to seek a transcendence that violates the boundaries by bringing about a re-entry of timelessness, of timeless justice, into time: "But we ask (with Creon, as it were): can there be such a re-entry in the temporal order of human existence, or only in death?"[51] We may ask, however, has Creon discovered the "abyss of 'non-relation' between mortal and divine," or the abyss of narcissistic denial of transcendence, of our relatedness to the divine?

It is clear to both Steiner and his readers that his interpretation of Creon's remark that "we can't defile the gods" is inconsistent with his various descriptions of Creon's pathology. Specifically, Creon's remark is made at the very moment when he is in a paroxysm of rage toward Tiresias. It requires quite a stretch of the imagination to believe that a person in such a state can attain an insight that is equivalent to "the ethics of *caritas* and compassion;" nevertheless, this is what Steiner maintains. It might be instructive, however, to consider an interpretation of Creon's remark that is more appropriate to the situation and to his character as a whole.

Even a cursory examination of *Antigone* shows that as the play unfolds, Creon's rages toward the Chorus and in his dialogues with the Sentry, Antigone, Haemon, and Tiresias increase both in frequency and intensity. Concepts from contemporary psychoanalysis reveal that Creon manifests a syndrome called "narcissistic rage," described by psychoanalyst Heinz Kohut as follows:

> In its undisguised form, narcissistic rage is a familiar experience which is in general easily identified by the empathic observer of human behavior. . . . It is self-evident that narcissistic rage belongs to the large psychological field of aggression, anger, and destructiveness. . . furthermore, it is clearly analogous to the fight component of the fight-flight reaction with which biological organisms respond to . . . actual (or anticipated) narcissistic injury. . . . Narcissistic rage occurs in many forms; they all share, however, a specific psychological flavor. . . The need for revenge, for righting a wrong, for undoing a hurt by whatever means, and a deeply anchored, unrelenting compulsion in the pursuit of all these aims,

which gives no rest. . . these are the characteristic features of narcissistic rage in all its forms and which set it apart from other kinds of aggression. . . . Deprived of the mediating function of the reality ego, they are therefore no longer modifiable by later external influences, be these ever so accepting or approving, i.e., there is no possibility of a "corrective emotional experience."[52]

On the basis of Kohut's detailed description, it is evident that Creon manifests not simply rage, but *narcissistic* rage. With this in view, we can now offer another, and more plausible, interpretation of Creon's remark that "we can't defile the gods."

Consistent with Creon's character as a whole, we can see that his remark indicates that his rage extends even, and perhaps especially, to the gods. For Creon, it is a narcissistic injury that the gods are all powerful, and he, a mere mortal, so powerless. Moreover, we die—the gods are immortal. Thus, his raging, anguished, and despairing cry which is at the same time a challenge to the gods: "we can't defile the gods;" that is, we have no power to affect the gods in any way, not positively, not even negatively.

Thus, rather than signaling the discovery of an "abyss of 'nonrelation'" between the human and the divine, Creon's remark is an expression of the rage evoked in him by the narcissistic injury of divine omnipotence. This is in complete synchrony with the mechanistic, opportunistic character of Creon's expressions whenever he speaks of the relation of humans to the divine. That is, Creon's relationship to the divine is the same as his relation to human beings:

> The shame-prone individual who is ready to experience setbacks as narcissistic injuries and to respond to them with insatiable rage does not recognize his opponent as a center of independent initiative with whom he happens to be at cross-purposes. . . . The narcissistically injured. . . cannot rest until he has blotted out a vaguely experienced offender who dared to oppose him, to disagree with him, or to outshine him. . . . The archaic mode of experience explains why those who are in the grip of narcissistic rage show a total lack of empathy towards the offender.[53]

The purpose of this section is to lead into a critique of Steiner's evaluation of Antigone as autonomous yet lacking in empathy by showing not only that Creon lacks empathy, but that his character structure is such as to render him incapable either of manifesting empathy, or *of receptivity to the empathic responses of others*. Moreover, Creon's psychic life is such that the absence of empathy results not just in an inability to communicate, but in denial of transcendence, of all possibility of human relatedness to the divine or to any transcendent ground of morality. What remains is to show that Antigone does indeed manifest empathy in the phenomenological-psychological sense, that is, as an autonomous subject within transcendental intersubjectivity. The goal is then to show that the tragedy occurs, not, as Steiner believes, because Antigone lacks empathy, but rather because Creon cannot respond to the empathy she displays and deploys.

The next section comprises an analysis of the first part of Antigone's *kommos,* her lamentation, in which she dialogues with the Chorus. This analysis will begin to generate an understanding of the nature of Antigone's intentionality as autonomous and empathetic.

ANTIGONE'S *KOMMOS*

In an extended exegesis of Holderlin's translation of *Antigone,* Steiner points out that in the *kommos,* Antigone's final lamentations, "the chorus, forced to clairvoyance by the overpowering pressure of Antigone's lament, rules that it is 'self-willed passion,' a wild autonomy of impulse—the word *autognotos* is graphic—which has driven Oedipus' child to her ruin."[54] For Steiner, then, Antigone's autonomy, that is, her individuality, is the cause of her ruin:

> Antigone's lament and farewell can best be understood as a desperate endeavor to come home to her own sole truth of being. This endeavour will enlist pathos and sophistry as well as a surpassing nakedness of appeal. If Antigone does not wholly succeed, it is precisely because the vehemence of her dissociations, of her cumulative exits from the compromising fabric of erotic, social, and civic life, have finally made her something of a stranger even to the initial certitudes and firmness of her own ego.[55]

Thus we find in Steiner's *Antigones* the playing out of the individuality-community *agon,* in all of the brutal irreconcilability alleged by Steiner, in terms of an empathy-autonomy duality within Antigone herself: if only Antigone had been less autonomous and more empathic! (Steiner's model of autonomy-empathy seems to be analogous to Freud's, but not Kohut's, model of self-love versus object love: increase of the one is depletion of the other.) Moreover, Steiner maintains that Antigone's individuality, her quest for "her own sole truth of being," leads her to sophistry and to fanatical self-isolation that renders impossible any empathic turn; that is, for Steiner, Antigone, not Creon, is the narcissist (despite his reference, quoted above, to "the ethics of *caritas* and compassion announced by Antigone")!

Steiner is not correct in interpreting Antigone's lament as the culmination of her cumulative exits from "the compromising fabric of erotic, social, and civic life," nor is he correct in interpreting her autonomy as an anti-community, individualistic choice of isolation and loneliness. He admits to a point that is crucial to a full understanding of Antigone's lament. He says that, "Nothing in her acquiesces in an Aeschylean theodicy, in the acceptance, proposed by the chorus, of unmerited doom or of the absence of divine help in consequence of some hereditary malediction. She wants to know. She is Oedipus' child, rebellious in knowledge."[56]

Steiner's point here is that Antigone's refusal to acquiesce in an "Aeschylean theodicy" is indicative of her final isolation from even the primordial sources of her own religious convictions, as well as from the primordial community. This comment by Steiner is extremely insightful; however, when brought to bear on a crucial passage, it will lead to very different conclusions.

At the outset of the *kommos,* the Chorus presents itself as sympathetic to Antigone, as weeping. Before long, however, Antigone accuses the members of the chorus of laughing at her and wanting to dance on her grave before she is dead. Her accusation flows from her perception that the Chorus wants to worship her after she is dead but care nothing either for her or for her convictions and suffering. In the same passage in which she accuses them, she begs them to bear witness to her fate as one unjustly judged and to have pity on her. It is at this point that the Chorus invokes the determinism of the curse as the cause of her deed:

> You have passed beyond human daring and come at last
> Into a place of stone where justice sits.
> I cannot tell
> What shape of your father's guilt appears in this.

The place of stone is Antigone's tomb. The Chorus refers to Antigone's resemblance to her father in the rashness of her act, and points out that Oedipus was punished by the curse on his descendants. Antigone responds in a manner that appears to echo the Chorus:

> You have touched it at last: that bridal bed
> Unspeakable, horror of son and mother mingling:
> Their crime, infection of all our family!
> O Oedipus, father and brother!
> Your marriage strikes from the grave to murder mine.
> I have been a stranger here in my own land:
> All my life
> The blasphemy of my birth has followed me.

For Steiner, Antigone cannot here be agreeing with the Chorus, for she refuses to accept the "Aeschylean theodicy . . . of unmerited doom" that the

Chorus has just invoked. Additional confirmation that she does not buy into the Chorus' fatalism and determinism is its reaction to her words:

> Reverence is a virtue, but strength
> Lives in established law: that must prevail.
> You have made your choice,
> Your death is the doing of your conscious hand.[57]

What is most interesting about this passage is that the Chorus seems to have dropped its reference to the determinism of the curse. The gentlemen of the chorus acknowledge that Antigone's reverence is virtuous, but insist that established law must prevail, that is, that Creon is right to punish those who break the laws of the state. They then insist that Antigone's deed was a matter of deliberate choice—it was self-willed, or "conscious."

How is it, we may ask at this juncture, that the Chorus does not seem to notice that it is contradictory to attribute Antigone's deed of burying Polyneices on one hand to the determinism of the curse, and on the other hand to a deliberate, self-willed action? One might argue that the reference to Antigone as self-willed does not contradict the curse-determinism explanation because it merely points out again that she is her father's daughter. But why would the Chorus need to repeat the point it has just made, and with no additional reference to the curse on the house of Oedipus?

In fact, consistent with Steiner's view that Antigone is too "autonomous," too self-ruled to accept the Aeschylean theodicy, the Chorus realized that Antigone *did not* accept their claim that she was the victim of the curse. Their subsequent cold insistence that she must be punished for choosing reverence over civic law indicates that they understood her reference to her family history to mean, not that she was the victim of a curse, but that no one in her community empathizes with her as the person she is, Antigone herself. Consequently, no one can comprehend her motives as autonomous in the positive sense of autonomy, and thus as empathic. The Chorus coldly denounces her because the elderly gentlemen who compose it do not wish to acknowledge that Antigone acted with positive autonomy, that is, on the basis of reasons that were her reasons, freely chosen as the motivational ground of her decision to act.

For the Chorus, for Creon, and for all who view autonomy in a negative light, autonomy is de facto equivalent to determinism because it is understood by them to be irrationally individualistic, rather than grounded in authentic freedom, which cannot exist in their worldview. Antigone's autonomy, her authentic freedom, is expressed in her refusal to acknowledge that she did anything wrong and in her implicit claim to have been motivated by reasons that she gave to herself, that she constituted as of sufficient weight to motivate her action. These reasons included her belief that non-burial is a violation of divine law as well as her compassion for her brother. In these respects, Antigone's *kommos* contrasts sharply with Creon's lamentations after the death of his wife and son. Creon pointedly reduplicates the Chorus' failure to constitute any contradiction between divine retribution and deliberate choice, between determinism and freedom. First, he cries out that "surely a god has crushed me between the hugest weights of heaven";[58] then, he insists that "I alone am guilty. I know it, and I say it."[59] Thus, unlike Antigone, Creon both accepts the Aeschylean theodicy (though in his perverse, mechanistic manner of relating to the divine) and is devoid of both autonomy and empathy. That he constitutes determinism and deliberate choice as non-contradictory reveals that he was not authentically free in the sense of having chosen, not merely to act, not merely this rather than that, but of having chosen the *reasons* for, the *motivational foundation* for his acts. Freedom in this sense is just what is meant by autonomy. Philosopher of law Gerald Dworkin makes this point neatly when he says that autonomy is "the attitude a man takes toward the reasons for which he acts, whether or not he identifies himself with these reasons, assimilates them to himself, which is crucial for determining whether or not he acts freely. . ."[60]

Thus, in her dialogue with the Chorus in the course of her final lamentations, Antigone conveys with great power that she is unrepentant, believes that she deserves great pity because she is dying for having done what is right, and that she chose to bury her brother not because of an external determinism, but because of the reasons that she *chose* as the basis for her actions. How then is all of this a manifestation of empathy?

It is quite clear in the *kommos* that the failure of the members of the chorus to empathize with her and to show pity for her regardless of their belief that she should not have acted as she did, and their open hostility, are both quite painful to Antigone. If, however, their pity is what she wanted and needed, could she not win it from them? For example, she could have appealed to their sympathy by conforming to their wish not to be challenged or threatened; they can express sympathy so long as they are not challenged directly. Antigone's empathy is expressed, rather, in her refusal to allow them to victimize her (and themselves) further by making compliance the price of affection. What they want to hear is that she *chose,* but did not *intend* that action; what is most important to Antigone is precisely that her choice was intentional—that it was constituted in and through her recognition and approbation of the feelings and beliefs that motivated it. In short, Antigone's empathy is manifest in that she appeals to the Chorus to pity her and witness her *unjust* death on the ground of her self-recognition as having her own reasons for her action, reasons that are principled and universalizable. Her empathy is her refusal to abandon her reasons and her appeal to the Chorus' autonomy, an autonomy that would, if deployed, be manifest as empathy for her. They coldly reject her because they realize that to empathize with her would mean to accept an absolute moral demand and responsibility, that is, to stand on one's own feet and knowingly accept the consequences of actions one chooses to do.

Thus, Steiner is mistaken in his belief that Antigone is autonomous in the sense of having chosen death over life and to cut herself off from the community. On the contrary, she loves life enough to plead, in her last moments, for the Chorus to witness to the injustice of her death, and she pleads for their pitying love. Why would she wish this if, as Steiner claims, her "daimon" is one of self-isolation?[61]

We now turn to Antigone's relationship to Ismene, which many scholars, including Steiner, view as the prime indication of Antigone's lack of empathy.

ANTIGONE AND ISMENE

Sophocles represents the relation and interaction between Antigone and Ismene in two scenes: the Prologue, in which Antigone asks Ismene to join her in the burial of Polyneices, and the scene in which Antigone, captured and condemned, refuses Ismene's plea to die with her sister. There is a critical tradition of interpretation of the latter scene which sees Antigone's behavior as devoid of empathy toward Ismene. That Steiner views Antigone's autonomy as anarchistic individualism, and that this view is a consequence of his separation of autonomy and empathy, is nowhere more clear than here.

Referring to Antigone's statements, in her dialogues with Creon, that Polyneices deserved burial even if he was a traitor and that the gods' law requiring burial of the dead transcends any human motivations, and to Antigone's powerful sense of family loyalty, Steiner remarks, "How, then, can she deny to Ismene that sense of *philia* which embraces Polyneices and gives validity to her own death? Sophocles gives no answer."[62] Steiner, however, has provided an answer in his characterization of Antigone as having made "cumulative exits from the compromising fabric of erotic, social, and civic life." That is, Antigone wants to die and to die alone; she never had any desire to comfort Ismene or see her point of view; Antigone lacks empathy and her choice of extreme, isolating autonomy, that is, individualism, is proof. However, as we shall see, it is just Steiner's presupposition of the separation of autonomy and empathy that prevents him from realizing that Antigone's behavior toward Ismene is profoundly empathic.

Antigone's interpretation of Ismene's motives for refusing to bury Polyneices shows that Antigone was deeply disappointed by that refusal. She says that Ismene's overriding motive is survival, protection of her own life. In effect, Antigone maintains that survival is at the apex of Ismene's hierarchy of values, and that, therefore, for her, survival supersedes divine law; indeed, it supersedes all other values. However, Ismene's refusal fails to secure her survival. Creon decides to accuse Ismene of guilt by association, an accusation that Antigone anticipated when, in the Prologue, she suggested to Ismene that she tell Creon of her plans to bury Polyneices. When Ismene is bought out, Creon asks her if she confesses and Ismene says yes, if Antigone will allow her to. Antigone coldly rejects Ismene's claim to be guilty, saying that Ismene did not help her then and that she does not want her help now.

Before offering an interpretation of Antigone's refusal to accept Ismene's claim of a right to die with her, it is important first to respond to certain efforts to defend Antigone's motive for her refusal. Those who see Antigone's rejection of Ismene as compassionate generally see it as a move to save Ismene's life, and a successful move at that, since Creon later, after his reversal, decides to spare Ismene. However, the claim that Antigone aims to save Ismene's life is prima facie untenable.

If saving Ismene's life was Antigone's motive, why did she ask Ismene to participate in the burial in the first place? What would be the point of both of them dying when the action of Antigone herself would make the point? One might maintain that saving Ismene's life was not Antigone's motive at the outset, but became her motive later on. Thus, Antigone wants to save Ismene's life because she considers it pointless, and not beneficial to Ismene or anyone else, for Ismene to die without moral understanding and commitment to the moral issue at stake, that is, without autonomy in the moral sense of the term. This comes closer, but does not yet reach the crucial insight.

If not to save Ismene's life, then why does Antigone refuse her help? What are Antigone's alternatives: she could accept her, or she could refuse her, but not coldly; rather, sympathetically explaining to Ismene that there is no point in both of them dying, and furthermore that since Ismene didn't bury Polyneices, this might compromise the meaning of Antigone's action. Given that Creon is privy to this discussion, this last alternative is not viable, for Creon has already decided, at that point, that Ismene is to die even though she did not participate in the burial. What Antigone aims to show Creon, rather, is that Ismene lacks the capacity to *intend* the burial of Polyneices. Even more, Antigone aims to show Ismene that there is no moral foundation to her existence and thus no foundation at all; that is, that Ismene is neither autonomous nor empathic. She lacked empathy for her dead brother when she refused to participate in his burial, and she lacks autonomy because her motive for wishing to die with Antigone is, as Ismene eventually reveals, that she cannot bear to live in Creon's Thebes without her sister. However, we have still not reached the main point.

Antigone has made clear her concern for her existence after death and for the judgment of the gods. Her concern is for the immortal life of Polyneices, and it is equally for the immortal life of Ismene. Antigone is not as much concerned with saving Ismene's life as she is with preventing Ismene from dying without first undergoing a moral transformation. Here is the essence of empathy: concern for the person's ethical being, *for that person's relatedness to transcendence.* Antigone's own empathy is profound, as is her manifest love for Ismene. That is to say, her empathy for Ismene is a directedness toward the autonomy of the other, toward the growth and transcendence of the other, which is at the same time a directedness toward stimulating the empathic capacity of the other. That is, empathy, as active grasping of the motivational structure of the psychic life of the other, is a directedness toward recognition of transcendental intersubjectivity, that is, that there is not "a multiplicity of separated souls. . . but rather. . . there is a sole psychic framework. . . of all souls, which are united. . . through the intentional interpenetration which is the communalization of their lives. . ."

CONCLUSION

In *Antigone,* Antigone says to Creon, "It is my nature to join in love, not hate."[63] Does this statement represent the "fatal interestedness," the "tragic partiality," that Steiner believes the play intends to expose as the enemy of peace? Or is it rather a premonition of the community of souls that comprise transcendental intersubjectivity, autonomous in their empathy, empathetic in their autonomy? The result of this investigation has been to show that Antigone's desire to join in love is either one or the other of these alternatives. It is no repudiation of that community of souls, rather an affirmation of it, to say that each of us must decide between the two alternatives, and we must do so through self-investigation.

EPILOGUE: LACAN'S *ANTIGONE*/ANTIGONE

A contemporary postmodern thinker who has written extensively on Antigone is Jacques Lacan, both philosopher and psychoanalyst. Lacan's views differ in the most significant respects from the views developed in this paper. For this reason, I have included here a response to the challenge of post-structuralism and postmodern thought as that thought is reflected in Lacan's interpretation of *Antigone,* the play, and Antigone, the character in the play. Indeed, Lacan's *Seminar VII: The Ethics of Psychoanalysis,*[64] which contains a forty-four page treatise on *Antigone,* is a magnificent contribution to the literature. There is hardly any point in terms of the critical points and interpretive tropes historically central to *Antigone* studies that Lacan overlooks. And, the integration of his interpretation of *Antigone* with his philosophy of psychoanalysis is a remarkable creation. Nevertheless, from the point of view of the interpretation made in the present essay, as contextualized by Husserlian phenomenology, Lacan's view of *Antigone* is, I believe, deeply flawed and profoundly misguided. Hopefully, a brief summary of the basis for this view will be plausible enough to stimulate interest. The following critique is intended to be suggestive; it is by no means a thorough or definitive presentation of the point of view it expresses, or of that which it critiques.

Lacan, deeply influenced by Heidegger, and in keeping with his poststructuralist stance, rejects humanism. In the words of the most renowned contemporary Lacanian, Slavoj Zizek,

> Lacan accomplishes the passage from theoretical to practical anti-humanism, i.e., to an ethics that goes beyond the dimension of what Nietzsche called "human, all too human," and confronts the inhuman core of humanity. This does not mean only an ethics which no longer denies, but fearlessly takes into account, the latent monstrosity of being-human, the diabolic dimension which exploded in phenomena usually covered by the concept-name "Auschwitz"—an ethics that would be still possible after Auschwitz, to paraphrase Adorno. This inhuman dimension is for Lacan at the same time the ultimate support of ethics.

Following Lacan's interpretation of *Antigone*, Zizek writes,

> . . . Antigone herself was inhuman (in contrast to Ismene, her "human, all too human" sister). One likes to quote the chorus from Antigone about man as the most "demoniac" of all creatures, as a being of excess, a being which violates all proper measures; however, it is crucial to bear in mind the exact location of these lines: the Chorus intervenes immediately after it becomes known that somebody (it is not yet known who this was) has defied Creon's order and performed the funeral ritual on his body. It is THIS act which is perceived as a "demonic" excessive act, and not Creon's . . . .[65]

For Husserl, on the other hand, the human and humanity are inherent in and as the telos of our existence, our individual and collective striving toward an ever more meaningful, more fulfilling life. This telos and striving were, for Husserl, an infinite task. Husserl's emphasis on human existence as the creation and bestowal of meaning, and his belief that human existence has a transcendental character, one that in no way conflicts with its existential character, show his thought to be a philosophical anthropology of the human as directed toward the enhancement of life, including freedom and ethical practice. Lacan's interpretation of *Antigone* focuses, on the contrary, on death, a focus that reaches its apotheosis in his exploration of the character of the protagonist (or antagonist) herself. For him, the focus on death indicates a necessary appropriation of human finitude. It is, for Lacan, in and through her appropriation of finitude that Antigone seeks death as she appropriates her own desire. Because she will not back down, will not give up a shred of her desire even in the face of certain death, she is for Lacan a paradigmatic example of the ethical being.

In at least two passages in Lacan's essay on *Antigone* (chapters xix–xxi of *The Ethics of Psychoanalysis*), he states his belief that Antigone desired death. On page 281 we read that, "In effect, Antigone herself has been declaring from the beginning: 'I am dead and I desire death.'"[66] Note that the text itself indicates that the material in quotation marks (double quote marks in Lacan's text) is not a direct quote of something that Antigone says; rather, it is Lacan's own words that he thinks summarize or encapsulate what Antigone has been saying. The second passage is as follows:

> Antigone appears as *autonomos* [in Greek alphabet in Lacan's text], as a pure and simple relationship of the human being to that of which he miraculously happens to be the bearer, namely, the signifying cut that confers on him the indomitable power of being what he is in the face of everything that may oppose him.
>
> Anything at all may be invoked in connection with this, and that's what the Chorus does in the fifth act when it evokes the god that saves.
>
> Dionysos is this god; otherwise why would he appear there? There is nothing Dionysiac about the act and the countenance of Antigone. Yet she pushes to the limit the realization of something that might be called the pure and simple desire of death as such. She incarnates that desire.[67]

Lacan goes on to associate Antigone's alleged desire for death to the curse on the house of Oedipus, the family *Ate* or destiny. Lacan writes that because the community had been unwilling to bury Polyneices, to forgive and forget, to cover over the criminal—i.e., incestuous, origins of the family, Antigone "is required to sacrifice her own being in order to maintain that essential being which is the family *Ate* . . . . Antigone perpetuates, eternalizes, immortalizes that *Ate*."[68] Here the unacknowledged contradiction between freedom and determinism which I analyzed and interpreted in the preceding essay in both the Chorus' statements in the *Kommos* and in Creon's final lament is reduplicated by Lacan: Antigone was for Lacan, as we will see, both a "self-willed victim" and a victim of the destiny of the family—the latter a force over which she had no control. Apparently, Lacan, like the Chorus of *Antigone* and Creon, sees no contradiction here.

What I call into question is, first, the relation between awareness of finitude, or awareness of limit and death, and desiring death for the human person. Lacan finds Antigone to be "splendid"—his section on the play is titled "The Splendor of Antigone." He loves her. But, he is unwilling or unable to account for her actions as ethical in any manner other than as associated with the view that she chose death in the sense that she *wished* to die. One can plausibly argue that Antigone actively chose death in the sense that she believed that Creon would execute anyone who buried Polyneices; yet, despite knowing this, she buried him. She performed that action that she believed would lead to her own death. Does this justify the claim that Antigone *wished* to, wanted to, die?

For Lacan, the appropriation of one's own desire is both the aim of psychoanalysis—that is, that patients gain the ability to do so, and it is the only ethical act. All other values or "goods" are dismissed by Lacan as bourgeois. In this way, Lacan's view conforms with a commonplace in the history of Antigone critique, and indeed with the initial reaction of many people to the play: Antigone wished to die; if not, she would not have acted as she did. This view presupposes that physical survival is the highest value and that the only way, therefore, to explain Antigone's action, since, 'objectively speaking' she need not have performed that action, is to conclude that she desired death. In my view, consistent with Husserlian phenomenology, this conclusion is reached only when the phenomenon of ideality or transcendence as inherent in human existence is either not understood, or suppressed and prohibited, as in the thought of Jacques Lacan.

That Antigone transgressed the law or *kerygma* promulgated by Creon, with the penalty of death for violation, is what happens in the play. That Antigone believed that she would be discovered and found to be the perpetrator of the forbidden burial of Polyneices, and that Creon would carry out the death sentence, is evident in the play. That Antigone manifested a clear apprehension of her own finitude her own words to Creon attest: "I knew I must die even without your decree. I am only mortal."[69] But that Antigone wished to die can only be inferred through a mental slight of hand, or shall we say a slight of mind.

Antigone, by her own testimony in her last dialogue with the chorus, believed that she was "unjustly judged"[70] (as did her betrothed, Haemon, Creon's son), and that if she were justly judged then the judges would have realized that her action was necessary to enable Polyneices' body to find rest, and that Creon's edict was beyond the pale of acceptable action for a head of state. Yet, that Antigone wished to die is a problematic view of her behavior and expressed thoughts. Are we to conclude that every human being who acts for what she believes though facing almost certain death wishes to die? Is desire for death a necessary component for ethical action in extreme circumstances, or in any circumstances? Or, is it that Lacan and others cannot conceive of, or have ruled out in advance, any transcendent values that would be "worth" one's death? Does this not indicate that, consistent with his psychoanalytic (Freudian) perspective, physical survival is at the apex of Lacan's hierarchy of values? As long as one is not facing death, that is, if one's survival is not in question, other values may guide one's actions (though it is not at all clear that Lacan believed in values at all). But, if one's options for survival approach zero, valorize, we are told, the inevitable: death.

It is my contention that none of the statements in the play by Antigone regarding death, for example, Antigone's assertion to Ismene: "You are alive, but I belong to death,"[71] can be interpreted as manifesting a desire to die. This statement by her is rather an expression of her conviction that Creon will make good on his threat of execution, and that she will not renounce her act. Rather than a desire to die, what is manifest is Antigone's sense that, for the sake her brother, and of Thebes and its people, whom, she maintains, would support her were their "lips not frozen shut in fear"[72] of Creon, someone must challenge Creon's despotic actions, even if faced with certain death, and that reverence and compassion for the dead are values defended in her actions that she views as worthy of her death, that is, that, in her view, her own survival was a lesser value ("this death of mine is of no importance"[73]) than defense of transcendent values, including love.[74] From this point of view, Antigone's actions were grounded in transcendent values that she chose to ground her own existence. Let us remember that Antigone did not promulgate an edict forbidding the burial of her brother: Creon did. So, in what sense does Lacan mean to say that Antigone desired death? In my view, Lacan's conviction that this is so reflects the prior abrogation of transcendence and the rejection of any version of humanism.

To show this, I will refer to a statement that Lacan makes in *The Ethics of Psychoanalysis* that is both consistent with his fundamental anti-humanism and with the kind of strictures that inhere in his writings (and in the writings of many structuralist, poststructuralist, and postmodern thinkers, as well as many 'analytic' philosophers) in order to control the field of investigation, and which, to my knowledge, has never been questioned in the literature on his book.

In chapter XXIII of *The Ethics of Psychoanalysis*, titled "The moral goals of psychoanalysis," Lacan, addressing the psychoanalysts attending the seminar, says (I have severely truncated this paragraph in the interests of space and getting to the point; readers may wish to read the entire paragraph):

> There is absolutely no reason why we should make ourselves the guarantors of
> the bourgeois dream. . . . The movement that the world we live in is caught up

in, of wanting to establish the universal spread of the service of goods ["Private goods, family goods, domestic goods, other goods that solicit us . . . "] . . . The establishment of the service of goods at the universal level does not in itself resolve the problem of the present relationship of each individual man to his desire in the short period of time between his birth and his death. The happiness of future generations is not at issue here.[75]

Consistently with this, Lacan had earlier written. "To put it in terms of Levi-Strauss... Antigone with relation to Creon finds herself in the place of synchrony in opposition to diachrony."[76]

Lacan's remark that "The happiness of future generations is not at issue here" is striking. On what basis is concern for future generations excluded? Why did Lacan find it so important to insert this comment? In declaring this exclusion, Lacan seems to think that he is performing a verbal fiat: "If I say it is excluded, so it is. That's the parameter of my thinking." But can saying it make it so? Is it actually possible (not to mention desirable) to meditate on the meaning of ethics while abstracting from considerations of the well-being of future generations? Can saying so make it possible? The ethical acts of individuals impact upon both contemporary and past generations. If I am concerned about the kind of world my infant son will encounter when he emerges into adulthood, must I not also be concerned about the world that his children whom he loves will emerge into, and their children, and so on? It would seem that Lacan's eagerness to announce the decisive exclusion of future generations is indicative that it is not possible to *live* such an exclusion. The suspicion of an attempt at verbal fiat is borne out, it seems to me, by Lacan's prior remark remanding Antigone to synchrony (the present) and Creon to diachrony (history)! Isn't the opposite more coherent: Creon wants to use state power to abrogate traditional values; Antigone stands in defense of the traditional belief that bodies must be buried for the souls to find rest? However, if Lacan were to acknowledge the diachronic elements of Antigone's existence and of her own self-understanding, she could not be what he wishes her to be: an exemplification of his anti-humanism, of his belief that the death drive governs life.

The question I pose can be restated in this way: Is ethics possible in the context of the peremptory exclusion of consideration of future generations and human historicity? Here I would say that Lacan abrogates the very consciousness of finitude, of death, that his theory believes itself, uniquely, to require. I say this because the emptiness of death is not adequate to the notion of finitude. Human finitude as experienced by living human beings is not an emptiness; rather, it is a determinate finitude. In his defense at his trial, in the *Apology*, Socrates stated that the jury expected him to beg for his life. Socrates' response to this is that were he to do so, to compromise the

values for which he had lived, to abandon those values, he would be acting as
if he thought that he would, having escaped the death penalty, live forever. He
would be denying his finitude.[77] Socrates' acute, all pervasive awareness of his
mortality forbade such a compromise, as did Antigone's stated awareness of
her own mortality. Thus, human finitude is determinate in that it necessitates
reflection on one's relation to those who live on. The deaths of Socrates and
Antigone were unwanted by them, yet preferable to a living death of meaninglessness, of valuelessness, a life lived in the searing fires of ceaseless shame
induced by betrayal of oneself, and of one's responsibility to all. *Thus, the
slight of mind constituted by Lacan is to equate the choice of a lesser evil with
choice of a positively desired, willed outcome of action.* Indeed, Socrates' and
Antigone's actions, their choice of the lesser evil, death, is evidence of their
belief, or hope, that the generations to come will benefit from their actions after their deaths. Even if one were to argue that they were mistaken in this view,
it still would not follow that they chose death for its own sake as death. For
them, finitude means not the emptiness of death, but the recognition that to be
human just is to be inserted in a historically generative community of persons.
For Lacan, all of ethics is embodied in the notion of appropriating one's own
desire, and death, valorized for Lacan as the correlate of awareness of finitude,
is, it seems to me, Lacan's attempt to obliterate concern for the continuity of
the generations of humanity. It is for this reason that he attempts a verbal fiat:
it would indeed be a miracle if the human could be adequately and insightfully
conceived as abstracted from our necessary embeddedness in our individual
and communal historicity of past, present, and future. Can one appropriate
one's own desire in the absence of a historically generative community? On
Lacanian grounds, one cannot argue that Antigone may have believed that she
was choosing the lesser of two evils, but in actuality, unbeknownst to herself,
she was "really" choosing death, she "really" wished to die. For Lacan, of
necessity, Antigone's wish for death was consciously willed, chosen, though
he describes her as enslaved to her destiny.

Finally, I will discuss the relevance of my critique of Lacan to the theme
of this volume, *Neither Victim nor Survivor.* Near the beginning of Lacan's
chapter on *Antigone,* he writes,

> We know very well that over and beyond the dialogue, over and beyond the
> question of family and country, over and beyond the moralizing arguments, it is
> Antigone herself who fascinates us, Antigone in her unbearable splendor. She
> has a quality that both attracts and startles us, in the sense of intimidates us: this
> terrible, self-willed victim disturbs us.[78]

Here at the outset we have Lacan referring to Antigone as a "self-willed
victim." I cannot attribute to Lacan the sort of notion of 'victim' that has re-

cently become current such that all victims are self-willed, that to be a victim no longer means to suffer at the hand of an other; rather, it means now to be the cause of one's own suffering. (For extensive elaboration of this point, see "What Is a Victim?" chapter one in this volume.) Yet, Lacan's phrase does suggest that for him Antigone was just such a victim—a victim of her own hand, not at the hand of an other.

The title of the present volume, *Neither Victim nor Survivor*, indicates that, on the contrary, a victim is one who has been victimized by an other. The point here is that victims of oppression, under extreme duress, often identify with their oppressor and become accomplices in their own oppression. To say this is not to blame the victim; rather, it is the only way to preclude blaming the victim. Victim blaming is the claim that victims will their own oppression. However, when under extreme duress people identify with their aggressors, they are not choosing to be oppressed; they are indeed choosing, but what they are choosing is, rather, the only means of coping with oppression that they believe to be available to them.

From this point of view, Lacan's claim that Antigone is awesome, indeed intimidating, as a self-willed victim in her splendor is in actuality a massive denial that Antigone rejected mere survival, and did so in the name of transcendent values. She was neither a self-willed victim nor a survivor. I say she was not a survivor not because in fact she died, but rather because survival would have meant rejecting her values, and, from this point of view, pace Lacan, it is the choice of mere physical survival that violates the possibility of ethics, of our humanity. What is intimidating? Those who, like Lacan, find Antigone to be intimidating are reacting to their perception that they themselves reject the moral demand that a real understanding of Antigone would open one to. Antigone intimidates because *she asks her family, her contemporaries, and us to be more than we have been*, to realize the potential of humanity to transgress extant norms, not to embrace death, but to move us all in the direction of the ideal, or, put another way, to help us to mature, to "grow up." Lacan's intense rejection of this sort of perspective is revealed when he says that Antigone is "inhuman." This is analogous to self-professed Christians who say that it would be inhuman to expect humans to be Christ-like in our lives, except, of course, that is exactly what Christ exhorted his followers to do! Or, taking the question from the other side, like mayor of Chicago Richard M. Daley who, when confronted with clear evidence of abuse of power by police officers, announced, during an interview broadcast on television, that the police are only human!—that is, it would be inhuman to expect better behavior from the police, or the police would be inhuman if they did not abuse their power! But this is not possible because only the very, very few can, like Christ and Antigone (who, for Hegel, was above Christ, ethically speaking), be inhuman!

Lacan seems to think that Antigone's deed was both inhuman and ethical, that being human precludes ethics. That Lacan believed that such valorized inhumanity is not within the scope of possibility for mere humans like himself is perhaps indicated by the fact that during the Nazi occupation of France, he never joined the Resistance, and furthermore, that he "had little sympathy for the Resistance, either" [and] " 'had had no hesitation about going to the Hotel Meurice and fraternizing with the German officers to get a permit to go and see Sylvie in the unoccupied zone.'"[79] Of course, had Lacan been a Jew, such behavior would have been impossible, to say the least.

Husserlian phenomenology is precisely a phenomenological account of the mediation of individual and community through an account of the developmental processes that synthesize, or, better, reveal the inseparability of synchrony and diachrony, of the horizonal structure of the present constituted by the living past of both the individual and the community, and by the protended horizon of the future. Indeed, the genetic phenomenological investigation of the horizonal structure of human being in the world and its transcendental constitutive origins is the meaning of Husserlian phenomenology.[80]

Finally, then, the advent of structuralist, poststructuralist, and postmodern thought takes to the limit the possibility and scope of the rejection of the human and of humanism. Paul Allen Miller adds a comment to one of the quotes from Lacan above, to the effect that, when Lacan says that Antigone fulfills "the pure and simple desire of death as such," Lacan means that this desire for death is desire for "that which is beyond the pleasure principle."[81] However, perhaps a word from Freud is in order here, to wit, the last lines of his *Civilization and Its Discontents* (a book on which Lacan placed great emphasis): "And now it is to be expected that the other of the two 'Heavenly Powers', eternal Eros, will make an effort to assert himself in the struggle with his equally immortal adversary [Thanatos]. But who can foresee with what success and with what result?"[82] Ignoring Freud's sexist language and his recourse to myth, which it seems to me was Freud's way out of acknowledging transcendence, it is indeed to be hoped that the human capacity for love, in all of its forms, including of course active resistance to real inhumanity, will motivate us toward a better future.

NOTES

1. The exact nature of the affront to prevailing religious practices is a matter of considerable controversy in the scholarly literature. A helpful summary with references can be found in S. Elden, "The Place of the Polis: Political Blindness in Judith Butler's *Antigone's Claim*," in *Theory and Event* 8, no. 1 (2005): 20. Elden remarks

that "the affront is the public display of the unburied body within the polis. . . ." The point here is that Creon refused to have Polyneices' body (which, while it was outside the walls of Thebes, was nevertheless on the soil of the polis) taken outside the polis where it could be buried.

2. R.P. Winnington-Ingram, *Sophocles: An Interpretation* (Cambridge, UK: Cambridge University Press, 1980), 148.

3. Judith Butler, *Antigone's Claim* (New York: Columbia University Press, 2000).

4. G.W.F. Hegel, *Lectures on the Philosophy of Religion*, vol. II, trans. and ed. by E. B. Spears (London: Routledge, 1974), 264.

5. Paul Ricoeur, *Oneself as Another*, trans. by K, Blamey (Chicago: University of Chicago Press, 1992), 244. Ricoeur refers to George Steiner's book, *Antigones* (Oxford: Oxford University Press, 1984), to be discussed at length below, as a "great book." Indeed, Ricoeur's views on the play seem to mirror Steiner's. Both acknowledge that "our preference" (Ricoeur, 245) goes to Antigone; yet, they maintain that both Creon and Antigone gave way to a "tragic partiality" (Steiner) and that the tragedy would not have occurred if they had just listened to one another. The interpretation in this paper is very different from this.

6. Edmund Husserl, *The Crisis of European Sciences and Transcendental Phenomenology*, trans. by D. Carr (Evanston, IL: Northwestern University Press, 1970), 276.

7. Edmund Husserl, *Ideas Pertaining to a Pure Phenomenology and to a Phenomenological Philosophy, First Book: General Introduction to a Pure Phenomenology*, trans. by F. Kersten (The Hague, The Netherlands: Nijhoff, 1983) (Originally published in 1913).

8. Paul Ricoeur, "The Problem of the Will and Philosophical Discourse," in *Patterns of the Life-World*, edited by J.M. Edie, et al. (Evanston, IL: Northwestern University Press, 1970), 277.

9. Immanuel Kant, *Foundations of the Metaphysics of Morals*, trans. by Lewis White Beck, (Indianapolis: Bobbs-Merrill, 1969), 73.

10. Kant, *Foundations*, 68–74.

11. Kant, *Foundations*, 74.

12. Sophocles, *Antigone*, in *The Oedipus Cycle*, trans. by Dudley Fitts and Robert Fitzgerald (New York: Harcourt, 1977), 208–9. All references to an English translation are to this edition unless otherwise noted.

13. Sophocles, *Antigone*, 203.

14. Kant, *Foundations*, 67.

15. Sophocles, *Antigone*, in *Sophocles: The Plays and Fragments, Part III: The Antigone*, ed. and trans. by Richard Jebb (Amsterdam: Hakkert, 1962), p. 150, line 821. All references to the Greek original are to this Jebb bilingual edition.

16. Jebb, 160, line 875.

17. Edmund Husserl, *Ideas Pertaining to a Pure Phenomenology and to a Phenomenological Philosophy, Second Book*, trans. by Richard Rojcewicz and Andre Schuwer (Dordrecht, The Netherlands: Kluwer, 1989; German originally published in 1952), 239–40.

18. Kant, *Foundations*, 12.

19. Sophocles, *Antigone,* 208.

20. Sophocles, *Antigone,* 203.

21. Husserl, *Crisis.*

22. Husserl, *Crisis,* 255. The grounding of empathy in primordial empathy, i.e., in the originary constitution in consciousness of the other as an alter ego, another self, is the condition for the possibility of empathy experiences. The locus classicus for the phenomenological constitution of primordial empathy is Edmund Husserl, *Cartesian Meditations* (The Hague, the Netherlands: Nijhoff, 1969) (German original published 1950).

23. Transcendental intersubjectivity and the community of persons as a phenomenon of everyday experience are a unity. To say that the unity of autonomy and empathy is the mundane correlate of transcendental intersubjectivity is to say that insofar as this unity inheres in persons, the community of persons is transcendental intersubjectivity.

24. George Steiner, *Antigones* (New York: Oxford University Press, 1984).

25. Steiner, *Antigones,* 108–9.

26. Steiner, *Antigones,* 271.

27. Steiner, *Antigones,* 231–32.

28. Steiner, *Antigones,* 284.

29. Steiner, *Antigones,* 300.

30. Steiner, *Antigones,* 290.

31. Steiner, *Antigones,* 261.

32. Elisabeth Ströker, "The Role of Psychology in Husserl's Phenomenology," in *Continental Philosophy in America,* H.J. Silverman, et al., eds. (Pittsburgh, PA: Duquesne University Press, 1983), 15.

33. Husserl, *Crisis,* 261.

34. Edmund Husserl, *Formal and Transcendental Logic,* translated by Dorian Cairns (The Hague, the Netherlands: Nijhoff, 1969), 248.

35. For a thorough discussion of Kohut's version of psychoanalysis, which he named "self-psychology," see my "Kohut and Husserl: The Empathic Bond" in *Self Psychology: Comparisons and Contrasts,* eds. Douglas Detrick and Susan Detrick (Hillsdale, NJ: The Analytic Press, 1989), 151–74.

36. Steiner, *Antigones,* 300.

37. Steiner, *Antigones,* 248.

38. Steiner, *Antigones,* 251.

39. Steiner, *Antigones,* 247.

40. Steiner, *Antigones,* 245.

41. Steiner, *Antigones,* 245.

42. Steiner, *Antigones,* 238.

43. Steiner, *Antigones,* 287.

44. Steiner, *Antigones,* 270.

45. Steiner, *Antigones,* 271.

46. Steiner, *Antigones,* 257.

47. Sophocles, *Antigone,* 226.

48. Steiner, *Antigones*, 274. Steiner states here that he is quoting from the Robert Fagles translation, but does not provide a reference to this translation anywhere in *Antigones*.

49. Steiner, *Antigones*, 275–76.

50. Sophocles, *Antigone*, 203.

51. Steiner, *Antigones*, 250.

52. Heinz Kohut, "Thoughts on Narcissism and Narcissistic Rage," in *Self-Psychology and the Humanities: Reflections on a New Psychoanalytic Approach*, ed. C. B. Strozier (New York: Norton, 1985), 124–60. The quotations covered by this endnote are a composite selected from paragraphs throughout the essay.

53. Kohut, *Thoughts*, 148.

54. Steiner, *Antigones*, 97.

55. Steiner, *Antigones*, 278.

56. Steiner, *Antigones*, 282.

57. *Antigone*, 220. Fitts and Fitzgerald translate *autognotos* as "conscious," whereas Jebb translates the same word as "self-willed."

58. Sophocles, *Antigone*, 237.

59. Sophocles, *Antigone*, 237.

60. Gerald Dworkin, "The Concept of Autonomy," in *The Inner Citadel: Essays on Individual Autonomy*, ed. John Christman (New York: Oxford University Press, 1989), 59.

61. Steiner, *Antigones*, 278.

62. Steiner, *Antigones*, 278.

63. Sophocles, *Antigone*, 206.

64. Jacques Lacan, *The Ethics of Psychoanalysis*, trans. with notes by Dennis Porter (New York: Norton, 1992).

65. Slavoj Zizek, "Badiou: Notes from an Ongoing Debate," *International Journal of Zizek Studies*, <http://www.lacan.com/zizou.htm> (08/12/2008).

66. Lacan, *The Ethics*, 281.

67. Lacan, *The Ethics*, 282.

68. Lacan, *The Ethics*, 283.

69. Sophocles, *Antigone*, 203.

70. Sophocles, *Antigone*, 220.

71. Sophocles, *Antigone*, 208.

72. Sophocles, *Antigone*, 204.

73. Sophocles, *Antigone*, 203.

74. Sophocles, *Antigone*, 188.

75. Lacan, *The Ethics*, 303.

76. Lacan, *The Ethics*, 285.

77. Plato, *Apology*, in Plato, *The Works of Plato*, trans. by Benjamin Jowett, ed. with an introduction by Irwin Edman (New York: Random House, 1956), 84–88.

78. Lacan, *The Ethics*, 247.

79. Elizabeth Roudinesco, *Jacques Lacan*, trans. by Barbara Bray (New York: Columbia University Press, 1997), 158.

80. Ludwig Landgrebe, "The Problem of a Transcendental Science of the A Priori of the Life-World," in Ludwig Landgrebe, *The Phenomenology of Edmund Husserl: Six Essays by Ludwig Landgrebe,* ed. with an introduction by Donn Welton (Ithaca, NY: Cornell University Press, 1981), 288–89. This entire essay is a magnificent explication of the essential character of Husserlian phenomenology.

81. Paul Allen Miller, "Lacan's Antigone: The Sublime Object and the Ethics of Interpretation"<http://www.apaclassics.org/AnnualMeeting/05mtg/abstracts/miller.html> 13 (8/14/08).

82. Sigmund Freud, *Civilization and Its Discontents,* trans. and ed. by James Strachey (New York: Norton, 1962), 92.

Chapter Eight

Neither Victim nor Survivor Be: Who Is Beloved's Baby?

The singing women recognized Sethe at once and surprised themselves by their absence of fear when they saw what stood next to her. The devil-child was clever, they thought. And beautiful. It had taken the form of a pregnant woman, naked and smiling in the heat of the afternoon sun. Thunderblack and glistening, she stood on long straight legs, her belly big and tight. Vines of hair twisted all over her head. Jesus. Her smile was dazzling.

Toni Morrison, *Beloved*[1]

. . . .Morrison develops the recurring theme of the quest for wholeness, which we must now deem the sine qua non of her canon.

Toni Morrison, Wilfred D. Samuels and Clenora Hudson-Weems[2]

INTRODUCTION: VICTIMS AND SURVIVORS

In August of the first year of the new millennium (2000), I attended hearings sponsored by the blue ribbon commission that then Governor George Ryan established to make recommendations for reform of the judicial process to en-sure that innocent people would not be executed in Illinois (Ryan also ordered a moratorium on executions that is still in effect, in 2009). Members of many community organizations testified. All said that the legal apparatus of the death penalty cannot be reformed and that capital punishment should be abol-ished. Some individuals not representing any organization testified as well; they, too, condemned the death penalty. Given the commission's mission, it is plausible to assume that this was not the sort of testimony its members were interested in hearing. Nevertheless, at one point an African-American

woman not representing any group went to the floor microphone and testified that her son had been executed for a crime that she believes he did not
commit. Toward the end of her brief statement, in which she, too, condemned
the death penalty, she said, with great intensity and personal presence, "I am
not a victim, I'm a survivor." This poignant declaration seems to posit an exclusive disjunction between victims and survivors: survivors are not victims
and victims are not survivors. However, is this not a contestable claim? Are
not victims also survivors? Are survivors not, also, victims, albeit ones who
have survived? And what of the victims, including the woman's son, who do
not survive?

Many sites of contestation converge and diverge in this woman's words.
She represented only herself, one person, but she did so in a public forum
sponsored by a quasi-governmental body; moreover, she testified seeking
redress from the state—a political act. Yet, victimage and survivorship also
threaten to transgress the easy and uneasy dichotomizing of the personal and
the political, their apparent convergence and divergence in bourgeois juridi-
cal systems and in the recent history of attempts to realign these historically
and culturally, more, or less, dichotomous poles. Consider, for example, the
influential but by now well-worn slogan of "second wave" feminism: "the
personal is the political." This slogan is usually deployed in hope of raising
awareness that the personal is always already politicized and that institutional
sexism and misogyny take root, and are transmitted across generations, in
personal relations as well as cultural, historical, and political lifeworlds.
However, is not the political also the personal, a manifestation, that is, of the
maturational levels attained or not attained by individual persons who are
not reducible in toto to processes of socialization, even massively oppressive
socialization? Along what non-reductive trajectory can we construe, dissent
from, or assent to these dichotomies, victim and survivor, personal and political? What of the sociogenic traumas suffered by individuals and groups
that both victimize persons and potentiate the strife of the personal and the
political? In what manner does or can trauma induce facing or flying from
one's self or other designation as victim, or one's segue into survival? Can the
trauma victim surpass survival and the strife of the personal and the political
to move toward recuperation of the wholeness of the self, even in fractured
times? If so, would this not call into question the status of the victim-survivor
binary by showing it to be a false dichotomy, a defensively motivated narrow-
ing of possibilities on the part of both trauma victims and trauma theorists? In
this paper, usages of both concepts and their cognates that connote reification
or colonization by ideologically interpellated[3] senses will be explored.

The lady who said, "I am not a victim, I'm a survivor" was, it seems
reasonable to assume, traumatized by the unjust execution and loss of her

son. She was a victim of injustice. Why did she believe it necessary to deny this, that she was a victim? In the contemporary lifeworld, at least in the United States, the term 'victim' now often connotes a person who has to one degree or another imposed victim status on her or himself, and it was this connotation, I believe, that the woman sought to evade. The victim blaming connotation of the term 'victim' is a salient instance of the ideological interpellation of sense. In pointing this out, it should be clear that it is not my intention to deny that there are victims. On the contrary, I affirm the existence of victims, and, in doing so, I deploy the term victim shorn of any connotations of victim blaming by either victims themselves, others, or social institutions: victims are not to blame for their victimization. Thus, the phrase "neither victim nor survivor be" is in no way meant as a denial of the existence of victims. On the contrary, one of the aims of this chapter is to reactivate a notion of victim that is prior to the ideological interpellation of sense noted here. Additionally, what is challenged here is not only victim blaming in all of its multifarious overt or covert forms; challenged as well is the notion that 'survival' is a meaningful, positive, or desirable outcome of or response to trauma or victimization. Of course, the point is not that failure to survive, for example, dying, is a preferred alternative. The point is, rather, to challenge reified notions of 'survival' that suggest that all we can ever do is just survive—that is, that survival is the terminus ad quem of human existence. This, too, is an ideological interpellation of sense. Such a view reflects social forces, for example in capitalist societies that manipulate resources and objectify persons in order to compel acceptance of permanent threat to one's survival.

The ideological sense of 'survival' depends on an implicit and explicit claim that survival as such is in itself a value. However, survival cannot, as such, be a value, for, it is the precondition for the possibility of the actualization of any and all values. In order to actualize values of freedom, justice, love, and so on, one must survive and so, too, must society survive. Thus, survival is of value only insofar as it actually or potentially grounds the possibility for the actualization of some or all other values. This does not mean, however, that values are relative to survival. On the contrary, what it does mean is that defending certain values may necessitate that one must endure not surviving, that is, that defending certain values in circumstances where no better options are available ethically supersedes survival. Antigone's defense of reverence, love, and justice for example, is a case in point. Thus, to believe that survival is the terminus ad quem, the only goal for human existence, is to believe that it is ethically sound to sacrifice any or all other values in the interest of survival: truth, justice, love, and so on. It is just this ideologically motivated doctrine that is challenged in this paper, and in this book.

We who are alive today are all survivors; yet, victimization of people and peoples, including ourselves, has accelerated everywhere, including in societies like the United States today where hyper-alienation and survivalist propaganda rob us of the joy of meaningful life and work. I maintain, moreover, that the segue from victim into survivor, taken as denial of victimization and as best outcome, rather than into acknowledgment of having been victimized that may potentiate demand for an end to victimization, is a function of forces of oppression and that it must be exposed as such. I argue that survival in its ideologically colonized sense, as terminus ad quem, is not, as the woman implied, incompatible with victim status in its ideological form as victim blaming; on the contrary, as we shall see below, it depends on it, and, for this reason, cannot point toward, or empower us to seek, transcendence, that is, a radical transformation of ourselves and of society.

We will return in the end of this essay to approach once again the woman's words, and the possibility or impossibility of survival as a renunciation or denunciation of victimization, or as a life enhancing goal. Most important, in following a trajectory that will engage the questions just posed, we will not fail at every moment to connect empathetically with the anguish and suffering of the person, and persons, before whom we stand to both witness an unholy injustice, the state sponsored murder of the innocent and the guilty, and seek a point of departure for our efforts to both reveal and reconstitute the personhood of the person; the person, that is, *before* victimization and *beyond* survival.

In this study, we will rely on two texts, the one an interpretation of the other. First, we have one of the novels of a woman whose awesome, incandescent genius illuminates the night sky like the wonder wheel of rotating, coruscated, many-colored lights at the end of the fireworks display. Beloved *Beloved*, Toni Morrison's visionary tale, will be our point of departure. The second of the texts that will assist me in generating a phenomenological *gedank-experiment* regarding the before and after of the victim-survivor binary is Naomi Morgenstern's finely wrought and challenging appreciation and critique of *Beloved*, titled "Mother's Milk and Sister's Blood: Trauma and the Neoslave Narrative."[4] Through the study of these texts, as well as others, we will discover who Beloved's baby, fathered by Paul D, is, the baby with whom Beloved is pregnant when she disappears near the end of the novel of which she is the eponym. Most importantly, *Beloved* enables us to experience and to understand non-ideologically colonized senses of victimization and survival, and to do so in the context of Morrison's profound exploration of the interplay of the personal and the political. The intention of this paper is to suggest that the meaning of *Beloved* as microcosm is by extension applicable to the macrocosm, humanity as a whole and each individual member of it as an individual.

TRAUMA AND THE NEOSLAVE NARRATIVE

Naomi Morgenstern, a professor of literature, is explicit regarding the goal of her essay, which is "to explore the connections and disjunctions between trauma and the neoslave narrative, the twentieth-century novel about slavery."[5] *Beloved* is, of course, just such a neoslave narrative. In order to discern the nature and consequences of the traumas experienced by Beloved and her mother, Sethe, Morgenstern emphasizes a distinction between trauma and repression. The tendency of the traumatized subject to relive the traumatic events, (as the people of *Beloved* incessantly do), is quite different from the effects of repression. "Repression," Morgenstern explains, "is a response to conflict: that which has been repressed returns . . . in a . . . distorted form." In contradistinction, she writes, "The traumatized past . . . has not been forgotten. . . . It is strangely concrete, forcefully present, literally there, not past at all."[6] The trauma victim does not experience the return of the repressed because there has been no repression. Thus, with respect to trauma, there is no past that might return, distorted or not. This, Morgenstern contends, is also the way in which trauma is present in neoslave narratives: "As fictional testimonial literature, neoslave narratives both stage a simple return of history and reinscribe it . . . they both return to an event and make it happen for the first time. . . ."[7] Most important, this characterization of the effects of trauma partially justifies (along with clinical evidence) Morgenstern's inference that traumatic experiences cannot be represented. They are not representable in that, due to the nature and severity of the trauma, rather than being repressed or forgotten and thus relegated to the past, they are chronically lived and relived by victims. Because victims experience their traumas in their present, no one, not even the victims themselves, can represent those experiences, for the victims "cannot simply remember what they never forgot."[8] For Morgenstern, then, trauma is "unrepresentable,"[9] and the notion of the unrepresentability of trauma is an important element of Morgenstern's critique of Morrison, which will be discussed below.

Thus far, as Morgenstern points out, we have been traversing the terrain of more or less orthodox trauma theory from Freud's repetition compulsion (*Beyond the Pleasure Principle*) to the invention of the diagnosis of post-traumatic stress disorder, or PTSD. Moving on to more recent work on trauma, Morgenstern refers to the work of noted trauma theorist Cathy Caruth, who wrote that, ". . . trauma is a repeated suffering of the event, but it is also a continual leaving of its site . . . trauma is not simply an effect of destruction [as orthodoxy would have it] but also, fundamentally, an enigma of survival."[10] Thus, Caruth's notion of traumatic reliving is that of reliving not merely the horrific events, even if one ascribes to this reliving, as did Freud and others, a motive of struggle for mastery of the traumatic experience; rather, for Caruth, there is also a reliving of the subject's *survival* of the horrific events.

While, on one hand, Caruth and Morgenstern imply that their view that trauma victims relive not only trauma but survival as well is more realistic and more constructive than prior views, on the other hand it seems that on their account the trauma victim relives two moments that are ineluctably linked. If trauma victims must continually relive their traumas in order to relive their survival of those traumas, in what way does this assist them to move beyond the crippling psychic effects of the trauma? Morgenstern concurs with Caruth's reading of trauma; however, as we shall see, inspired by *Beloved,* Morgenstern moves beyond Caruth to a terrain that invokes, in my reading of the novel, *though not in Morgenstern's,* the primordial before of traumatic victimization, and, taking the primordial before traumatization as my *point de départ,* I will attempt to point to its connection to the possibilities beyond survival, indeed beyond the trauma (victim)-survivor binary, that are creatively engendered by Morrison in *Beloved.* Morgenstern, as we shall see, casts a cold eye on these possibilities.

Morgenstern writes that, "the narrative begins when Paul D, another ex-slave from Sweet Home, arrives at Sethe's address. . . . If Paul D walks out of the past, he nevertheless represents the possibility of a future of a story that can go on. . . ."[11] Thus, Morgenstern points out, Paul D represents, at least ostensibly, a position beyond survival, for, mere survival is not "a story that can go on," not a future in, shall we say, the pregnant sense, inasmuch as in this paper we are involved in a project of not throwing out the baby (Beloved's baby) with the bathwater.[12]

Morgenstern is, however, skeptical regarding the possibility of a meaningful future for Sethe and Paul D, a future beyond survival. Regarding the end of the story of Sethe and Paul D near the end of the novel, an ending which begins with Sethe's second reunion with Paul D which occurs after the disappearance of pregnant Beloved, Morgenstern comments that, "Indeed it is only in moments of willful optimism (the sentimental ending with Sethe and Paul D is, after all, 'much happier than what really happened' [a reference by Morrison to the real story of Margaret Garner on which the novel is based]) that the precariousness of testimony itself seems to disappear."[13] Morgenstern holds, quite plausibly, and with an implicit critique of psychoanalysis, that witnessing the testimony of trauma victims can have a curative effect on the traumatized. For Morgenstern, witnessing is the function of the neoslave genre as such. Her critical point here is that the alleged "sentimental ending" of *Beloved* subverts the novel's proper testimonial function as a neoslave narrative that presents testimony and at the same time bears witness to it. Morgenstern's critique of the ending of *Beloved* will be critically addressed in the concluding section of this paper.

CONFLATING MATERNAL AND
HISTORICAL TRAUMA IN *BELOVED*

Morgenstern's primary interest is not directly focused on the problematic of the novel's ending; rather, she is interested in discerning who the true traumatized subject of *Beloved* is, and her views on this are determinative, as we shall see, of her interpretation of the ending. Morgenstern writes: "Since it is Beloved who returns to represent a traumatic resistance to narrative, the temptation is to locate the novel's traumatic center at the site of the infanticide, of Sethe's murder of Beloved to save her from slavery. Yet it is not this scene, or at least not the actual killing, that returns to haunt Sethe."[14] Morgenstern maintains that though the infanticide was traumatic for both Beloved and Sethe, Sethe's most significant trauma was, rather, her abandonment by her own mother when she was a young child: "The unspeakable secret in *Beloved*, what Sethe can never say, is that her own mother deserted her."[15] Sethe does not know why her mother, who was lynched after being caught running away, possibly while attempting to escape, left her. Sethe is shocked when, still a very young child, she was told by another, older, slave child that her mother was caught running away without her and wondered why her mother did not take her with her or why her mother didn't just stay with her, as mothers do. (We also learn that Sethe barely knew her mother, who rarely even slept in the same place as Sethe. Indeed, Sethe's mother had to be pointed out to her. Thus, Sethe's trauma, rather than maternal abandonment, may have been never having had a mother.) Regarding the traumatic effect of the infanticide on Beloved, Morgenstern argues that it was not that her mother killed her, for Beloved never reproaches Sethe for this act.[16] Rather, for Morgenstern, the trauma for Beloved was that in killing her in her infancy (Beloved was less than two years old when killed), Sethe abandoned her as Sethe herself had been abandoned by her own mother.

Morgenstern then enunciates her central theme: "If the infanticide is not *the* trauma, neither is Sethe *the* traumatized subject. *Beloved* is about a traumatized, gothicized culture. If there is an original trauma in *Beloved*, it is the trauma of Middle Passage which establishes a pattern of separation and desertion. *Beloved* is about its conflation of maternal and historical thematics . . ."[17](Morgenstern's emphases). In her usage of the term 'conflation' here, it does not have pejorative connotations as it does in some usages in which it connotes confusion rather than fusion. For Morgenstern then, the Middle Passage was the *"original"* trauma. With respect to Morgenstern's use of the term "original" in this context, I do not believe that she is open either to the charge that she commits the genetic fallacy, that is, that of claiming that origin is cause, or the fallacy of *post hoc ergo propter hoc*. It seems that

Morgenstern does believe, and correctly so, that the traumas suffered by the people of the Middle Passage did indeed result in the development of a pattern of deficient parenting in the form of maternal abandonment: mothers who were abandoned tend to be mothers who abandon their children one way or another, physically or emotionally or both, and in slavery, of course, mothers were sold away from their children and vice versa, and children understandably experience such events as abandonment. Morgenstern goes on to say that Sethe's abandonment by her own mother together with Beloved's abandonment by Sethe is a metaphor for the true traumatized subject: the many millions of victims of the Middle Passage and the ensuing "traumatized, gothicized" culture. This is just what Morgenstern means when she writes that the novel is "about its conflation of maternal and historical. . . ." For Morgenstern, this is the greatest strength of the novel. However, though this conflation or fusion of the maternal and the historical is a feature of the novel, in referring to Middle Passage as the "original" trauma, Morgenstern, I contend, marginalizes the traumas suffered by the people of *Beloved* as individuals.

Consequently, I will attempt to show in this paper that the novel is centrally not just about its conflation of the maternal and the historical (I take Morgenstern to mean that the novel is about its theory that the traumatic impact of slavery itself was due to the institutionalized dehumanization that produced a history of maternal abandonment). Rather, *Beloved* is also, with equal significance, about the struggle of individuals to transcend the victim-survivor binary, where "survive" means just that and nothing more, not surviving *and* living well, living a fulfilling, human life. It is just this dimension of the novel that Morgenstern misses. Owing to this lacuna, Morgenstern's view regarding the conflation of the maternal and historical bears within it no resistance to devolution into historical reductionism and determinism, even if these stances are not consistent with her views.

CRITIQUE OF MORGENSTERN: PERSONAL AGENCY IN *BELOVED*

In arriving at her interpretation of *Beloved* as a site of conflation of maternal and historical, we arrive at both Morgenstern's critical appreciation of the novel and our own critique of her interpretation. Initially, let us raise this question: in showing that maternal and historical, personal and political, (Morgenstern does not make this analogy directly in just these terms, but I believe it to be in keeping with her views), are conflated in *Beloved*, why does Morgenstern find it necessary to aver that Sethe is *not THE* traumatized subject, whereas she previously referred to Sethe's experience of abandonment by her mother as an unspeakable, that is, traumatic secret? The answer lies in the manner in which Morgenstern deploys and interprets Sethe's abandonment by her mother. As we have seen, for Morgenstern the personal trauma that Sethe experienced, abandonment by her mother, was not only symptomatic of the entire institution and history of slavery; in addition, Sethe's abandonment is a metaphor, a literary trope, that itself stands for the entire Middle Passage and post-Middle Passage, traumatized culture. For Morgenstern, it seems, Sethe's personal trauma (or traumas, depicted in the novel with extraordinary intensity in their effects on her), is subordinated to the trauma of Middle Passage that it both enacts and symbolizes, or metaphorically represents.

Of course, Morgenstern does not deny that Sethe was *a* traumatized subject. Indeed, Morgenstern parses "maternal" as "the trauma of subject formation" and "historical" as "the trauma of slavery."[18] Thus, Morgenstern does see that Sethe, Paul D and others in the novel experience personal traumas and crises of subject formation, and this dimension of the novel is referred to several times in her essay; but, it is never thematized as such. Morgenstern's main point is that *THE* traumatized subject, by which I take her to refer to the subject proper of the novel, is the history of the slaves as a traumatized people from the Middle Passage on, a traumatic history which engendered the transmission of maternal abandonment, including, of course, Sethe's abandonment of Beloved (by killing her). Thus, Morgenstern, having claimed that "*Beloved* is about its conflation of maternal and historical," infers from this that *Beloved's* central subject is, not, for example, Beloved or Sethe (who is the protagonist of the novel), but is rather the entire culture, the traumatized, gothicized culture.

Morgenstern is certainly correct in pointing out that Beloved herself, in her inchoate way, describes her experiences prior to her appearance at 124 Bluestone Street in utterances highly suggestive of the horrific conditions of the Middle Passage, and she is certainly correct to maintain that Beloved is a representation of all the "Sixty Million or more" murdered human beings of the Middle Passage to whom Morrison dedicates the novel. Equally significant is the fact that *Beloved* was an attempt by Morrison, and a successful attempt indeed, to convey, from the slaves' point of view, from the perspective of their inner lives, these experiences, and thus to convey them in a manner not previously achieved in slave narratives. Morrison stated that she intended Beloved to function on two levels—as Sethe's murdered daughter, and as a child who came over on a slave ship.[19] As the latter, however, Beloved cannot be Sethe's murdered daughter because Beloved was born at Sweet Home, the slave plantation. What is contestable in Morgenstern's interpretation is, however, her apparent view that the novel *privileges* the trauma of the Middle

Passage and its consequences, an historical-political event with historical-political consequences, as *the* trauma of the novel, over the trauma *for* Sethe, the personal trauma for Sethe the person, indeed, of Sethe's entire life, including both her abandonment by her mother and her murder of her daughter to save her from slavery. I do not at all wish to suggest that Morgenstern is not empathetic regarding Sethe's inner life as an individual human being, depicting which, as Morgenstern does point out, was one of Morrison's primary motives in writing the novel. I am suggesting, though, that in her interpretation of *Beloved*, Morgenstern conveys the sense that Morrison's novel privileges the collective trauma so that Sethe's tragedy is secondary, or is exhausted by its metaphorical function. *I say this because Sethe's agency as an individual person is not addressed by Morgenstern.* It is just this underestimation of the significance of Sethe's (and others') agency, their being as individuals and their agentic struggle for wholeness, that is a manifestation of Morgenstern's one-sided view of the novel.

Morgenstern deploys Sethe's trauma of abandonment by her mother as Sethe's original and most devastating trauma, a trauma that can be laid at the door of slavery and the Middle Passage. However, this was an event that occurred *without any willed action at all on the part of Sethe*: she was indeed a helpless victim, a very young girl born into a slave society. However, it seems that Morgenstern's emphasis on the historical aspects of the conflation of the maternal and the historical in *Beloved* induced her to under-appreciate and thus fail to integrate into her understanding of the novel Sethe's agency as an individual human being. Thus Sethe's murder of her daughter is divested of significance, as if that act were passive, equivalent with Sethe's own victimization as a helpless child. In an interview with Toni Morrison, after suggesting a comparison between events in Morrison's novel *Jazz* and Sethe's act of infanticide, Salmon Rushdie asked Morrison "So what's that about?" Morrison responded,

> How to own your own body and love somebody else. Under historical duress, where one fights for agency, the problem is how to be an individual, how to exert individual agency under this huge umbrella of determined historical life. In the case of Sethe, the story was based on the real story of a slave woman who did indeed kill her children rather than have them go back to slavery. Her claim is grotesque, but it comes out of a determination to nurture and be a parent. So the beloved for her was the best thing she was, which were her children.[20]

Clearly, then, Morrison indicates that an important dimension of the novel is the individual's struggle for agency, to exert individual agency even in the face of a "huge umbrella of determined historical life." In slavery, of course, Sethe's options as to means of asserting her agency were few indeed, yet she struggled to do so nonetheless. While it is true that Sethe's murder of Beloved can, and should, also be laid at the door of slavery in the sense that saving her daughter from slavery motivated it, killing Beloved was an action consciously willed by Sethe, as it was for her prototype, Margaret Garner, as an action for their children and against slavery, whether effectively so or not. Therefore, that act should not be elided, nor should its cost to Sethe be elided. It is likely that had Sethe been taken back into slavery, she would have suffered the same fate as Margaret Garner—since neither the murdered child nor his mother was considered to be a human being, Garner suffered no legally imposed penalty additional to being returned to slavery. Sethe, on the other hand, who was not taken back into slavery, and as a free person living in free Ohio, was given a prison sentence. (She was saved from the gallows by the intervention of a white abolitionist, Mr. Bodwin.) This dimension of Sethe's infanticide is neither discussed nor alluded to by Morgenstern.

In the historical context of Middle Passage, slaves, owing to the circumstances of their capture, were victims. Yet they found ways to assert agency. In Morrison's depiction of the Middle Passage, based on extensive research, Sethe's grandmother, Sethe's mother's mother, acted agentically when she committed suicide by jumping off the slave ship, and there are other examples given of agentic action on the slave ship, and in slavery, for example both Sethe's and Paul D's much-more-than-arduous escapes. In the case of Sethe's murder of Beloved, Sethe was active—she acted intentionally in a situation based on her beliefs and values. For Sethe, as for her prototype Margaret Garner, slavery was worse than death—and she, deeply invested in her role as mother, a role Sethe agentically claimed though it was denied by slavery, refused to allow her children to suffer a fate she clearly believed was worse than death. Sethe acted in accordance with what she viewed, correctly or not, as in the best interest of her children, and thus of herself. This actionality in its existential depth and searing revelation of the intolerable suffering of persons who always already are subjects beyond and before all objectification, all dehumanizing forces, consistently with what I take to be Morrison's creative vision, should not be subsumed in a conflation of the maternal and the historical, and was not, I aver, so subsumed in Morrison's novel. That is, subsumption of the personal in the political, or in the present instance, of the crisis of subjectivity for individuals in the historical crisis of a culture, is not a necessary consequence of the conflation of the maternal and the historical in *Beloved*. If Morgenstern is right that the novel is about its own conflation of the maternal in the historical, and I believe she is right, it is necessary to add that the novel is also, with equal gravitas, about the capacity of individuals to transcend both their psychic and physical traumas, their own crises of subjectivity, however imbricated they are with oppressive forces of history. Unless this is acknowledged, we are in danger of falling into historical reductionism or determinism, or at least we pose no plausible countervailing factor.

But, Morrison's tale is no sentimental tale of "triumph over adversity," as if to say, "no adversity, no triumph." On the contrary, in its depiction of the inwardness of human beings and their insistent need to strive for wholeness and inner connectedness with others and with a community, a need, that is, to claim subjecthood for themselves, the novel makes all the more glaring, all the more morally compelling, all the more a claim on our own humanity, the need to eliminate from human existence all forces and forms of dehumanization.

MORGENSTERN'S CRITIQUE OF MORRISON AND *BELOVED*

Morgenstern sees what she takes to be Morrison's conflation of maternal and historical in *Beloved* as the greatest strength of the novel. However, she also expresses what I take to be a severe critique of it which, if correct, would be devastating. She emphasizes that *Beloved* as a neoslave narrative belongs also in the genre of testimonial, which does not at all mean representing the unrepresentatable, the trauma as lived by the victims. Morrison has stated, as Morgenstern points out, that *Beloved* seeks to represent that which has been *underrepresented*, and what has been underrepresented is the trauma of slavery as presented in slave narratives. Morrison maintains that the authors of such narratives underrepresented the trauma of slavery because readers would not be able to deal with its horrible reality. Morrison wrote that, ". . . most important for me—there was [in slave narratives] no mention of their interior life. . . . My job becomes how to rip that veil drawn over 'proceedings too terrible to relate.' The exercise is also critical for any person who is black, or who belongs to any marginalized category, for . . . we were seldom invited to participate in the discourse even when we were its topic." [21] What Morgenstern objects to is an aspect of *Beloved* in which, Morgenstern contends, what is conflated is "the concept of the unrepresentable and the *under*represented. . . ." She insists "that there is a difference between what has not yet been said and what is constitutively excluded from the possibility of saying." [22] Following Caruth and other trauma theorists, as we saw above, Morgenstern holds that trauma is not repressed; rather, it is chronically relived and thus unrepresentable, in that the one experiencing the trauma experiences it as present and thus has no temporal distance from it that would allow for representation because the trauma experience has no temporal location. She explicitly voices her critique of *Beloved* when she says that, "This is the enabling fantasy of Morrison's text: the unrepresentable can be approached as if it were only a problem of not yet being represented. In this depiction, the forceful and literal return of the past is domesticated and used."[23] Thus, the novel has what we might call a fatal flaw—it fails to acknowledge the unrepresentability of the trauma of slavery, of the Middle Passage, and in so doing, betrays it, i.e., domesticates and uses it.[24]

According to Morgenstern, then, the novel itself is just one more manifestation of the symptomatology of PTSD. Indeed, in the last sentence of her paper, she says that, "While *Beloved* . . . repeats the story of slavery, then, it also asserts that it is only through an account of traumatic repetition that the story of slavery ever gets told."[25] I take this to mean that since *Beloved* does not, because it cannot, represent the unrepresentable, it is just one more neoslave novel, one more traumatic repetition that functions, or should function, as testimonial (although, as we have seen, Morgenstern believes that the "sentimental" ending of the novel undermines its testimonial function). Morgenstern implies that Morrison believed that in exposing or representing the inner lives of slaves in a way that slaves themselves did not do, that the entire traumatic experience is laid bare and that nothing of it is deemed to be unrepresentable. Morgenstern however maintains that Morrison conflates (here in the pejorative sense of confuses rather than fuses) the (concept of the) unrepresentable with the (concept of the) underrepresented. However, it seems that Morgenstern herself conflates Morrison's goal of correcting the slave narrative's underrepresentation of trauma with an alleged claim by Morrison that there is nothing about traumatic experience that is unrepresentable. Yet, there is no indication that Morrison makes such a claim. Moreover, Morgenstern seems to think that any effort to represent traumatic suffering and its consequences beyond just repetition of trauma-survival, e.g., Morrison's "willfully optimistic" ending, is betrayal, if not of the victims themselves, at the very least betrayal or subversion of the capacity of literature to testify, to witness to their fate.

For Morgenstern, the unrepresentable is twofold: first, it is the trauma itself, which can never be represented, but only survived. Here we might add that this formulation seems to imply: no trauma, no survival (in the sense noted above: just survival, not living a human life); and the corollary: trauma and survival, nothing else. For Morgenstern, "*Beloved* is both the text that has been excluded from the canon . . . and the story of its own impossibility: how can there be a story of trauma?" There cannot be a story of trauma because trauma is not what has not yet been said; rather, it is what is "constitutively excluded from the possibility of saying."[26]

Her view that *Beloved, pace* Morrison, shows the problem to be not the underrepresentation but rather the unrepresentability of trauma is reinforced for Morgenstern by the fact that the return of Beloved is precisely not the return of something that had been repressed, but is rather the return of an infant,

Morgenstern emphasizes, who is on the preverbal, preoedipal stage of development, as Beloved patently is. Thus, Beloved's impossibility of representing linguistically her own trauma of abandonment is conflated by Morgenstern (assuming that this is what happens in the novel itself) with the impossibility of representing the trauma of the Middle Passage. Morgenstern expresses this as follows, including also Morrison's own contrasting view:

> . . . in the case of *Beloved*, trying to separate out an account of trauma from an account of the mother child dyad proves difficult . . . [because] *Beloved* is about its conflation of maternal and historical themes. . . . The infant's experience is the trauma of Middle Passage and vice versa. Beloved does not haunt Sethe because Sethe killed her—the infanticide is not traumatic in this sense—but because she left her, deserted her repeatedly: the infanticide is one more desertion. . . . While it sounds too simple to say that *Beloved* is guided by a regressive dynamic, it does seem fair to say that it is a novel about a crisis of subjectivity, a crisis inseparable from the traumatic legacy of slave culture . . . the novel's dramatization of pre-Oedipal dynamics provides the metaphorical vehicle for its depiction of the experience of slavery. Morrison herself would seem to reverse the emphasis. She claims the slavery presented an "ideal situation" for discussing the intricacies of the mother-child relationship. Neither assertion wholly accounts for the novel's pattern of figuration.[27]

The first point to be noted is one that we have already seen: Morgenstern assumes, correctly, as Morrison has attested, that Beloved is Sethe's murdered child. Morgenstern is correct that Beloved does not reproach Sethe for killing her, thus leading Morgenstern to conclude that not the killing but maternal abandonment was Beloved's (and Sethe's) greatest trauma, and she contends further, it was the Middle Passage that resulted in the history of separation and abandonment. Thus, the culture of the surviving victims of the Middle Passage is the true traumatized "subject" in the novel. However, though she maintains that the novel is about a "crisis of subjectivity that is inseparable from the traumatic legacy of slave culture," Morgenstern does not at all address the crisis or crises of subjectivity of the people of the novel, as if inseparability means that the legacy of slave culture is the only, or the most significant determining factor that brings about the crises of subjectivity. Morrison's contrary point implies that certain dimensions of crises of subjectivity correlate with the "intricacies of the mother-child relationship," intricacies that are, it is safe to say, a universal dimension of human psychosocial development. Thus, Morgenstern comes perilously close to reduplicating the ideologically interpellated senses of both victim and survivor. The former, the victim blaming sense of victimization, is not ruled out, not because of any assertion by Morgenstern, but rather by exclusion of the agency and irreducibility of individual subjects that Morrison sought to represent in the context of the horrific oppression of subjects in slavery. The latter, the ideological sense of surviving as terminus ad quem is reduplicated by Morgenstern when she maintains that in the end of the novel, excluding the "willfully optimistic" aspect, Sethe and Paul D are broken and defeated, just survivors of trauma.

REBUTTAL OF MORGENSTERN'S CRITIQUE OF *BELOVED*

A preliminary critique can take the following form: on one hand, that Beloved does not reproach Sethe for the infanticide suggests the possibility that Beloved is not, or rather, is not only the daughter whom Sethe killed. On the other hand, even assuming that Beloved is only Sethe's murdered daughter, why would Beloved reproach Sethe for killing her? One of the signal characteristics of Morrison's novel is that nowhere in it is judgment passed on Sethe for killing her child, with the exception of Paul D who nevertheless, as a consequence of working through his own personal crisis of subjectivity, later revisits and revises his judgment. Moreover, it is well known that abandonment can be experienced as death, or even as a fate worse than death, and likewise death as abandonment, either of or by the deceased. That Beloved experienced Sethe's murder of her as abandonment does not rule out that Sethe did not wish to abandon her daughter—only to kill her in order to spare her the horrors of slavery, which in all likelihood would have included forced abandonment. Moreover, as noted above, Sethe attempts to explain to Beloved that she killed her not to abandon her, but to spare her worse suffering. Most important, however, had Beloved, whether she is, or is only, Sethe's daughter or not, reproached Sethe for murdering her, this would introduce an element of judgment that would be discordant with the finely tuned non-moralistic, non-judgmental tenor of the novel as a whole. It would suggest that Beloved thinks that Sethe made the wrong decision, and since Beloved never reproaches Sethe for killing her, we do not know whether or not Beloved thought it was the wrong decision. When asked whether or not she, Morrison, or the novel "takes a moral position on the infanticide," Morrison responded,

> The novel admits that it cannot negotiate the morality of that act, that there's no one qualified who can, except the dead child. That is why her presence, or the belief in her presence, is so important. She alone can ask that question with any hope of a meaningful answer. I personally don't know. I can't think of anything worse than to kill one's children. On the other hand, I can't think of anything worse than to turn them over to a living death. It was that question that destroyed Baby Suggs.[28]

Thus, we can see that Beloved herself, the only one entitled to judge, does not take a stand on the morality of Sethe's killing of her, and thus does not reproach her for specifically that action, though Beloved does indeed reproach her mother for abandoning her. Since Beloved was less than two years old when killed, she could not possibly grasp that her mother's intent was not to abandon her but, as an act of love, spare her a fate worse than death. This constitutive gap between the meanings bestowed on parental actions by infants and young children, and the parents' actual motives as well as the extended internal and external circumstances that obtained at the time, is a crucial dimension of human psychosocial development that is deeply imbricated in the relationship between Beloved and Sethe. There is no doubt that Morgenstern is correct to point out both that a severe trauma to both Beloved, whomever she is, and Sethe is that of maternal abandonment, and that this is a metaphor for the history of the Middle Passage and its devastating consequences in slavery. However, what Morgenstern overlooks is that in the novel not only is no negative judgment passed on Sethe by anyone important to her, not even by herself, but, in addition, through reliving her own traumas with great intensity and great courage in and through her relationship with Beloved, Sethe begins to reclaim herself as subject thus enabling herself, as we shall see, to have a meaningful future.

Who Is *Beloved*?

The straightforward view that Beloved is only Sethe's murdered daughter (the view of most readers of *Beloved*) has been strongly contested. Though Morgenstern assumes throughout that Beloved is just Sethe's daughter, she does entertain the notion that Beloved might have multiple identities. In contradistinction to the view that Beloved is only Sethe's murdered daughter, Jennifer L. Holden-Kirwan, in her powerful and persuasive essay, "Looking into the Self that Is No Self: An Examination of Subjectivity in *Beloved*,"[29] presents an impressive abundance of textual evidence to show that Beloved is not at all Sethe's murdered daughter but is, rather, Sethe's mother.

As Sethe's mother, Beloved has many memories of "life" on board the slave ship. Sethe's mother was indeed abandoned by her own mother, Sethe's grandmother, when the latter committed suicide by jumping off the slave ship. This accords well with Morgenstern's claim that the Middle Passage inaugurated a history of maternal separation and abandonment. However, Holden-Kirwan shows that this does not get us to the core of the novel or even to the core meaning of the conflation of maternal and historical in *Beloved* that Morgenstern has emphasized, or of the crises of subjectivity that Morgenstern acknowledges.

Holden-Kirwan's interpretive analysis focuses on the consequences for individuals of maternal abandonment. Thus, while nothing in Holden-Kirwan's views argues for rejecting the conflation of maternal and historical, her essay emphasizes that the theme of *Beloved* is rather the impact of intergenerational maternal deprivation on individuals, in particular the way in which such deprivation severely compromises the ability of individuals to develop subjectivity, or, put another way, to experience themselves in the subject position: as subjects, or selves, not objects. Holden-Kirwan shows that the novel is about the dehumanizing consequences of slavery for individual human beings.

Holden-Kirwan writes that, "Since the child that Sethe murders is born in America and never travels the Middle Passage, the proposal that Beloved is solely the reincarnated baby seems highly unlikely, if not impossible."[30] This is followed by a complex analysis of Beloved based on Freudian and Lacanian psychoanalytic notions, in particular regarding the meaning for individuals of their "primal scene." Holden-Kirwan summarizes these findings by quoting from an article by Barbara Shapiro: "If from the earliest years on, one's fundamental need to be recognized and affirmed as a human subject is denied, that need can take on fantastic and destructive proportions in the inner world: the intense hunger, the fantasized fear of either being swallowed or exploding, can tyrannize one's life even when one is freed from the external bonds of oppression. (|*Beloved*| 209)"[31] Needless to say, Shapiro's explanation of the consequences of maternal abandonment is not confined to what happened in Middle Passage and slavery. Holden-Kirwan further maintains that, "For Sethe, Beloved's disappearance [at the end of the novel] means the dissolution of her own subjectivity."[32] While Holden-Kirwan does not elaborate directly on this statement, she apparently means to say that what undergoes dissolution is not Sethe's subjectivity as such; rather, what undergoes dissolution is slavery's entrapment, fixation, and objectification of Sethe's inherent subjectivity. Sethe's slavery-induced confinement of her subjectivity in the fantastic imago of motherhood is what is dissolved, as Holden-Kirwan indicates in the following remark: "Only Paul D can begin to convince her *that she has access to subjectivity outside of the maternal* [my emphasis], as he insists, 'You [not your dead daughter, not your children] your best thing, Sethe. You are.' Sethe's closing response, 'Me? Me?' seems to imply that she may in time come to recognize and claim her own subjectivity."[33]

The point here is not to claim that Holden-Kirwan's view that Beloved is Sethe's mother is definitive; not at all—Beloved's identity remains a highly contested issue in Morrison criticism, though Morrison herself said that Beloved functions as Sethe's murdered daughter. Nevertheless, there is considerable sentiment in the literature that Beloved's identity cannot, and ought not, to be viewed as singular, and this is not incompatible with Morrison's own statements. The point is, however, that in Holden-Kirwan's highly plausible account the emphasis is on the traumatic suffering of individual human beings *as individuals* and on a means of comprehending the nature of that suffering. From this point of view, the emphasis is not so much on attempting to represent the intensity of the victims' suffering: no one can live another's suffering with the immediacy of the victim's experiencing of it. Moreover, the victim's constant reliving of the traumatic events, the fact, that is, that these events are not consigned to memory but are relived as if in the present, which is an aspect of why Morgenstern and others deem them to be unrepresentable, is consistent with the fact that no one can ever live events the way the one experiencing them does. This is not to deny the unique intensity and severely debilitating consequences of that suffering in cases of severe trauma, but it is to deny that there is a qualitative difference from suffering as such, for, all suffering is traumatic, to greater or lesser degrees. In this sense, no one's experience is representable. As Morrison points out, the slave narratives did underrepresent the inner lives of the slaves, perhaps because the authors themselves were still traumatized, and, they were still living in the deeply racist, post-bellum society. Morrison points out in the essay cited above that as a contemporary African-American, female novelist her task is to present those experiences and their consequences *from the slaves' point of view*, something that she believed had not been achieved in the slave literature on slavery. In the light of this focus on the slaves' inner lives, what Holden-Kirwan shows is that the novel enables us to consider the consequences for the victims and to see that they can be comprehended in terms of psychic, developmental factors as these were imbricated with oppression. That the novel enables us to do this enhances both our ability to empathize with the victims as individuals and thereby enhance our motivation to seek redress for all victims of dehumanization, where dehumanization means what Holden-Kirwan refers to, and illustrates extensively, as the conditions that generate failure to attain subject status.

Most important, however, the point for Morrison was not just to reveal the intensity of the suffering of the slaves; the point was to reveal that indeed they were human beings and as such *had, as all oppressed people do have, inner lives, i.e., that they are human subjects.* In his characterization of the dehumanization suffered by black people, Frantz Fanon emphasized that the dehumanizing practices of racists and colonizers reflect that they did not experience their victims as human beings precisely in the sense that they did not experience them as having inner lives at all. In Fanon's words,

> Ontology—once it is finally admitted as leaving existence by the wayside—does not permit us to understand the being of the black man. For not only must the black man be black; he must be black in relation to the white man. Some critics will take it on themselves to remind us that this proposition has a converse. I say that this is false. The black man has no ontological resistance in the eyes of the white man.[34]

That is to say, in the eyes of the white man the black man has no inside, no inner life, no subjective being: he is his black skin which is present only as an absence, visible only in its invisibility.

Thus, the difficult path to the attainment of subject status, personal autonomy in community, can be derailed not only by historical-political conditions of oppression but also by the intrinsic complexities of mother-child relations. We see, then, that behaviors that may appear to a colonized consciousness to be self-destructive acts or acts of self-victimization, for example, the slaves' and abolitionists' relative inability (despite numerous efforts by individuals, numerous escapes, and numerous slave rebellions) to end slavery, was not due to self-destructive acts of either commission or omission; rather, as Fanon describes and explains regarding colonized peoples, failure was in part due to efforts to cope with the inner fragmentation brought about by destruction of, or failure to attain, subject status under conditions of servitude. Sethe's struggle to cope with her inner fragmentation and become inwardly more coherent is enacted in her monumental struggles with Beloved in the house on 124 Bluestone Road. In other words and most important, as we experience these struggles either as observers of Sethe or in the context of our own life experiences, we begin to gain a deeper insight into the fact that the victims are neither wholly determined by external forces nor to blame for their own suffering and that victims always struggle one way or another for coherence and realized subject status. This sense of the meaning of the whole of *Beloved,* and of its existential gravitas, is in accordance with Morrison's stated desire to depict the slaves as subjects rather than as the objects they were constituted to be by slavery. Only an object is wholly determined from without, and, objects cannot be enslaved, only human beings can be enslaved. The point is that in depicting victims as wholly determined from without, we have to explain why some who endured the same conditions fared so much better than others.

Morgenstern points out quite astutely that,

> Trauma theory (at its best) refuses the "choice" between self division and external force and asks us to consider the psychopathology of the historical subject....The difficulty that trauma theory then encounters is that of articulating the specificity of violence against the psyche. This is a difficulty that can be bypassed ("trauma" or "psychoanalysis" can be posited as the answer), but it is not a difficulty that will go away . . . [35]

However, having rejected, much to her credit, a simplistic inside-outside formulation as well as the "solutions" offered by trauma theory (outside) and psychoanalysis (inside), Morgenstern then avers that the most promising approach is through "the psychopathology of the historical subject," which approach, apparently, she understands to transcend the self-division vs. external force dichotomy. However, in her essay, by emphasizing as she does the conflation of maternal and historical, by marginalizing the struggles of individuals, and by undervaluing Morrison's desire to represent the inner lives of the slaves, Morgenstern nevertheless bypasses a non-reductive consideration of individual persons as individuals. For, the formulation "the psychopathology of the historical subject" seems to foreclose input from any dimension of the person or subject that, if not historically determined, is at the very least historically conditioned or constructed. Morrison in all of her writings manifests her interest in understanding why some "survive" and others do not (I take Morrison to mean "survive" in the sense of living a human life, moving beyond the victim-survivor binary. For, as has been pointed out by many, the living-dead collaborators of the Nazi concentration camps also survived.)

Morgenstern is quite correct to note that Beloved has many of the characteristics of the pre-verbal, pre-oedipal child and that the relationships among Beloved, Sethe, and Paul D follow some of the psychic dynamics of such a child. She seems to suggest that only a child on the preverbal level would be able to reveal the memories of the Middle Passage that make her also an embodiment of the people and the intergenerational memories of the Middle Passage itself. Beloved here, as a preverbal child, is a metaphor for the experiences of people during Middle Passage because the preverbal child cannot express herself or her trauma, and thus represents the fact that those experiences are unsayable, therefore unrepresentable. However, is this all that Beloved is in the novel? The pre-verbal, pre-oedipal developmental level is a developmental level experienced by all human beings. Does Morrison use it only as a metaphor for the unrepresentable, that is, unspeakable character of the traumatic experience of millions of slaves of the Middle Passage, though Beloved herself, as Sethe's daughter, was never on a slave ship?

Regarding Morgenstern's claim that Morrison conflates what ought not to be conflated—the unrepresentatable and the underrepresented, in actuality nothing in *Beloved* contests that elements of traumatic experience may be unrepresentable. There is no contradiction between acceptance that elements are unrepresentable and that the traumatic experiences people endured in slavery have been underrepresented. If one goes to a museum which brings together artifacts, videos, and testimony of victims of the Jewish holocaust, one may feel deeply that the suffering of the victims, the traumatic force of their experience, cannot ever be wholly represented, while, at the same time, one may feel intensely that at least they have not been underrepresented, i.e., that they have been represented insofar as is possible. So, too, Morrison's novel is profoundly moving and disturbing as she brings to life the terrible sufferings of slaves, and brings them to life through the stories and testimony of persons in the novel who actually experienced those horrors, and does this so that they will no longer be underrepresented, particularly their inner lives. From this magnificent achievement we need not conclude that the author believes that there are no aspects of such traumas that are "constitutively unrepresentatable" or that the author set out to represent the unrepresentatable rather than to do what she said she wanted to do: correct the underrepresentation of the experience of slaves from their point of view as persons with inner lives. Morrison points out that actual slave narratives did not at all portray the inner lives of slaves and it is precisely this underrepresentation of the slave experience that Morrison wants "to extend, fill in and complement. . . ."[36] It seems as though Morgenstern recoils from the power of Morrison's depiction of the inner lives of the slaves and their traumas, and it is terrible indeed.

In view of this, we can now see that Morgenstern, perhaps against her own intentions, actually represents the relation of maternal and historical, personal and political, in the novel not as a conflation, for this would mean that each element contributes vitally to the fusion; what Morgenstern describes, is, rather, the subsumption of the personal in the political (historical) or the colonization of the personal by the political. It is this overlooking of the primordial irreducibility of the person that, it seems to me, induced Morgenstern to subordinate both Sethe's abandonment by her mother and the trauma of Sethe's murder of her daughter to the collective trauma of the Middle Passage. One consequence of Morgenstern's view is that the immense struggle between Sethe and Beloved, and the role reversals they undergo, are not thematized, though they are one of the most significant and most extensively portrayed aspects of the novel.

Regarding additional dimensions of Beloved's role in the novel, her preverbal and pre-oedipal developmental stage and her struggle for self-expression can open up just that which children also in more favorable circumstances open up within us. The preverbal child is both immensely vulnerable and immensely open, as are children throughout early childhood. People who have either witnessed grandparents with their grandchildren or are grandparents themselves may have experienced the enchanted dimension of the grandparent-grandchild relationship—children make us young again, enable us to open ourselves to our inherent potential to grow, our *physis*. Many parents, those who are fortunate, know that with children they have the remarkable opportunity to grow up all over again, or for the first time. This will be an important consideration in our effort to discern who Beloved's baby is.

Though at the end of the novel Morrison portrays Sethe as broken and defeated by her struggles and by Beloved's disappearance, with the arrival of Paul D she is offered the possibility of a future, once again. The first time Paul D came and offered Sethe that possibility she was not ready, she had not yet battled her demons, had not yet experienced recrudescence of her own potential for growth, and so Beloved had reappeared. Paul D leaves when Sethe tells him that she murdered her daughter to save her from slavery. He is shattered by the revelation that Sethe committed what he viewed as a monstrous act. When he returns after learning that Beloved was gone, Paul D has come to understand that Sethe's murder of her own child, all things considered, could be set aside in that it did not constitute an all-encompassing evil in her character.

Morgenstern denies that Paul D as created in the novel holds the possibility of reconstituting and continuing the narrative, that he can be an agent of a new future for Sethe and himself. Morgenstern's interpretation of *Beloved* seems to be a response to, or defense against, a perceived threat emanating from the novel: the threat that our authentic challenge, as human beings, is to call upon the resources of our primordial, irreducible personhood to bring about the final revolution—the world-constituting instantiation of the primordial lived experience that human existence is human only if at its very core, not peripherally, it transcends mere survival, or, put another way, when survival is not terminus ad quem but the ground for the possibility of living a human life. This notion can be explored in the light of Morgenstern's interpretations of the end of the novel and my contrasting view.

WHO IS BELOVED'S BABY?

Morgenstern comments,

> If *Beloved* is about the literalization, personification and reanimation of the past, it not only shows repetition compulsion at work, but is also a fantasy realized, a wish fulfilled. . . . This fantasy, of course, is also the fantasy of successful testimonial, and *Beloved* certainly moves in the direction of restoring the possibility of witnessing to the world it depicts . . . . Morrison's novel is about history as trauma insofar as it is about what happens when your past wants you. Indeed, it is only in its moments of willful optimism (the sentimental ending with Sethe and Paul D. is, after all, "much much happier than what really happened") that the precariousness of testimony itself seems to disappear. . . . With its depiction of testimonies that do not and cannot succeed . . . *Beloved* . . . allows for no easy cure.[37]

Later, Morgenstern writes that, "what most needs to be said in the novel defies narrative form. Instead it is said through the unlocatability of trauma, the conflation of the maternal and the historical, and the ambivalence of an ending that repudiates Beloved...even as it conjures her once more."[38] In what follows, I will show that the ending of the novel does not at all repudiate Beloved.

Many interpretive readings of *Beloved* speak of what is referred to as the first ending of the novel as a "fairy-tale" ending (the ending that Morgenstern says is "sentimental" and a product of Morrison's "willful optimism"): Beloved, Paul D, and Denver all live happily ever after as a traditional heterosexual couple and as a family. These writers generally interpret Sethe's response, "Me? Me?", to Paul D's remark that she herself "is her best thing" as Morrison casting doubt that Sethe can attain the level of subjectivity, of being a subject to herself, a self. Yet Sethe's response, as we have seen in Holden-Kirwan's interpretation, can just as readily be understood to be surprise, the dawning within her of an incipient self or lived subjectivity. I reject the notion that the possibility of a future for these victims of the horrors of slavery is a "fairy tale," that is, that it is devoid of plausibility, and that it manifests an otiose sentimentality. It is true that Morrison provides what has been referred to as a second ending to the novel, and it is grim indeed, but, it is not a repudiation of the first ending.

Rather than a second ending to the novel, the last two pages of *Beloved* have the character of an epilogue, a sequel to the denouement of the story. It is a sequel that is bathed in ambiguity. On one hand there is a tone of subtle chastisement: the voice of the epilogue tells us that Sethe and others who knew her forgot Beloved: "So, in the end, they forgot her too. Remembering seemed unwise." Beloved was then "disremembered."[39] This act of disremembering, of an almost willful act of forgetting or refusing to remember suggests that the horrors of slavery and Middle Passage are forgotten and that this is an act of abandonment.

Does this narrator chide the people of *Beloved*, and through them chide us all for our disremembering of the Middle Passage, of slavery and the continued existence of antiblack racism in the United States and the world? This seems likely. Commentators have pointed out that since some witnesses say, quite plausibly, that they saw Beloved running away, that this is the ultimate representation of the horrors of slavery—another pregnant black woman on the run, abused and abandoned. This, too, is a plausible inference. For, Morrison's story is indeed a soul-wrenching depiction of the horrific brutality of slavery and of the suffering of its victims and their descendents. Our own humanity is at stake in forgetting and in remembering.

However, at the same time as we are made to confront the forgetting of what really happened as incarnated in Beloved, the narrator does not erase the ambiguity of Beloved's existence:

Down by the stream in back of 124 her footprints come and go, come and go. They are so familiar. Should a child, an adult place his feet in them, they will fit. Take them out and they disappear again as though nobody ever walked there.

By and by all trace is gone, and what is forgotten is not only the footprints but the water too and what it is down there.[40]

What does it mean to say that both a child's and an adult's feet will fit in Beloved's footprints? Beloved herself was both child and adult, and, she had a nascent child within her; yet, physically, one cannot be both simultaneously, and Beloved was physically an adult woman. Moreover, *our* feet will fit in Beloved's footprints, too. And, as noted above, Beloved, as a pre-verbal, pre-oedipal child stirs up our own early developmental capacity for growth. Are we all Beloved? Did not Beloved desire the love and recognition that we all sought, and seek?

Throughout the novel, Sethe speaks of her children as "her best thing." She, a slave woman, has nothing; under slavery, she cannot even claim her own children as her own. Sethe dared to do this and grounded her very being in her devotion to her own children. She killed her infant daughter, she maintains throughout, because she loved her and therefore could not allow her to grow up in slavery. When Beloved arrives and is claimed as Sethe's dead daughter, Sethe again reiterates that Beloved is "her best thing." Then, the immense struggles between Beloved and Sethe ensue, struggles in which the two women undergo several mother-daughter role reversals and in which they become victims of the insatiability of the demand for absolute, total devotion, devotion that is incompatible with the separateness of individual human beings. All of this Sethe endures until her final delusion that Mr. Bodwin came to take her and Beloved back to slavery and her attempt in this delusional state to kill Mr. Bodwin with an ice pick, the same white man who saved Sethe from the gallows after she murdered her daughter. But, she attacks Bodwin, the delusional persecutor, not her daughter.

At this point, Morrison depicts Beloved's interior state as feeling again abandoned by Sethe when Sethe lets go of her hand in order to attack Mr. Bodwin. Anguished because of feeling abandoned again, Beloved disappears. However, in letting go of Beloved's hand, Sethe did not at all abandon Beloved, either in intention or in physically moving away from her; rather, in her delusional state Sethe believed that she was defending Beloved and, rather than attacking her child, Beloved herself, attacking the person whom she believed would take Beloved back to slavery. Beloved's instantaneous misreading of Sethe's actions speaks to Beloved's own symbiotic attachment to and non-separation from Sethe. This is to say that a reading which takes at face value Beloved's own interior life when she felt again abandoned by Sethe as if to imply that she actually was abandoned by Sethe—such a reading is simplistic. Beloved's regressed psychosocial developmental level was determinative for generating the feeling of abandonment that gripped her during these events. These developmental processes, for example symbiosis and separation-individuation and their exquisite responsiveness to parental attitudes and actions[41] can take many different forms in different cultural, historical, and political circumstances, but their inherence in human life is one of the structural presuppositions of *Beloved*.

Beloved's distress when Sethe lets go of her hand shows Beloved to be a preverbal child who has not yet attained the level of object (mother) constancy: she lacks the inner structure that would give her confidence that her mother will return. At the same time, Beloved disappears just as Sethe, again fearing the worst (this time delusionally)—having her child taken back into slavery, attacks, not Beloved again, but the imagined oppressor. This assertive act suggests that Sethe herself has become freed from the developmental arrest imposed by the psychosocial and material forces that acted on slaves' psychosocial development. There is hope, then, that Sethe will no longer be prey to such delusions. Thus, Beloved's disappearance signals that Sethe has worked through some of the most crippling inner constraints that precluded her attainment of subject status, her appropriation of her own subjectivity and self.

Who, then, is Beloved's baby? In what follows, I will offer an interpretation of the role and meaning of Beloved's baby in this novel. My interpretation is speculative; however, *Beloved* is a novel that is imbued with powerful psychic currents that run through it that are at times almost unchecked by the controlling function of authorial presence. Indeed, Morrison has said that the endings of her novels have a quality of openness. Though my interpretation is speculative, I believe that it is a speculation that emerged within me and can do so in other readers stimulated by those psychic currents set in motion by the creative ferment within the novel.

Beloved's baby, Morrison has attested, was fathered by Paul D during his affair with Beloved which he ended before he left the family after learning of the infanticide. Now, after Beloved's disappearance, Paul D returns, with his nurturant masculinity, to help Sethe to live and to create a shared future. Why does the event of Beloved's pregnancy by Paul D occur in this novel? On one hand, Paul D enacts an aspect of his own crisis of subjectivity when he allows himself to be repeatedly seduced by Beloved, even though he loves and has always loved Sethe. On the other hand, that Beloved becomes pregnant adds nothing to Paul D's own story (though he did tell Sethe that he wanted to father their child). There is in the novel a disconnect between Paul D and Sethe, on one hand, and Beloved's pregnancy, the baby in her womb on the other hand. After Paul D's return subsequent to the disappearance of Beloved, Beloved's pregnancy is never again mentioned. This absence signals a presence in another register, another mode of existence. Beloved's baby, I suggest, enters into Sethe as the return of her own primordial self reborn within her. Since one can plausibly see Beloved as Sethe's mother, or at least as an embodiment of Sethe's ancestors, her baby can be seen as Sethe herself, reborn in her mother (Beloved as Sethe's mother), and entering into Sethe as her reborn self after Beloved disappears. From this perspective, Beloved's baby in her womb, fathered by Paul D, is the physically represented ground for the transmission of a transcendental, intersubjective phenomenon: Paul D's mediation, not cause, but midwifery, of Sethe's recovery of her self, her subject status. While Beloved's pregnancy makes all the more traumatic and symbolic her flight, it also, as all pregnancy does, portends the future, and, as noted above, portends not only birth but the possibility of rebirth. Is this why Beloved's "smile was dazzling" as she stood, naked and pregnant, before the assembled crowd?

CONCLUSION

It is true, as Morrison tells us, that the past is disremembered. It is also tragic that this forgetting of immense human suffering seems to be heretofore concomitant with our need to move forward and integrate or reintegrate ourselves. To this extent, we are all compromised, all condemned to repeat history. Far, far better it would be to remember, and in remembering be, not traumatized, but rather empowered to create the conditions for the possibility of a future for humanity such that there will be no more victims, no more holocausts, and thus no more survivors. The paralysis and total devastation brought about by surviving in a perpetual state of trauma—that is, by not forgetting, is, of course, not a solution either for in such a state constructive or transformative action is impossible. This should not be taken as a critique of the traumatized, for that would indeed be to blame the victims, and doing so is both incorrect and ethically anathema. Rather, it is meant as a critique of those who think that traumatized persons have no resources within that can enable them to move beyond survival toward personal wholeness, even in conjunction with "forgetting." To deny this is to blame the victims by setting them apart as a special category—those condemned perpetually to relive their trauma and survival of it. If the "fairy tale" ending of Beloved is ambiguous, and I believe it is, it is not because it is marked by trauma denying implausibility, but precisely because it is not a "fairy tale" in the pejorative sense or an act of "willful optimism." Sethe can achieve subject status. She can become a self through her own struggles and with the intervention of Beloved, Beloved's baby, and Paul D. For Sethe, life can now, after living for eighteen years in a free state, be more than mere survival for she has reconnected with her self before her most devastating traumas, and this enables her to reconnect with the people whom she loves and who love her. Moreover, there is no indication whatsoever in the novel that Sethe and Paul D's future in this world will be a blissful happily-ever-after, even if it is much, much happier than what really happened to Margaret Garner and the Sixty-Million victims of the Middle Passage. What really would be a "fairy tale" in the pejorative sense, a fairy tale that is not at all represented in *Beloved,* is the notion that we, any and all of us, can fully realize our humanity, can become whole, no matter how favorable our circumstances, in a world of continued, pervasive inhumanity. The ending of *Beloved* shows, therefore, that Paul D and Sethe are enabled to live a meaningful life together because they understood from all of their struggles to survive that they survived partly in virtue of their implicit realization that just surviving was not enough; they were implicitly aware that they are not the animals that slavery held them to be, but human beings. For, they might have survived in slavery, but not living human lives. Just so, Frederick Douglass asserted himself and turned on his overseer Covey when he realized that not his survival but his humanity, his dignity as a human being, was at stake.

"I am not the slave of the Slavery that dehumanized my ancestors," wrote Fanon. [42] How can we throw off this slavery? Fanon has his own ideas about this, ideas that are not very different from Toni Morrison's in *Beloved.* We must abandon the abstract, reified victim-survivor binary, the dialectic of false consciousness. We, as both individual persons and as the human community, must trace the line of fusion that connects our best things—our personhood before victimization and our human future beyond mere survival.

"I am not a victim, I'm a survivor," said the lady at the hearings. Read one way, this statement can intimate victim blaming, for, what of those who do not survive? We do not know exactly what the woman who made this statement at the hearing meant; we do not know what the terms 'victim' and 'survivor' meant to her. Nevertheless, this statement is uttered all too often in a culture that has now predetermined that the term 'victim' means that one's suffering is self-imposed, and that all we can ever do is survive; we are always struggling, no matter what our life circumstance are, rich or poor, powerful or powerless, struggling for survival. Presumably, in rejecting the description of oneself as 'victim' one is asserting one's ability to succeed in the struggle against adversity, succeed, that is, 'survive,' that is, refuse to defeat oneself. But then, if one is always already a 'survivor,' when does one move beyond just survival into a more human future? Thus, the propaganda in a society like ours that impels us to blame the victims, ourselves and others, is a function of the profound inhumanity of the socioeconomic system in which we are embedded, a system that must be changed through a liberatory praxis, or what Fanon conceived as mature actionality.

What I have attempted to show in this paper is that in *Beloved* Morrison has created a novel imbued with what I have referred to as a radical, existential humanism.[43] The existential moment is the novel's presentation of individual, embodied human beings in situations that have cultural and historical density, but that have meaning only in and through the inwardness, or consciousness, of each person. The sort existential humanism I have in mind is not of the Sartrean kind that repudiated Husserl's transcendental subject and transcendental intersubjectivity, but is, rather, the Husserlian mode of existential being in becoming where the subject, or self, or consciousness is shown to be the repository of the open, non-essentialized, *a priori*, transcendental ground of being and becoming human in an intersubjectively constituted lifeworld. From this point of view, the non-ideologically colonized senses of victim and survivor can be recuperated through the phenomenological suspension of ontological commitments and the methodology of genetic phenomenology. I hardly maintain that this interpretation of the existential dimension of our existence is what Morrison had in mind. I do however hold that it is consistent with her manner of representing human existence. Morrison seems to be attempting to discern the elements that mediate the relation between the individual qua individual and the intersubjective, historical community without subsuming either pole of the relation in the other. It is just this problematic that is most adequately encompassed by Husserlian phenomenology.[44]

Nor should the perspective embedded in this paper be interpreted as a repudiation of awareness that historical events and institutional, political, and cultural factors are the locus of the conditions that generate the horrific crimes against humanity that have occurred throughout recorded history; nor is this perspective denial of the value of collective action or active struggle to create a more human world for all persons. On the contrary, my hope is that heightened awareness of the crippling effects of the pervasiveness in our lives of the ideologically constituted functioning of the victim-survivor binary will empower us, will release our capacity for mature actionality. Is this not the meaning of Fanon's life and work? What is shown by Morrison and by a large body of postcolonial literature and theory is that the principal factor associated with crimes against humanity is the attempt to deny, through an attempt to eradicate, the humanity of the victim. Dehumanization is a victim blaming stance in that it places responsibility for the abuse on the alleged non-human status of the victims: they get what they "deserve." And the rationale of the perpetrators (witness Guantánamo Bay) is always that these crimes were necessary so that "we" will survive.

If we are to survive, and if we are to work toward eliminating the conditions for the possibility of such crimes against humanity, we must realize that the goal of mere survival is a betrayal of our humanity that generates crises which threaten our very survival. Our humanness is openness to all that which lies before and beyond survival, and beyond the victim blaming that imposes survival as our only possible goal, the only one that we as finite, incomplete beings "deserve." To believe this, however, is to leave the chain of dehumanization intact. This chain must be broken, for what we deserve is, rather, justice, wholeness, and liberation.

NOTES

1. Toni Morrison, *Beloved* (New York: Plume, 1988), 261.

2. Wilfred D. Samuels and Clenora Hudson-Weems, *Toni Morrison* (New York: Twayne, 1990), 79.

3. The concept of interpellation entered scholarly discourse through Louis Althusser's justly celebrated essay, "Ideology and Ideological State Apparatuses," in *Lenin and Philosophy and Other Essays,* trans. by Ben Brewster (New York: Monthly Review Press, 1971), 127–86. Althusser maintained that a scientific discourse on ideology must be "subjectless" (173), and that it is exactly the subject that is ideologically interpellated, i.e., that ideology "transforms" individuals into subjects (174). While I find the notion of interpellation useful and explanatory, I do not share Althusser's view that a social science must be subjectless and that the subject as such is ideologically constituted. Like many structuralist and post-structuralist perspectives, Althusser throws out the baby (subjectivity) with the bathwater (alienated modes of subjectivity). That there is an originary, non-alienated mode of subjectivity and intersubjectivity is shown in and by Husserlian phenomenology.

4. Naomi Morgenstern, "Mother's Milk and Sister's Blood: Trauma and the Neoslave Narrative," *Differences* 8, no. 2 (1996), 101–26. This essay consists in an introduction followed by, first a discussion of Gayle Jones' novel *Corregidora,* and then, second, a discussion of Toni Morrison's novel, *Beloved.* In this paper, *Corregidora* will not be discussed.

5. Morgenstern, *Mother's Milk,* 101.

6. Morgenstern, *Mother's Milk,* 103.

7. Morgenstern, *Mother's Milk,* 105.

8. Morgenstern, *Mother's Milk,* 102

9. Morgenstern, *Mother's Milk,* 114

10. Quoted in Morgenstern, *Mother's Milk,* 106.

11. Morgenstern, *Mother's Milk,* 111.

12. In my necessarily limited survey of the vast critical literature on *Beloved,* there is very little discussion of the meaning or role of Beloved's pregnancy in the narrative. It is remarkable that there is a huge literature on the discussion of the identity of Beloved, of who Beloved is, yet that literature does not include discussion of Beloved's pregnancy, of her baby, since by the end of the novel, just before she disappears, Beloved is described as having a very large belly, indicative of advanced pregnancy. In the literature as a whole there is remarkably little discussion of this pregnancy.

Indeed, I would say that there has been abandonment of Beloved's baby by literary, philosophical, psychological, and so on interpreters of the novel. And, in abandoning Beloved's baby, interpreters have, I believe, abandoned a more subtle, more exquisite, more integral, and more hopeful interpretation of the denouement of the novel. The present paper is an attempt to reclaim that baby, to undo the abandonment, to be its midwife. One commentator on the novel who does discuss and interpret the meaning of Beloved's baby is Mary Panniccia Garden in her essay, "Models of Memory and Romance: The Dual Endings of Toni Morrison's *Beloved*," in *Twentieth Century Literature* (Winter, 1999), 1–21. Garden's interpretation of the meaning in the novel of Beloved's baby is entirely different from the interpretation in this paper; however, though the two interpretations are extremely different, they are both tenable. Indeed, my interpretation is more speculative, and more psychological, than Garden's.

13. Morgenstern, *Mother's Milk*, 117.

14. Morgenstern, *Mother's Milk*, 112.

15. Morgenstern, *Mother's Milk*, 114.

16. Although, in the novel, Denver, Sethe's younger daughter, points out that Sethe attempted to convince Beloved that the murder was an act of love, and this is indicative that the murder was a trauma for Sethe, a trauma that Morgenstern acknowledges as such, but does not deal with further).

17. Morgenstern, *Mother's Milk*, 113–14.

18. Morgenstern, *Mother's Milk*, 116.

19. Danille Taylor-Guthrie, ed., *Conversations with Toni Morrison* (Jackson: University Press of Mississippi), 247.

20. Carolyn C. Bernard, ed., *Toni Morrison: Conversations* (Jackson: University Press of Mississippi, 2008), 56.

21. Toni Morrison, "The Site of Memory," in *Out There: Marginalization and Contemporary Culture*, edited by Russell Ferguson, et al. (Cambridge, MA: MIT Press, 1990), 302.

22. Morgenstern, *Mother's Milk*, 116

23. Morgenstern, *Mother's Milk*, 116.

24. Morgenstern's general attitude toward neoslave narratives, including both novels that are examined in her paper, Gayle Jones' *Corregidora* and *Beloved*, is difficult to discern. She concludes her essay by saying that "While *Beloved*, like *Corregidora*, repeats the story of slavery, then, it also asserts that it is only through an account of traumatic repetition that the story of slavery ever gets told." Morgenstern maintains that the novels are not manifestations of trauma, but they are efforts to "theorize and control" it. Yet, Morgenstern also points out that both novels complexify the story of slavery. *Corregidora* does so "in that it is also a story of conflict, a story of the fraught relationship between desire and survival," and *Beloved* does so by including an ending of "willful optimism," the fairy tale ending, the romance of Paul D and Sethe. Morgenstern seems to suggest that by including these elements the novels "use" trauma in a way that compromises the possibility of readers' experiencing them as testimony to what really happened.

25. Morgenstern, *Mother's Milk*, 118.

26. Morgenstern, *Mother's Milk*, 116.

27. Morgenstern, *Mother's Milk*, 115–16.

28. Denard, *Toni*, 46.

29. Jennifer L. Holden-Kirwan, "Looking into the Self that Is No Self: An Examination of Subjectivity in '*Beloved,*'" *African American Review* 32 (Fall, 1998): 415–426. The pagination used in the present paper is based on the downloaded version of Holden-Kirwan's paper: http://www.thefreelibrary.com/_/print/PrintArticle. aspx?id=21232162, 1-17 (9/29/08).

30. Holden-Kirwan, Locating, 5.

31. Quoted in Holden-Kirwan, Locating, 14.

32. Holden-Kirwan, Locating, 14.

33. Holden-Kirwan, Locating, 14.

34. Frantz Fanon, *Black Skin White Masks* (New York: Grove Press, 1967), 110.

35. Morgenstern, *Mother's Milk*, 104.

36. Morrison, The Site, 305.

37. Morgenstern, *Mother's Milk*, 116–17.

38. Morgenstern, *Mother's Milk*, 118.

39. Morrison, *Beloved*, 274

40. Morrison, *Beloved*, 275.

41. See Margaret Mahler, *The Psychological Birth of the Human Infant: Symbiosis and Individuation* (New York: Basic Books, 1975).

42. Fanon, *Black Skin*, 230.

43. Samuels and Hudson-Weems, *Toni*, passim. This book is an excellent contribution to the discussion of the existential dimension of Morrison's work.

44. Lewis R. Gordon, in his essay, "Sociality and Community in Black: A Phenomenological Essay," in Robert E. Birt, ed. *The Quest for Community and Identity: Critical Essays in Africana Social Philosophy* (Lanham, MD: Rowman & Littlefield, 2002), presents a superb discussion of the way in which Husserlian phenomenology enables conceptualization of the relationality of individuals in community. In this essay, Gordon also includes a critique of Sartre showing that in his writings Sartre presupposed the transcendental character of the relationality between individual and community. For a detailed exegesis and critique of Gordon's seminal essay, see Marilyn Nissim-Sabat, "Lewis Gordon: Avatar of Post-Colonial Humanism," in *The C.L.R. James Journal* 14, no.1 (Spring 2008): 46–70.

Bibliography

Althusser, Louis. "Ideology and Ideological State Apparatuses." Pp. 127–86 in *Lenin and Philosophy and Other Essays,* trans. by Ben Brewster. New York: Monthly Review Press, 1994.

Anderson, Kevin. *Lenin, Hegel, and Western Marxism: A Critical Study.* Urbana: University of Illinois Press, 1995.

Aristotle. *Politics*, ed. and trans. Ernest Becker. Oxford, UK: Oxford University Press, 1969.

Bernard, Carolyn C., ed. *Toni Morrison: Conversations.* Jackson: University of Mississippi Press, 2008.

Bernheimer, Charles and Kahane, Claire B., eds. *In Dora's Case: Freud-Hysteria-Feminism.* New York: Columbia University Press, 1985.

Blatt, Sidney J. "Minding the Gap between Positivism and Hermeneutics in Psychoanalytic Research." *Journal of the American Psychoanalytic Association* 54, 2 (2006): 571–610.

Brooks, Peter and Woloch, Alex, eds. *Whose Freud; The Place of Psychoanalysis in Contemporary Culture.* New Haven, CT: Yale University Press, 2000.

Bulhan, Hussein Abdilahi. *Frantz Fanon and the Psychology of Oppression.* New York: Plenum, 1985.

Bunge, Mario. *Causality and Modern Science.* New York: Dover, 1979.

Butler, Judith. *Antigone's Claim.* New York: Columbia University Press, 2000.

Cherki, Alice. *Frantz Fanon: A Portrait*, trans. by Nadia Benabid. Ithaca, NY: Cornell University Press, 2006.

Collins, Jerre, et al. "Questioning the Unconscious: The Dora Archive." Pp. 243–53 in *In Dora's Case: Freud-Hysteria-Feminism*, eds. Charles Bernheimer and Claire Kahane. New York: Columbia University Press, 1985.

Domanski, Olga. "Two Contributions by Olga Domanski." Pp. 91–109 in *Woman's Liberation and the Dialectics of Revolution,* ed. Raya Dunayevskaya. Detroit, MI: Wayne State University Press.

Dreyfus, H. L. and Rabinow, P. *Michel Foucault: Beyond Structuralism and Herme-neutics.* Chicago: University of Chicago Press, 1982.

Dunayevskaya, Raya. *Marxism and Freedom.* New York: Columbia University Press, 1988.

——. *The Philosophical Moment of Marxist-Humanism.* Chicago: News and Letters, 1989.

——. *Philosophy and Revolution.* New York: Columbia University Press, 1989.

——. *Rosa Luxemburg, Women's Liberation, and Marx's Philosophy of Revolution.* 2nd ed. with a foreword by Adrienne Rich. Urbana: University of Illinois Press, 1991.

——. *The Marxist-Humanist Theory of State-Capitalism.* Chicago: News and Letters, 1992.

——. *Women's Liberation and the Dialectics of Revolution.* Detroit, MI: Wayne State University Press, 1996.

Dworkin, Gerald. "The Concept of Autonomy." pp. 54–62 In *The Inner Citadel: Essays on Individual Autonomy,* ed. John Christman. New York: Oxford University Press, 1989.

Elden, Stuart. "The Place of the Polis: Political Blindness in Judith Butler's *Antigone's Claim.*" *Theory and Event* 8, no. 1 (2005).

Ellison, Ralph. *The Invisible Man.* New York: Vintage, 1947.

Ellman, Stephen J. and Moskowitz, Michael. "An Examination of Some Recent Criticisms of Metapsychology." *Psychoanalytic Quarterly* 49 (1980): 641–46.

Fabrega Jr., Horacio. "Cultural Relativism and Psychiatric Illness." *Journal of Nervous and Mental Disease* 177, 7 (1989): 415–25.

Fanon, Frantz. *The Wretched of the Earth,* trans. by Constance Parrington. New York: Grove Press, 1963 (Fr. original pub. in 1961).

Feffer, Melvin. *Black Skin, White Masks,* trans. by Charles Lam Markman. New York: Grove Press, 1967 (Fr. original pub. in 1952).

——. *The Structure of Freudian Thought.* New York: International Universities Press, 1982.

Fernando, Suman, Ndegwa, David, and Wilson, Melba. *Forensic Psychiatry, Race and Culture.* London: Routledge, 1998.

Foucault, Michel. *Mental Illness and Psychology,* trans. by Alan Sheridan. New York: Harper and Row, 1976. (French version originally published in 1954).

——.The *History of Sexuality,* 1. Translated by R. Hurly. New York: Pantheon, 1978 (French original published in 1976).

——. "Afterward." Pp. 208–26 in H. L. Dreyfus and P. Rabinow, *Michel Foucault.* Chicago: University of Chicago Press, 1982.

Freud, Sigmund. *The Interpretation of Dreams.* Standard Edition, v. 4-5. London: Hogarth Press, 1900/1953.

——. *New Introductory Lectures on Psychoanalysis.* Standard Edition, v. 22. London: Hogarth Press, 1933/1955.

——. *Psychoanalysis and Telepathy.* Standard Edition, v. 18. London: Hogarth Press, 1922/1955.

———. *The Claims of Psychoanalysis to Scientific Interest.* Standard Edition, v. 13. London: Hogarth Press, 1913/1958.

———. *Civilization and Its Discontents.* Standard Edition, v. 21. London: Hogarth Press, 1930/1961.

———. *Civilization and Its Discontents.* New York: Norton, 1961.

———. *The Complete Introductory Lectures on Psychoanalysis,* trans. by James Strachey. New York: Norton, 1966.

———. "Femininity." Pp. 576–99 in *The Complete Introductory Lectures on Psychoanalysis,* trans. by James Strachey. New York: Norton, 1966.

———. *Project for a Scientific Psychology.* Standard Edition, v. 1. London: Hogarth Press, 1895/1966.

———. *The Interpretation of Dreams,* trans. by Joyce Crick. Oxford: Oxford University Press, 1999.

Freundlieb, Dieter. "Foucault's Theory of Discourse and Human Agency." Pp. 152–80 in *Reassessing Foucault,* edited by Colin Jones and Roy Porter. London: Routledge, 1994.

Friedlander, Stephen. "The Confluence of Psychoanalysis and Religion." Pp. 147–62 in *Soul on the Couch: Spirituality, Religion, and Morality in Contemporary Psychoanalysis,* edited by Charles Spezzano and G. Gargiulo. Hillsdale, NJ: The Analytic Press, 1997.

Fuss, Diana. *Identification Papers.* New York: Routledge, 1995.

Garden, Mary Panniccia. "Models of Memory and Romance: The Dual Endings of Toni Morrison's *Beloved.*" *Twentieth Century Literature,*(Winter, 1999), 1–23.

Gay, Peter. *Freud: A Life for Our Time.* New York: Norton, 1988.

Gedo, John E. *Beyond Interpretation.* New York: International Universities Press, 1979.

Gill, Merton. "Metapsychology Is Not Psychology." Pp. 71–105 in Merton Gill and Philip S. Holzman, *Psychology versus Metapsychology.* New York: International Universities Press, 1976.

Gill, Merton and Holzman, Philip. *Psychology versus Metapsychology.* New York: International Universities Press, 1976.

Gordon, Lewis R. *Bad Faith and Antiblack Racism.* Atlantic Highlands, NJ: Humanities Press, 1995.

———. *Fanon and the Crisis of European Man.* New York: Routledge, 1995.

———, ed. *Fanon: A Critical Reader.* Oxford: Blackwell, 1996.

———. *Her Majesty's Other Children.* Lanham, MD: Rowman & Littlefield, 1997.

———. *Existentia Africana.* New York: Routledge, 2000.

———. "Identity and Liberation: A Phenomenological Approach." Pp. 189–205 n *Phenomenology of the Political,* edited by Kevin Thompson and Lester Embree. Dordrecht, the Netherlands: Kluwer Academic Publishers, 2000.

———. "Sociality and Community in Black: A Phenomenological Essay." Pp. 105–23 in *The Quest for Community and Identity: Critical essays in Africana Social Philosophy,* edited by Robert E. Birt. Lanham, MD: Rowman & Littlefield, 2002.

———. *Disciplinary Decadence: Living Thought in Trying Times.* Boulder, Colorado: Paradigm Publishers, 2006.

———. *Introduction to Africana Philosophy.* Cambridge: Cambridge University Press, 2008.

Grgic, Filip. "Aristotle on the Akratic's Knowledge." *Phronesis,* XLII, 4 (2002): 336–58.

Grier, William H. and Cobbs, Price, M. *Black Rage.* New York: Bantam, 1968.

Harding, Sandra. *The Science Question in Feminism.* Ithaca, NY: Cornell University Press, 1986.

Harrell, Camara Jules P. *Manichean Psychology: Racism and the Minds of People of African Descent.* Washington, DC: Howard University Press, 1999.

Hegel, Georg W.F. *Lectures on the Philosophy of Religion,* vol. II, trans. and ed. by E. B. Spears. London: Routledge, 1974.

Herrera, J. M., et al, eds. *Cross Cultural Psychiatry.* New York: Wiley, 1989.

Hoffman, Irwin Z. *Ritual and Spontaneity in the Psychoanalytic Process: A Dialectical-Constructivist View.* Hillsdale, NJ: The Analytic Press, 1998.

Holden-Kirwin, Jennifer L. "Looking into the Self that Is No Self: An Examination of Subjectivity in Beloved." *African American Review* 32 (Fall, 1998): 415–26.

Hudis, Peter. "Introduction." Pp. vii–xxvi in Raya Dunayevskaya, *The Marxist-Humanist Theory of State Capitalism: Selected Writings.* Chicago: News and Letters, 1992.

Husserl, Edmund. *Cartesian Meditations,* trans. by Dorian Cairns. The Hague, The Netherlands: Nijhoff, 1969 (Original Ger. pub. in 1950).

———. *Formal and Transcendental Logic,* trans. by Dorian Cairns. The Hague, The Netherlands: Nijhoff, 1969.

———. *The Crisis of Human Sciences and Transcendental Phenomenology,* trans. by David Carr. Evanston, IL: Northwestern University Press, 1970.

———. "The Vienna Lecture." Pp. 269–99 in Edmund Husserl, *The Crisis of European Sciences and Transcendental Phenomenology,* trans. by David Carr. Evanston, IL: Northwestern University Press, 1970.

———. "Prolegomena to Pure Logic." Pp. 53–247 in *Logical Investigations,* vol. I, trans. by J. N. Findlay. New York: Humanities Press, 1970.

———. *Ideas Pertaining to a Pure Phenomenology and to a Phenomenological Philosophy, Third Book.* The Hague, The Netherlands: Nijhoff, 1980.

———. *Ideas Pertaining to a Pure Phenomenology and to a Phenomenological Philosophy, Second Book,* trans. by R. Rojcewicz and A. Schuwer. Dordrecht, the Netherlands: Kluwer, 1989.

———. Ms 3 III, p. 26a. Cited and translated by James Mensch in "Freedom and Selfhood," *Husserl Studies* 14, no. 1 (1997): 41–59.

Kant, Immanuel. *Foundations of the Metaphysics of Morals,* trans. by Lewis White Beck. Indianapolis, IN: Bobbs-Merrill, 1969.

Keller, Evelyn Fox. *Reflections on Gender and Science.* New Haven, CT: Yale University Press, 1985

Kleinman, Arthur. *Rethinking Psychiatry.* New York: Macmillan, 1988.

Kohut, Heinz. *The Analysis of the Self: A Systematic Approach to the Treatment of Narcissistic Personality Disorders.* New York: International Universities Press, 1971.

——. *How Does Analysis Cure?*, edited by Arnold Goldberg and Paul Stepanski. Chicago: University of Chicago Press, 1984.

——. "Thoughts on Narcissism and Narcissistic Rage." Pp. 124–60 in *Self Psychology and the Humanities: Reflections on a New Psychoanalytic Approach,* edited by C. B. Strozier. New York: Norton, 1985.

Kraus, A. "Phenomenological-Anthropological Psychiatry." Pp. 339–55 in *Contemporary Psychiatry,* edited by F. Henn, N. Satorius, H. Helmchen, and H. Lauter. New York: Springer-Verlag, 2001.

Lacan, Jacques. *The Ethics of Psychoanalysis,* trans. with notes by Dennis Porter. New York: Norton, 1992.

Lamb, Sharon. *The Trouble with Blame.* Cambridge, MA: Harvard University Press, 1996.

Landgrebe, Ludwig. "The Problem of a Transcendental Science of the A Priori of the Life-World." Pp. 176–200 in Ludwig Landgrebe, *The Phenomenology of Edmund Husserl: Six Essays by Ludwig Landgrebe,* ed. with an introduction by Donn Welton. Ithaca, NY: Cornell University Press, 1981.

Lawson, W. B. "The Art and Science of Ethnopharmacotherapy." Pp. 67–73 in *Cross Cultural Psychiatry,* edited by John M. Herrera, William B. Lawson, and John J. Srawek. New York: Wiley, 1999.

Leavey, John P. "Preface: Undecidables and Old Names." Pp. 1–21 in *Edmund Husserl's The Origin of Geometry: An Introduction, by Jacques Derrida.* New York: Nicholas Hays, Ltd., 1978.

Levin, Jerome D. *Treatment of Alcoholism and Other Addictions: A Self-Psychology Approach.* Northvale, NJ: Jason Aronson, 1991.

Lifton, Robert Jay. *The Protean Self.* New York: Basic Books, 1993.

Loevinger, Jane. "Origins of Conscience," Pp. 265–97 in *Psychology versus Metapsychology: Psychoanalytic Essays in Memory of George S. Klein,* edited by Merton M. Gill and Philip S. Holzman. New York: International Universities Press, 1976.

Mahler, Margaret. *The Psychological Birth of the Human Infant: Symbiosis and Individuation.* New York: Basic Books, 1973.

Marx, Karl and Engels, Frederick. *The Communist Manifesto.* Norton Critical Edition, ed. S. Bender; translated by S. Moore. Norton: New York, 1988. (Ger. orig. pub. in 1872.)

——. "The Communist Manifesto." Pp. 1–41 in *Marx and Engels: Basic Writings on Politics and Philosophy,* ed. Lewis S. Feuer. New York: Doubleday, 1959.

Masson, Jeffrey. *The Assault on Truth: Freud's Suppression of the Seduction Theory.* Toronto: Farrar, Straus, and Giroux, 1984.

Medical Murder. City of Hamburg, Germany. PP. 1–9. Retrieved from http://www.ITZ.uni-ham burg.de/rz3a03 5/psychiatry. html (3/15/2002).

Mele, Alfred. *Autonomous Agents: From Self-Control to Autonomy.* Oxford: Oxford University Press, 1995.

Miller, Paul Allen. "Lacan's Antigone: The Sublime Object and the Ethics of Interpretation" Retrieved from: http://www.apaclassics.org/AnnualMeeting/05mtg/abstracts/miller. html,13 (8/14/08).

Mitchell, Juliet. *Psychoanalysis and Feminism: Freud, Reich, Laing and Women.* New York: Random House, 1974.

Mitchell, Stephen A. *Influence and Autonomy in Psychoanalysis.* Hillsdale, NJ: The Analytic Press, 1997

Morgenstern, Naomi. "Mother's Milk and Sister's Blood: Trauma and the Neoslave Narrative." *Differences* 8, no. 2, (1986): 101–26.

Morrison, Toni. *Beloved.* New York: Plume, 1988.

——. "The Site of Memory." Pp. 299-306 in *Out There: Marginalization and Contemporary Culture, 4,* edited by Russell Ferguson, Martha Gever, Trinh T. Minhha, and Cornel West. Cambridge, MA: MIT Press, 1990.

Mouffe, Chantal. *The Return of the Political.* London: Verso, 1993 (reprinted 2005).

Nature Genetics. *Editorial.* 29, no. 3 (2001): 239–40.

Nissim-Sabat, Marilyn. "Edmund Husserl's Theory of Motivation." Ph.D. diss. De Paul University, 1977.

——. "Review of *The Structure of Freudian Thought* by Melvin Feffer," *Review of Psychoanalytic Books* 2, no. 3 (1983): 429–39.

——. "Psychoanalysis and Phenomenology: A New Synthesis." *The Psychoanalytic Review* 73, no. 3 (1986): 273–99.

——. "Psychoanalysis, Phenomenology, and Feminism." Unpublished paper presented at meetings of the Husserl Circle, 1988.

——. "Kohut and Husserl: The Empathic Bond." Pp. 151–74 in *Self Psychology: Comparisons and Contrasts*, edited by Douglas Detrick and Susan Detrick. Hillsdale, NJ: Analytic Press, 1989.

——. "The Role of the Unconscious in Critical Social Theory." Unpublished paper presented at meetings of the Society for Phenomenology and the Human Sciences, 1989.

——. "An Appreciation and Interpretation of the Thought of Lewis Gordon." *The CLR James Journal* 5, no. 1, 1997.

——. "Lewis Gordon: Avatar of Postcolonial Humanism." *The CLR James Journal,* 14, no. 2 (Spring, 2008): 46–70.

Ouimette, Paige and Brown, Pamela, eds. *Trauma and Substance Abuse: Causes, Consequences and Treatment of Comorbid Disorders.* Washington, DC: American Psychological Association.

Palmer, Robert E. *Hermeneutics.* Evanston: Northwestern University Press, 1969.

Pandina, R.J., Johnson, V., and Labouvie, E.W. "Affectivity: Central Mechanism in the development of Drug Dependence." Pp. 179–210 in *Vulnerability to Drug Abuse*, edited by M.D. Glantz and R.W. Pickens. Washington, DC: American Psychological Association Press, 1992.

Parnas, Josef., Sass, Louis A., and Zahavi, Dan. "Recent Developments in Philosophy of Psychopathology." *Current Opinion in Psychiatry*, 21 (2008): 1–7.

Pizen, S. A. *Building Bridges: The Negotiation of Paradox in Psychoanalysis.* Hillsdale, NJ: Analytic Press, 1998.

Plato, *Apology*. Pp. 59–88 in Plato, *The Works of Plato*, trans. by Benjamin Jowett, ed. with an introduction by Irwin Edman. New York: Random House, 1956.

Plato. *Protagoras*, edited and with an introduction by Gregory Vlastos. Indianapolis: Bobbs Merrill, 1956.

Radhakrishnan, Rajagopalan. "Poststructuralist Politics: Towards a Theory of Coalition." Pp. 301–32 in *Postmodernism/Jameson/Critique*. Washington, DC: Maisoneuve Press, 1989.

Ricoeur, Paul. *Freud and Philosophy*. New Haven, CT: Yale University Press, 1970.

———. "The Problem of the Will and Philosophical Discourse." Pp. 273–89 in *Patterns of the Life-World*, edited by J. M. Edie, et al. Evanston, IL: Northwestern University Press, 1970.

———. *Oneself as Another*, trans. by K, Blamey. Chicago: University of Chicago Press, 1992.

Rieff, Philip. *Freud, the Mind of the Moralist*. Chicago: University of Chicago Press, 1979.

Roudinesco, Elizabeth. *Jacques Lacan*, trans. Barbara Bray. New York: Columbia University Press, 1997.

Rowe, Christopher J. "Hedonism in the *Protagoras* Again." Pp. 133–47 in *Plato's Protagoras: Proceedings of the Third Symposium Platonicum Pragense*, edited by Alex Havlicek and Filip Karfik. Prague, Czech Republic: OIKOYMENH, 2003.

Ryan, William. *Blaming the Victim*. New York: Random House, 1976.

Samuels, Wilfred D. and Hudson-Weems, Clenora. *Toni Morrison*. New York: Twayne, 1970.

Sartre, Jean-Paul. *Being and Nothingness: An Essay in Phenomenological Ontology*. Translated by Hazel E. Barnes. New York: Routledge, 1969.

Schafer, Roy. *A New Language for Psychoanalysis*. New Haven, CT: Yale University Press, 1979.

———. *The Analytic Attitude*. New York: Basic Books, 1983.

Schwartz, Michael A. and Wiggins, Osborne. "Science, Humanism, and the Nature of Medical Practice: A Phenomenological View." *Perspectives in Biology and Medicine* 28 (1985): 231–61.

Schwartz, R. S. "Racial Profiling in Medical Research." *New England Journal of Medicine*, 334, no. 18 (2001): 1392–93.

Sophocles. *Antigone*. In *Sophocles: The Plays and Fragments, Part III: The Antigone*, ed. and trans. by Richard Jebb. Amsterdam, the Netherlands: Hakkert, 1962.

Sophocles. *Antigone*. Pp. 186–245 in *The Oedipus Cycle*, trans. by Dudley Fitts and Robert Fitzgerald. New York: Harcourt, 1977.

Spence, Donald P. *Narrative Truth and Historical Truth*. New York: Norton, 1982.

Spiegelberg, Herbert. *Phenomenology in Psychology and Psychiatry: A Historical Introduction*. Evanston, IL: Northwestern University Press, 1972.

Stanley, Liz and Wise, Sue. *Feminist Consciousness and Feminist Research*. London: Routledge and Kegan Paul, 1983

Steiner, George. *Antigones*. Oxford: Oxford University Press, 1984.

Stewart, Jon. *The Hegel Myths and Legends.* Evanston, IL: Northwestern University Press, 1996.

Stoler, Ann Laura. *Race and the Education of Desire: Foucault's History of Sexuality and the Colonial Order of Things.* Durham, NC: Duke University Press, 1995.

Stolorow, Robert and Atwood, George. *Faces in a Cloud.* New York: Jason Aronson, 1979.

———. *Structures of Subjectivity.* Hillsdale, NJ: The Analytic Press, 1984.

Ströker, Elisabeth. "The Role of Psychology in Husserl's Phenomenology." Pp. 3–15 in *Continental Philosophy in America,* edited by Hugh J. Silverman, et al. Pittsburgh: Dusquesne University Press, 1983.

Sullaway, Frank J. *Freud, Biologist of the Mind: Beyond the Psychoanalytic Legend.* New York: Basic Books, 1979.

Taylor-Guthrie, Danille, ed. *Conversations with Toni Morrison.* Jackson: University Press of Mississippi, 1994.

Thomas, Audrey and Sillen, Samuel. *Racism and Psychiatry.* New York: Carol Publishing Group, 1972, 1991.

Turner, Lou. "On the Difference between the Hegelian and Fanonian Dialectic of Lordship and Bondage." Pp. 134–51 in *Fanon: A Critical Reader,* ed. Lewis R. Gordon, et al. Oxford: Blackwell, 1996.

Van Herik, Judith. *Freud on Femininity and Faith.* Berkeley: University of California Press, 1982.

Wallace, Edwin R. *Historiography and Causation in Psychoanalysis.* New Haven, CT: Yale University Press, 1985.

Walton, Jean. *Fair Sex, Savage Dreams: Race, Psychoanalysis, Sexual Difference.* Durham, NC: Duke University Press, 2001.

Weinsheimer, Joel. *Gadamer's Hermeneutics.* New Haven, CT: Yale University Press, 1985.

Winnington-Ingram, Reginald Pepys. *Sophocles: An Interpretation.* Cambridge, UK: Cambridge University Press, 1980.

Wolfenstein, Eugene Victor. *The Victims of Democracy: Malcolm X and the Black Revolution.* London: Free Associations, 1990.

———. *Psychoanalytic Marxism.* London: Free Association Books, 1993.

Zack, Naomi. "Race, Life, Death, Identity, Tragedy and Good Faith." Pp. 98–109 in *Existence in Black,* edited by Lewis R. Gordon. New York: Routledge, 1977.

Zimmerman, Michael E. *Eclipse of the Self: The Development of Heidegger's Concept of Authenticity.* Athens: Ohio University Press, 1982.

Zizek, Slavoj. "Badiou: Notes from an Ongoing Debate." *International Journal of Zizek Studies,* <http://www.lacan.com/zizou.htm> (08/12/2008).

Index

agency, xi, xvii, xxii, 4, 104,
117–18, 123; and bad faith, 106;
and phenomenology, 106; and
psychoanalysis, 60, 92; and race,
113; and victim blaming, 113;
atomized, 112; Fanon and, 119;
Foucault, and 117; in *Beloved*,
170–76
akrasia, 81–96
Althusser, Louis, 3, 108n9, 191n3
Antigone, 129–62. *See also* Sophocles
Antigone, xxii, 87, 129–62; and death,
151–53, 156; as victim, 156–58. *See
also* Lacan, and *Antigone*
Appiah, Anthony, 107
Aristotle, 88
autonomy, 129–58; and anarchy,
136; Antigone's, 138, 144,
148; as *autognotos*, 144; and
Chorus (*Antigone*), 146, 148;
and community, 181; and
Creon (*Antigone*), 138–40; and
determinism, 146, 147; and
empathy, 133, 134, 135, 139,
144, 146, 148, 149; and freedom,
146, 147; and Ismene (*Antigone*),
149; and Freud, 144; and Kant,
132, 133; and moral claims, 133;
and transcendence, 150; and

transcendental intersubjectivity,
150, 160n23; Steiner's view of, 137

bad faith:and agency, 104; claim to be
victims, 107, 109; critique of, 107;
and essentialism, 107; forms of, 100,
103, 106, 107; and ideology, 107;
and racism, 105; and universality,
102, 103, 105
Bosnia, 2
Bunge, Mario, 61
Bush, George W., 99
Butler, Judith, 130

Carnap, Rudolf, 105
Caruth, Cathy, 167, 174
Cesaire, Aimee, 98
Chiapas (Mexico), 2
Chartists, 1
Cherki, Alice, 102
Chicago Tribune, 8
Cobbs, Price, 114
colonialism, 100, 118, 120
Cusick, Carolyn, xii, xiii, xxii

Daly, Richard M., 157
Darwinism, social 6, 36; and Freud, 29,
33, 35, 36, 39,n17, 39n19, 40–41n24,
48

203